# Whatever the Future Holds

Heidi E.V. McCann

Green Heart Living Press

Whatever the Future Holds

ISBN Paperback: 978-1-954493-26-1
Cover design: Teresa Hnat

This is a work of creative nonfiction. The events are portrayed to the best of the author's memory. While all the stories in this book are true, some names and identifying details have been changed to protect the privacy of the people involved.

# *Dedication*

To my Curtis

All that I am I give to you,
and all that I have I share with you.
Whatever the future holds,
I will love you and stand by you.
We will be united for all eternity.
This is my solemn vow.

# Table of Contents

# Introduction

We experience life through the individual lens of our own biases. This is a story written from and based on the perspective of my memory.

The more time I spend alone recollecting moments from before, during, and after the disease, the louder the memory of the sound of Curtis' respiratory aid reverberates in my ears. When the vivid memories of our past appear with no warning, I believe that Curtis is still alive. The excitement, as well as the shock, suffocates me. When my mind carefully places the memories in between blocks of time and my consciousness forces my body to breathe during the designated periods of rest, survival is an option. I do want to live. My present path is speckled with moments from the past; I would never wipe the path clean of these remnants. As I travel through time, the past must be revisited in order to pick up the pieces that harbor the potential to destroy me, hold them close to my heart and then allow them to fly away.

I promised Curtis that I would document our love and our journey with ALS. I didn't think that it would take me 22 years to complete our project. One of the reasons it has taken me so long is because I feared that once complete, our story would end. As time has moved forward, as it always does, I have grown to realize that there are no endings: not to love, not to grief. Love and grief have a lot in common. They are both ever-changing journeys.

I have taken the past 22 years to process our experience and to gain perspective. We lived a lifetime of love in a short period of time, traveled through a year-long near-death experience, flirted with continuing to exist together even after his death, and then grappled with letting one another go. I was 24-years-old when Curtis died. I needed time to place that part of my life within a larger framework and to understand that our love and my grief would never be able to be compartmentalized. Both are a part of me. Forever. I also needed to live my life, which I have done and continue to do, with passion, optimism, faith, and love.

I suppose that in order to feel a ray of hope, see the light, you have to have first lived in darkness. There have been moments when I have wondered what my life would have been like if I had never met Curtis or if I had walked away after the diagnosis or if I had not cared for Curtis. And each time I come up with the same answer: I would have missed out on the incredible journey. At the time, I never questioned my decision to care for him because there was never a decision to be made. It just happened. All that mattered to me was that I loved him and I loved being with him. Looking back, I realize that if I hadn't met Curtis and later become his caretaker, we would not have experienced the year as it happened. He would not have depended on me to live, and I would not have depended on him to make me feel alive.

# Curtis Roger Vance

I love to think because my thoughts amaze me. And I love to be alone so that I can think. Most of all, I love to be alone, thinking amazing thoughts, because then I am in the company of those I love. I do my best thinking when I am at the pond. Joe's Pond. *My* pond. I've always thought of Joe's Pond as my pond because it is the backdrop to my family's summer cottage: the gray cottage that used to be red that faces a 400-acre pond, located in the town of West Danville, Vermont, the home of 650 Northeast Kingdom dwellers. As a child, I spent a lot of time floating on my back in the cool water of Joe's Pond, looking north at the Green Mountains that seemed to beckon me. Although my innocent mind journeyed toward their call, I never understood their pleading. I always saw that the pond's blue water appears green when the sun's light and the Green Mountains reflect off the crests of the pond's waves. The reflection of the sun also created tiny rainbows, appearing everywhere and seeming to reveal a magical and serene land.

If it weren't for Joe's Pond, I would have never met Curtis, who was born and raised in Danville, a few miles east of my pond. Curtis Roger Vance was born in August of 1973, weighing 11 pounds and 2 ounces. He was the middle son in a family of five boys. From a very early age, Curtis played and worked hard. During his younger teenage years, Curtis' favorite hobbies included showing his father's Belgian horses and being a member of his brother's racecar pit crew. He played varsity baseball and basketball as well as the drum in the marching band in high school. He served as student council vice president for two years. He also played varsity soccer until he took up cross-country in the fall of his senior year, the same year he was voted "class clown." Fishing, car racing, and riding his snowmobile became important activities to Curtis in his older teenage years, and his love for these activities increased, as did the drinking that accompanied all three of these popular Vermont sports.

I was first introduced to Curtis through stories. I met Curtis in the summer of 1990, just before my sophomore year and his senior year. I heard stories about Curtis from Curtis himself, who painted me scenes with his voice, allowing me to get to know him deeply, as if we had known one another since we were born.

My older sister, Heather, brought me to a fourth of July party at her friend's house that summer of 1990. It was the first time she allowed me to be seen with her after the sun went down. I had made friends with other Joe's Pond summer kids, whereas she had gelled with the real Vermonters the summer I was six and she was nine. This was the first season that we had taken swimming lessons at the Joe's Pond beach: a quarter of an acre of land consisting of grass, picnic benches, a parking lot, and a strip of sand. Heather had begged Mom to bring her to the beach before her lesson and to let her stay after it was over. Heather needed to be social; she always had the desire to feel part of a group. I, on the other hand, had screamed before every lesson that first summer. When I was a child, I was terrified of new places, people, and things.

I experienced both excitement and anxiety when Heather told me that she was bringing me to a party. We entered the white farmhouse and the crowd yelled, "Heather!" I watched as she was greeted by dozens of friends, most of whom were her age or older. The party was fun; being sober was even more fun. Drunken teenagers were fascinating to watch. Heather had a great time.

She was always happy at parties. As we prepared to leave, I heard a car engine soar and wheels spin. Heather pulled me toward the bay window, out of which we had a perfect view of the front lawn. There, in the spotlight, was a red Chevy Blazer tearing up the lawn.

"Oh," Heather said. "It's Curtis again."

I sat on the window seat with my face to the glass watching a boy with brown hair drive back and forth across the lawn. I could barely make out his face in the dark. I had never heard his name before. I felt as though I couldn't wait to meet him but wondered how since I was so shy. Little did I know what would transpire over the next few weeks.

That summer was also the first summer I helped teach swimming lessons at the Joe's Pond beach and met Laurie, the lead swimming instructor, who was in her mid-twenties. She was shorter than my height of five foot three and heavier than my child-like frame of one hundred and ten pounds. She had red hair; mine is brown. She had ice blue eyes; mine are dark brown, almost black. Her skin got blisters from walking in the sun from her car to her house; my skin tanned to a reddish brown color after just a few days. But we both have freckles, and that, she said, was why she knew we'd get along so well. Over the next two weeks, Laurie and Melissa, the other swimmer's aide, gossiped about the boys in Danville, most of whom I had only recently met at the parties. They knew so much about them that I began to think of them as my friends, too. In my 15 years, my family had moved three times, always just when I was feeling at home. As I listened to them, I thought, maybe Vermont was home? After all, there would never be a year without a summer.

On the second to last day of swimming lessons, Laurie and Melissa told me that since I was leaving a week early, they'd throw me a going away party. "And you can choose the guy you want that night," Laurie stated.

"What makes you think that I can choose the one I want?" I asked.

"Because you're a summer girl," Melissa explained.

We spent my last day of work in Laurie's car drinking hot chocolate, listening to the rain pound on the roof of the car, and talking about the Danville boys. Curtis' name was the last one mentioned.

"Adorable. The nicest guy. Loves to party. A lot of fun. And he's going to get out of this godforsaken town and make something of himself. His girlfriend recently broke up with him, so he's acting a little crazy, but once he meets you, he'll forget all about her," Melissa said.

Laurie smiled, "Curtie is my little cousin. You guys are perfect for one another."

We called it a day at 4 pm. We had to get ready for my party. Laurie told me she'd drive me home. After making the right turn out of the beach, she took a sharp left into the Joe's Pond Country Store's parking area.

"He's here. Come on," Laurie said.

"Who?" I asked.

"Curtis."

Laurie barreled through the wooden screen door, "Hey Curtie!"

I hid behind her but caught a glimpse of his smile out of the corner of my eye. He had dark hair, was wearing a red Budweiser T-shirt, and when he smiled his left eye squinted so that it appeared smaller than the other. His baby face made him look younger than 17 but his six-foot, 160-pound frame towered over us as he stood up from the kitchen barstool. I imagined what Curtis thought of me: my clothes were damp, my hair was wet and I was hiding behind his older cousin.

Laurie begged Curtis to come to our party even though it was destined to be a wash out.

"How much beer you got?" he asked.

"Two kegs. And the party is for this little lady."

Laurie pulled me out from behind her.

I looked up.

He smiled.

My knees weakened, my heart pulsated, my face flushed. He was the one. I smile every time I remember the moment Curtis and I met. It was a moment in time that seemed to last much longer than a minute or two. It was a defining moment during which I felt as though I stepped outside of myself and viewed the world from a new perspective. Seeing him forced me over the threshold from a child to a young adult. There was something familiar about him; it was as if we had known one another for a long time. The moment I met Curtis I felt as though I discovered where I belonged.

"I'll be there, Laur, and I'll bring the town," Curtis said.

Two hours later, I was in the passenger seat of Laurie's car at the designated "meeting place," the parking lot across from The Joe's Pond Country Store. Laurie was outside talking to the others as they waited for the rest of the crew to appear. We were headed to The Swamp, an area in the woods that had been cleared by loggers years ago and was set back from civilization.

Tap. Tap.

I jumped. It was not like me to have lied to my parents about where I was going and what I was doing.

Curtis motioned for me to roll down the window, "So, this party is for you? Should be a good time."

"Do you think that people will come?" I asked.

"For you? Hell, yeah. The whole town will come."

"But the whole town doesn't know me."

"They all know me. Where ya going, anyways?" Curtis asked.

"London. My hometown soccer team was invited to a tournament."

"You must be pretty good."

"No, not really. I mean, the team is, but I'm not."

"Are you always so hard on yourself?" Curtis asked.

Moments later Laurie and I followed Curtis' red Chevy Blazer to The Swamp. An hour after that I was watching Curtis do keg stands, and then at one point I remember Melissa asking me which boy I had chosen.

"Curtis," I confided.

She grabbed my hand and led me toward the center of the crowd. The air was cool – the average summer evening temperature remained below 60 degrees in the Northeast Kingdom of Vermont. I wished I had worn another layer for I felt the wind through my Joe's Pond long sleeve T-shirt as we zig zagged through the clusters of people. I had had a beer or two. I couldn't decipher who was who as we dodged in and out of the groups of people making our way toward the heat. I heard laughter and shouting and music blaring. As we ran, I saw thousands of stars in the clear sky when I looked up and puddles around my feet when I looked down. And then we stopped. I wish I could remember what Melissa said to Curtis or what Curtis said to me or what I said to either of them. All I remember is stopping and then sitting and talking with Curtis on a log by the bonfire. *Did he kiss me or did I kiss him that first time?* The image is blurred, but I do remember that after our first kiss we talked for a while. It was so easy to talk to Curtis. He listened to me. He made me feel important, special. When Laurie told me that it was time to go, Curtis told her that he'd bring me home.

I asked Curtis if he was okay to drive and without hesitation, he replied, "Don't worry. Everything is going to be okay."

# The First Summer

The yellow blanket protected the white cotton sheet that covered my tanned skin. Mom's intruding voice called attention to the pounding inside my head. Afraid to move, too scared to open my eyes, I had been through the routine before, but not enough to master the art of deception. Hearing Mom's footsteps on the side porch, I crept down the stairs to the bathroom to try to brush my teeth before seeing her. Avoiding my hungover reflection, I rinsed the stale beer taste from my mouth. Mom's interrogation traveled through the front screen door, past the latched bathroom door, "How was last night, honey?"

Usually honest with Mom, I surprised myself with an inaccurate reply, "It was okay."

*HIM! Did it really happen or was it just a dream? I hope it wasn't a dream; he was so nice and cute... and OH, I can't believe I kissed him! I don't even know him. I'll never see him again, so it doesn't really matter; he probably doesn't even remember my name.*

Thirty minutes later Laurie and Curtis' youngest brother entered the cottage.

Laurie pounced, "Sooo, how was last night?"

Shrugging, I muttered, "I don't know. We had a good time." I knew that I had had a great time and that I really liked Curtis but I was nervous that he may not feel the same.

Laurie expressed concern, "Did he tell you he'd call?"

"He told me his number."

"You have to call him," Laurie encouraged.

The phone terrified me. I even had trouble calling my friends. I didn't like talking to people without seeing their expressions. A person's voice could feign emotion but most people's eyes couldn't conceal their soul's true feelings.

Laurie continued, "Just call."

I sat with the phone on my lap, the receiver up to my ear, my finger in ready position.

*What will I say? Okay. I can do it. Just dial the number, and say, "Hello, is Curtis there?"*

"Hello?" answered a foreign voice.

"Hi. Is Curtis there?" I prayed that he wouldn't be.

"Hello?" a male voice responded.

"Hi. Is this Curtis?" I asked. My heart was pulsating, my hands were sweating and my eyes remained focused on my baby toe's deformed nail.

"Yeah, this is Curtis, who's this?"

I wanted to cry. I couldn't see that he was joking.

Curtis stopped the tears from falling, "How are you feeling this morning?"

The year that Curtis was sick, he and I recalled this first phone conversation. He told me that he knew how hard it had been for me to call him. After one attempt, he ignored his natural tendency to joke around; he knew I wouldn't find it funny.

"Great," I answered.

"Tell him we're coming over in a few," demanded Laurie.

"Curtis, we're coming over in a few minutes, okay?"

"Sure. See ya."

Forty-two hours after I met Curtis, I left him for the first time. Before I went to London to play soccer for 12 days, he picked me up at my cottage early Sunday morning to take me fishing. We sat side by side on pages of the *Caledonian Record* so that we would not stick to the railroad track's black tar. My sandaled and his sneakered feet, as well as our bare legs, dangled freely over the trestle as we talked.

"Are you learning to drive this summer?" he asked.

"Yes." In Vermont, you only had to be 15 to get your driver's permit and take driver's ed.

Curtis had only brought one pole, so we took turns casting the line. He, though, was the only one to thread the worms onto the hook; I didn't have the heart to witness them squirm.

"This is the best place to learn how to drive. We have back roads, main roads, and a highway all within about eight miles. Have you learned how to drive a stick?" Curtis asked.

"No," I replied.

"I'll teach you when you get back home. I'll take you to North Danville – we have miles and miles of back roads. I learned how to drive before I was ten. All of us boys started on tractors, then snowmobiles, cars, and trucks."

"That's amazing. My first time behind a wheel was this year. I feel like I have no idea what I'm doing. Are you looking forward to your senior year of high school? What will you do when you graduate?"

Curtis laughed, "I don't know. I'm going to enjoy my last year and figure it out as I go. Why, what are you going to do?"

"I will go to college."

"I was joking when I asked you. You have three years until then. How could you possibly know what you're going to be doing in three years?"

"I know that I'll be going to college."

"Cool. There are a lot of colleges in Vermont, you know?"

Since we met on Friday night, we had spent Friday evening,

all day Saturday, Saturday night, and now Sunday morning together, and we spent most of our time talking and laughing, but mostly laughing. When Curtis laughed, his small, green eyes disappeared into the slight creases of skin, his mouth opened and his tongue jutted out just below the top set of his teeth, making it look as though he had no bottom teeth. I laughed at this odd expression, and then slowly his eyes opened and his tongue retracted into his mouth. I stared at his serious countenance. Since we were sitting so close, I noticed two thin, soft yellow circles around the green of his eyes. They reminded me of the way Joe's Pond reflected the sun's rays and the Green Mountains. I thought he was beautiful.

Late in the afternoon, I stood beside Curtis' red Chevy Blazer as he loaded up the remaining gear, and after he slammed the back hatch, he walked up behind me, ran his finger along my spine from the small of my back, where the material of my bathing suit started, up to my shoulder blades, and whispered, "I'll miss you."

"Twelve days. I'll be back in 12 days."

"Twelve days is a long time," Curtis said as he turned me around to face him and kissed me.

A sensational tingle shot up from my toes, to my stomach, and out to the tips of my fingers, and at that time, I could not imagine anything sweeter.

The evening I returned to Joe's Pond from Europe, Mom insisted that I call Curtis immediately, "He's already called four times today. Don't keep him waiting any longer!"

Mom knew how much I hated the phone; she didn't know, though, how I felt about Curtis. She didn't know that I was in love. I had spent the majority of my time in Europe thinking about Curtis while most of my girlfriends spent their free time flirting, talking, passing notes, and fooling around with the boys whom we met from around the world.

I spoke about Curtis to anyone who would listen and confided in my closest friend, "I think that I am going to marry this guy."

"How in the world can you say that?" she asked. "You don't even know him."

Despite my strong feelings, I doubted whether or not I should call him upon my return. I wasn't sure how and if it would work out between us. He lived in Vermont. I lived in Connecticut. But I couldn't ignore how I felt when I saw his smile or heard his voice, so I called him and he appeared within 15 minutes.

Curtis and I spent every day of August together, and although the exact events of that month are recorded in my journal, I mostly recall the laughter. And many, many tingles. But I also recall two distinct feelings: absolute bewilderment and awesome panic. The absolute bewilderment came first.

Two weeks after I returned from Europe, Curtis and I sat on a dock on Harvey's Lake, a much smaller body of water than Joe's Pond, located in a town a few miles south of Danville. We dunked chocolate-striped cookies into a pint of chocolate milk, and ate blueberry yogurt with our fingers until Curtis' closest childhood friend, Justin, and his girlfriend arrived. Once the bonfire was roaring, I rested my body in between Curtis' legs. His fingers created circles on my bare shoulders and neck. When the cool night air had swallowed almost all of the heat from the fire, Curtis started up the driveway toward the woodpile alone.

"So, what are your plans at the end of the summer?" Justin asked.

"I have to go back to Connecticut."

"What about Curt?"

"I don't know. We haven't really talked about that, yet."

Justin looked at his girlfriend as she spoke. "Right before Curt met you, he was hurt really bad by his ex-girlfriend. He was really crushed."

I had heard about Curtis' ex-girlfriend from his cousin, his friends, his brother and others in Danville who I barely knew but Curtis didn't talk about her to me. He never even mentioned her name. This worried me. If he couldn't talk about her, I was sure he wasn't over her. He was spending all of his time with me, though. I was hopeful that perhaps my assumption was wrong.

"You know how much he likes you, don't you?" Justin's smile was trying to reach across the dwindling flames. "I've never seen him so happy."

"I need your help." My ears followed Curtis' sweet echo until I found him beside the woodpile. He grabbed me, held my waist tightly, and buried his face in between my neck and shoulder. As he kissed me softly, my fingers searched for the wisps of dark hair that fell in a v-shape along the nape of his neck.

*Twenty days. Only 20 days.*

I laid my hands on either side of his chest and pushed him away, gently.

"What's wrong?" he asked.

"Nothing."

"It has to be something."

"Curtis, what will we do in September?"

"September? It's only August? Why are you worrying about September?"

"Because school starts in September."

"And...it is only August, now."

"Did you know that I am leaving in 20 days?"

"Yes. We have 20 whole days."

His arms drew my body toward his, and although my mind resisted the touch, my body sank heavily into his. I could not imagine living without his warm embrace. As his fingers reached around my cheeks and his pinkies supported my chin, he kissed my forehead, and then my ears heard the words, "Love me?"

I have often thought about why Curtis asked me if I loved him before he told me that he loved me. On an August day, nine years after the fact, the summer he was sick, Curtis told me that he was shocked by how quickly he had fallen for me that first summer. He could not comprehend how and why he felt the way he did about me; we had known one another for such a short period of time. Because he had doubted that I would feel the same about him, he had asked me first.

Love? I had written I LOVE U with a permanent red marker on my love notes to my fifth-grade boyfriend. I had told my eighth-grade boyfriend that I adored him. When Mom ended our phone conversations with, "I love you," I said, "Okay." I loved Curtis' touch, his kisses, his smile, and his stories. I loved that he made me laugh, and how his sweet voice called my name. His touch made me tingle. Did I love him? I was sure that I did but the feelings were so foreign to me. The prospect of saying the words scared me. It was not natural for me to express my feelings.

His sweet voice called again, "Love me?"

"Uh-huh."

Curtis' face rested gently between the soft of my neck and my shoulder bone, and his hot breath whispered, "Love you."

Once Curtis told me that he loved me the second time, I recited the words to him, too. And after he asked me to wear his high school ring, I really loved him. A lot.

And I thought that love lasts forever.

A week and two days before my departure date, Mom and Dad and my baby sister, Tricia, who is six years younger than I, drove Heather to college. I stayed home at the cottage because there wasn't room for all of Heather's stuff and me in our red Toyota Landcruiser. I had the entire evening planned. Curtis would arrive at 6 pm. We would have hamburgers with melted American cheese on a plain Lender's bagel and Kraft macaroni on the side, the only meal I knew how to make. We would sit. Sit and talk. We would talk about our plans for the next school year.

I sat.

I waited.

One. Two. Three. Four.

Five hours. And then I cried.

It was 11 pm. The hamburgers were burnt, the twice-toasted bagels were in the trash, and the macaroni and cheese had solidified to the bottom of Mom's pan.

Curtis banged on the door at 11:30 pm, just minutes after I had put in my retainer and shut off the front lights.

As I opened the screen door, Curtis fell into my arms and Justin stumbled into the kitchen.

I led Curtis to the couch, and because he clung to me, both of our bodies crowded into the crevice where the two pieces of the L-shaped couch barely touched. He held me tighter than I had ever been held. I raised myself off of Curtis and sat on the shorter part of the couch.

"I'm starved. Got anything to eat?" Curtis asked.

"No," I said.

"What's wrong with you?" Curtis asked.

"Curtis, you were supposed to be here at six. It is now almost midnight, and yes, there was food."

"So, what'd you do, eat it all?"

I smiled, even though what he said wasn't funny. I wanted to pout and scream, and I even thought about crying in front of him but the look on his face, one of boyhood mischievousness, made me smile. I wanted him more than I had ever wanted him before.

Curtis sat up and kissed my forehead.

"I'm still mad, you know," I said.

"I know."

After Justin passed out on the couch, I led Curtis upstairs. I urged his body toward the first bedroom on the left, my bedroom. I watched him unbuckle his belt, unbutton his jeans and then fall onto the bed. He asked me to help him pull off his pants, and so I did. He asked me to take off my shirt, and so I did. He asked me to turn off the light, and so I did.

Beside him, I rested my head on his chest. I allowed my hand to slip under his T-shirt and remain on his baby-like skin. He took off his shirt and pulled me on top of him. As my legs spread open his hands grasped the small of my back, and I let my lower body sink on top of his lower abdomen. My ears listened to his pleas and then to his steady heartbeat, until his soft snores began. When one of his arms slipped off of my back, I reached around, and placed it back around me.

I had never felt so warm or safe, and yet, as I lay there in my cottage with the boy that I loved, a feeling of awesome panic invaded my mind. At first, I thought it was from the thoughts of Mom and Dad coming home early but then I realized that it was the feeling that had lived inside of my heart ever since we had kissed the first time by the bonfire: the knowledge that I would have to leave him. And, it was the fear that he would not wait for me to come back home that next summer. I raised my upper body by placing my palms against his chest. I felt my face flush when I looked and saw my own breasts. I tapped him gently on the shoulder. "Curtis. Curtis. Wake up." He didn't stir. I shook him, "Curtis, come on. I want to ask you something." A sudden jump, a flicker of the eyes, and then out cold, again. I smothered him with kisses. No reaction. My tongue played with his ear. Not even a smile. Exhausted, I fell beside him.

Five days later, Curtis and I sat next to one another in the corner of the L-shaped couch watching TV, alone. We snuggled and kissed, and then like the few other times that we had been together over the past week, he made me feel like I had never felt before by touching me in places I had no idea could ever feel so good. Like the other times over the past week, he asked me to have sex with him. I was terrified but his reassuring voice repeated, "Everything is going to be okay." I trusted him. I loved him. So, I allowed him to get on top of me. After some uncomfortable moments of him shifting his body and using his voice and his hands to urge me to relax, I felt pain. Then it was over. A part of me was relieved that I had finally done it and a part of me mourned the fact that I had let him do it. He left a few minutes later but promised he'd be back that night. He did return that evening, and after cuddling and kissing, he asked me, again, to have sex with him. I said, "no." I had time to think. Although I was sure that I loved Curtis, I wasn't sure that I was ready for the possible consequences that I had heard could result from having sex.

I sat at the kitchen table listening for Curtis' red Chevy Blazer to cross the railroad tracks and stop in front of our cottage less than a week later. Autumn was on its way. The days were shorter. The big birch tree at the end of the dirt road had been taken over by magical colors – bright yellows, blazing oranges, deep dark reds. The pond's water was frigid. It was time to go back to school. Curtis and I had known each other for six weeks and three days. After Curtis finally appeared, he helped us move the sailboat into the garage, secure the storm windows and pack the car, and then he and I stayed outside while my family went inside.

"Listen, we haven't had a chance to really talk about the school year," I started.

"What's there to talk about?"

"Us. My mom said that you are more than welcome to visit us anytime in Connecticut and she said that maybe we can spend Thanksgiving or Christmas at my aunt's and uncle's. Their house is only about an hour from here. I'll be back next summer."

He kissed me. Once. Twice. Three times. "I love you, you know," he said.

I wanted to believe that we could stay together. *Why not, right? I'd be busy at school with classes and sports. His senior year would be full of activities. Neither one of us would have the time to dedicate to another, right? We would have just enough time to talk on the phone with each other and, hopefully, he'd drive down to see me, and I'd figure out how to make a few trips up north. We could do it. I knew we could.*

"I love you, too," I said.

Mom and Dad came outside, "It's time to go."

As we drove away, I turned and stared at Curtis as he watched me leave.

# *Around and Around*

Curtis and I called one another weekly in September. And, I worked very hard to arrange a weekend free from school obligations and convinced my parents to drive me up to my aunt and uncle's in Westford, Vermont, the last weekend of that month. We arrived late Friday evening, and once I awoke the next morning, I called Curtis immediately. All I could think about was finally seeing him after not seeing him for almost a whole month.

"Hey," he answered.

"I'm here."

"Where?"

"Westford."

"Westford. Vermont?"

"Yes. Curtis, remember? You were going to come see me."

"Oh, yeah. Listen, I'm really sorry but I can't come see you. I was with the boys really early this morning. We're on this new job. I've been installing insulation and I just got home and I'm feeling pretty sick. Must be from the fumes. I don't think I can drive an hour to see you. I'm really sorry. Next time?"

*Next time? Does he have any idea what it took for me to get out of my soccer game; how hard I worked to convince my parents to drive over four hours up one day and back the next; how long it's going to take me to make up a weekend's worth of homework?*

I believed that he wasn't feeling well. I was crushed that I couldn't see him. Most of all, though, I was devastated because I needed to talk to him in person about something very important.

My parents drove me home to Connecticut the next day and for the next two weeks I was crushed over not being able to see him and very worried about possibly being pregnant. I had not gotten my period since May. This was not unusual. I had always been irregular: since I was 12, I had maybe three cycles a year. I was feeling nauseous the past few weeks and I was getting headaches, both of which were unusual. I didn't think it was probable that I had gotten pregnant from that one time with Curtis over the summer but it was possible. I couldn't help but hear my fifth grade health teacher's voice in my head, "It only takes one time of unprotected sex and your whole life will be changed."

One evening, my mom knocked on my bedroom door and asked me what was wrong. "You seem so preoccupied," she said.

Silence.

"Are you pregnant?" Mom asked.

I looked up at her, "I'm not sure."

"Wait right here. Don't go anywhere," Mom instructed.

My mother returned from the drugstore with a pink box in a plastic bag. I went into my Pepto Bismol pink tiled bathroom, peed on a stick, and waited. The five minutes seemed like a lifetime and I cried until the five minutes were up and the second line hadn't appeared. And then I took the second test. Again, I cried until enough time had elapsed and the second line still didn't appear. I stepped out of the bathroom, ran to my room, and shut the door. Mom knocked on my door, and I opened it to a look I had only seen on my mother's face when she was worried about something that Heather had done.

"I'm not pregnant," I said.

"Thank God." She hugged me. Then she said, "So, I'm assuming that you didn't use protection?"

"No."

"Dear, I think that you need to call Curtis," my mother replied.

"Why?"

"Isn't he worried?"

"He doesn't know I was worried."

"Well, whatever you do… You do know there are things you can use, right, the next time?"

And that was the first and last sex talk my mother and I had.

I didn't call Curtis that night but when he called me three days later I confided in him that I had thought that maybe I was pregnant but not to worry, I wasn't. It had taken me 30 minutes into the conversation to build up the courage to tell him.

He responded with a snicker, "Are you kidding? How could you have been pregnant?"

"What do you mean, how could I be pregnant? I know how these things work, Curtis. Even if it's just once, it can happen."

Silence.

And, then, he laughed, "Wait, you thought we actually had sex?"

"But, I thought…"

I was mortified. I felt like a complete fool.

I never did tell my mom that Curtis and I never even had sex. I did call Heather, though, at her dorm room. She listened as I cried to her for almost an hour.


Curtis and I only spoke on the phone that one time in October and another time in November. I spoke about him constantly, though, to my friends. As a result of my urging, our family spent Christmas week in Westford, and I called Curtis the minute we arrived.

"Hey, you made it."

"My sister can drive me over to Danville whenever it works for you," I replied excitedly.

"Listen. About that. We haven't spoken in awhile so you wouldn't know. My basketball team qualified for a tournament in Waterbury. It's going to be going on all week."

"Cool. I'll come watch. Waterbury is closer to here than Danville. My sister will drive me to the game instead."

"You don't want to do that," he stated. "The weather is too unpredictable."

"Waterbury is so much closer than Danville and it's all major roads. We'll be fine."

"I don't think it's a good idea."

I was irate and knew that something wasn't right. But I was in love. Did I truly understand love? No. But I had experienced the most intense, incredible feelings that I had ever felt in my short life throughout my time with Curtis that past summer and I didn't know what to think now that he was being so distant. So I thought what my friends thought: if I had had sex with him, he would still be mine. If I had been able to give him what he had wanted, what he had asked for, he would still want me. These thoughts depressed me. How could it all come down to sex? It didn't. I was sure of this. As strong as it was, there had been something more than just physical attraction between us. I had recognized that it was something greater than us, something that I couldn't understand, but I didn't know what. So I just held on. For dear life.

After the Christmas week when he and I didn't see one another, I refused to call him. And, he didn't call me. In February, I visited Heather at her college for a long weekend. We partied with Curtis' cousin at his fraternity, and within hours I learned that

Curtis was back with the girl he had been dating before we met and had been since the fall. I felt like an idiot. Once Heather and I returned to her dorm room, I called him and drunkenly berated him for lying to me. He told me that he didn't lie; he just never told me the whole truth. I told him that I hated him.

A week later he called me in Connecticut and told me that he was sorry. "I never meant to hurt you," he said.

I remember crying; I was wrapped in my own arms.

In March, Curtis called me to wish me a Happy Sweet 16. We talked for an hour but never mentioned his girlfriend. I was still angry and hurt. I didn't want to know if they were still together. I missed my boyfriend. Even more importantly, though, I didn't want to lose our friendship. I missed our talks: nothing seemed real until I told him about it. I called him once or twice in April but he didn't return my calls which was upsetting but I ignored my feelings and instead focused on my classes and tennis at school. And, at this point in time, my highschool friends were trying to convince me to try dating someone from school.

"It'll help you forget all about him," they said.

There was this one boy who asked me to our spring dance. I said, "no." I couldn't stop thinking about Curtis, and didn't think it would be fair to the other boy.

In late May, I returned to our family's cottage for the weekend to help my parents open it for the season. I now had my license and so drove myself to the party in Danville on Saturday night. I saw Curtis at the party. He appeared to be so sad.

Justin pulled me aside early in the evening, "Curtis and his girlfriend broke up, again."

An hour later, Curtis asked me to go outside with him. He took my hand and led me away from the house. Holding both of my hands in his, he looked down at me. I could once again see his soul in his eyes. He spoke slowly and deliberately, "I've missed you so much. I am so glad that you're home." And then he kissed me gently.

Although I was deeply hurt, once we kissed for the first time since the summer before, I could only think about our future.

Later that night, I told him that I'd be back in three weeks.

"I can wait three weeks," he replied.

"You sure?" I smiled, although I was serious.

"Yes, I can wait three weeks because then we have all summer. It's going to be an amazing summer."

I went home to Connecticut and wished the days away until school vacation.

I tried to call him a few times over those three weeks. He left me a voicemail once. I was a little bit worried but hoped that he was just really busy; I knew that I was. Exactly 22 days from when we had last seen and spoken with one another, Heather and I drove up to Vermont alone. Mom had to stay in Connecticut until her and Tricia's last days of school, and Dad had to work. Heather was going to spend the summer nannying our cousins who were arriving from Canada in a few days and I was going to be nannying our other cousins who were arriving from Westford, Vermont in a few weeks. With no parental supervision or young cousins to watch, I envisioned that Curtis and I would have a few days to spend lots of time together. Toward the end of our trip up north, I asked Heather if we could drive the back roads to West Danville. She agreed. As we drove by Curtis' house, I saw his brand-new, cherry-red 5.0 Ford Mustang in his driveway but it was too late at night to just stop by. I called him the next day and waited by the phone for his return call. It never came. That second night, I made Heather come with me as I drove by his house again. I noticed that his car was parked in a different spot in his driveway.

The next day, Heather sat on the low end of the teeter-totter smoking a cigarette as I twirled around and around on the tire swing at the Danville school's playground. I whined, "He told me he'd wait. He kissed me goodbye. Why haven't I heard from him?"

"You will. Don't worry," Heather replied. She had convinced me to hang out in the schoolyard with her. She knew that Curtis would notice our car with its Connecticut plates.

A raindrop landed on my tanned shoulder. Then the rain fell faster and the first bolt of lightning struck. We scrambled toward the car. Before I put the car into drive, I checked my rear-view mirror and saw the reflection of a boy under the awning in front of the school's main entrance. *There he is!* I cautiously reversed the car towards him, keeping an eye on him the entire way. The boy was not looking at me. *Here! Here! Here I am!* Curtis opened the large high school doors. *No! Don't leave. I am right here.* I rolled down my window, and prepared my voice to shout, but the rain drowned out my futile attempt. Curtis disappeared into the building.

"Go after him!" Heather shouted.

As I opened the car door, the boy emerged, with a girl. They were hand in hand. *It can't be.* I shut the door. They stopped under the awning. The girl's black hair touched her tight, cropped tank as she looked up at the tall, dark-haired boy who wore an AC/DC T-shirt. *Does Curtis have a black AC/DC T-shirt?* I turned around and watched through the rear-view mirror, again. The girl kissed the boy. No, the boy kissed the girl. *He only had to wait three weeks.*

Heather whipped around in her seat and faced the couple,

"That horny bastard couldn't even wait three weeks."

I stepped on the accelerator.

My shoulders shook, my voice raged, "I can't believe this is happening."

Twenty minutes later, I stood by the phone which sat upon the stacked hollow wooden crates which served as our bookcase in the living room of our cottage. I dialed his number a few times with the receiver still on the hook while I stared at the stenciled border. I recalled how many days it had taken my mother to paint the brown cardboard-like walls white with BIN primer paint after we bought the cottage and the numerous times she repainted the light blue, pink, and yellow flower stencils so that they were straight. *Why couldn't he wait?*

I walked away from the phone because I couldn't decide what I would say if he answered my call. In the shower, I scrubbed every inch of my skin. I recalled how her jean shorts had revealed her model-like legs as I shaved my own chicken legs. I attempted to catch the salt that my eyes released; the soap from my short hair intruded. I spat out the soap and tried to keep the tears inside. I didn't even like to cry when I was alone.

I brushed my hair while staring at my body in the long mirror in the hallway. My legs were a bit skinny, but "running will improve their strength," my school's varsity soccer coach had suggested. My breasts weren't full, and they certainly wouldn't have looked like hers under a tight, cropped tank top, but at least the boys at school didn't refer to me as "the board." My tummy, well, Mom said I have always had a tummy, even when I was 36 pounds entering kindergarten. I could try sit-ups. I had always done the most in one minute for the President's Physical Fitness Test in junior high. No more chocolate chip cookies for breakfast.

Forget the ice-cream-cookie sandwiches for lunch. Just because the word s-a-n-d-w-i-c-h was printed on the plastic wrapper did not mean these treats made up a balanced meal. Vegetables? Definitely not zucchini. Cauliflower and broccoli were out of the question, too, but I could try carrots. Everyone always said I ate like a rabbit.

I heard Curtis' car coming from the highway. The 5.0 liter engine shifted down to second, and the wheels glided gently off the pavement and onto my dirt road. His Ford Mustang spat the rocks out from under itself. It had no tolerance for intrusion. He shifted the red beauty into third so that it could take the S-curve. And then I heard the gentle hum of the idle Ford Mustang in the rock driveway. I really didn't think he'd come. Not so soon, anyhow.

I heard a soft click as he closed the car door gently. And then I heard his calm tapping on the cottage's door frame.

Two louder taps.

Three successive firm knocks.

Heather called up the stairs to me in her you-know-who-it-is-but-I'll-pretend-you-don't-so-you-don't-look-desperate voice.

"Yeah?"

"Curtis is here to see you."

I wanted to yell that I was busy, that I didn't want to see him. But I couldn't lie. Not to him. Descending the steps slowly, I rehearsed over and over again, *Curtis, I never want to see you again. I hate you. I never want to see you again. I hate you.*

I noticed his broad shoulders and wisps of dark hair that covered the nape of his neck in a v-shape. My fingers had played with those wisps while my tongue had played with his ear. The black T-shirt hung loosely on his lean body, and the dark green jeans emphasized "his adorable butt," as Heather had pointed out the first time she had met him.

He turned around when the sound of my footsteps stopped. "Hi."

I didn't answer him.

"Hey, Heather Feather," Curtis punched my sister's arm lightly.

Turning her back toward Curtis, she stated, "I'm going. You need anything?"

"No, I think I'm all set." I tried not to stare at his AC/DC T-shirt.

"Call if you think of anything you need, okay?"

"Okay," I whispered.

After the screen door slammed, and we were alone in the cottage, I sat down cross-legged on the shorter part of the L-shaped couch. I watched Curtis follow and sit down on the longer side. I noticed he was holding his hands awkwardly by his sides, as if he couldn't decide whether to shift his baby down to second, or rev the engine and take the curve. I watched his eyes scan the magazines on the small brown table. I wanted him to suffer and to feel the pain that accompanied waiting and wondering, but I also wanted to crawl next to him, lay my head gently on his lap, so that I could hear the words, "Everything is going to be okay."

"You and your sister having a good time up here alone?" Curtis began.

I didn't know whether or not he actually saw our tan Camry with the Connecticut plates but his facial expression – one of manhood deviousness instead of his usual boyhood mischievousness – gave him away.

"We've only been here for two nights. We were tired last night, so we just went out to the movies," I replied.

Curtis looked at me for the first time as he forced out the words, "Yeah, I tried to call you last night. Must have been that you were at the movies." He chose two magazines from the table.

"You did?" My mind wanted to spit the words right back at him.

"Oh, have I got a story for you." Curtis leaned against the couch. "Last weekend, me and the boys were down at Harvey's Lake drinking a few beers, and it was the after prom party..."

I studied his face as he spoke. *He had said he never meant to hurt me. He had said he loved me. He gave me his high school ring and called me in Connecticut, and let me wreck his Chevy Blazer's clutch. He just needs to remember, to remember how much fun we had, how I made him laugh, how I made him forget how much she hurt him, and how much he needs me.*

As he finished, I smiled my too-wide and plastered smile, "You two are back together again, aren't you?"

He sat up straight and stared at me the way he did the summer before when I had refused a beer at the party full of strangers. "I'm really sorry. I was going to call you. I wanted to tell you. I never thought you'd know."

"Just answer me one thing, Curtis. Are you happy?"

Even though I didn't know any particulars about their relationship before he and I met, or afterwards, I did know that she had been his first love. That's all I really needed to know because I imagined he felt as strongly for her as I did for him and that scared me.

I watched his eyes demand the answer from mine. A hint?

Anything?

My black eyes stared blankly at his.

"It's different this time. She's over him," Curtis began. "We had made plans for the prom over the winter, because, as you found out, we were together then, and so even though we broke up in March, we decided to go since everything was paid for. Who else would I have gone with? You were in Connecticut, busy with exams. And then, well, you know, that night, prom night, we got back..."

I didn't want to hear anymore.

He told me another story, and I sat, and listened, and smiled, and laughed at his animated facial expressions and exaggerated hand motions. He was so full of life and so wonderful. He had so much to give. But then I thought, *I will be here all summer and yet he still has chosen her.* I didn't want to hear his incessant noise or my circular thoughts. But his words, along with the voices inside my head, continued to twirl around and around:

*We were supposed to have picnics,* I thought as Curtis spoke.

"I wish you had been here to snowmobile this winter."

*Go for walks.*

"We could have had so much fun," Curtis continued.

*I waited nine months.*

I didn't want him to see me cry.

He stood up and hovered over me. "Band practice."

The voices told me to end it. "Wait a minute. I have something for you."

I felt as though I had no control over my body's movements as my legs ran up the stairs, my fingers grabbed his high-school ring, and my smile greeted him as he stood on the front stoop, holding open the front screen door.

"I think someone else should be wearing this." My heart ached and I barely recognized the whisper that had escaped.

"Oh. I won't give it to her. I mean, I told her that I lost it. I wanted you to have it."

"You'd better go."

He balanced the ring in the middle of his palm, where I had placed it. He asked me if I'd be around all summer. I wanted to say "no" but I said "yes." I wanted to push him aside and leave, now that he no longer needed me, now that he was no longer mine. I was lost. I wanted him to leave for good. But Vermont is his home. He told me he'd stop by sometime. I knew he would, after she broke it off again.

He turned to leave, and I heard his voice. A voice that I knew was coming from his heart, not his head. "I'm sorry. Any other time. Any other place. It would have been different. If you ever need anything."

*Time and circumstance. They rule the world.*

At the time, I believed that if we were just a little bit older, if we lived a little bit closer, we'd be together. Forever.

Remorse crept into his green eyes, darkening them. He smiled as he bent down and kissed my forehead. The ring dug into my palm as his hand squeezed mine. I hated him for teasing me with his touch. I wanted to close my palm over the ring, but the voices forced the palm to remain open. He took the ring. I wanted to ask him to stay.

"Take care of yourself," I said.

He turned his back towards me and walked away.

As he opened his car's red door, he looked back at me, "See ya."

My lips smiled.

Alone, I cried.

Twenty minutes later I called him. He answered the phone. I knew that he didn't have band practice. I told him that I needed him to know how much I cared for him. How special he was. How he had made me so happy. I told him how much I loved him. "I just need you to know," I said.

"I know," he said.

I avoided him for a while by not going out to any parties. My feelings were too strong, though, to avoid him for too long. A few weeks later, at a party, I sat at a table pretending to play a drinking game waiting for Curtis to appear. Once he did, he spent the first hour ignoring me and then asked me if I would go outside with him. I did. The second we were alone he told me that I was the only thing in his life worth living for. Just as suddenly, he walked back inside and continued to drink.

Hours later I stopped him as he stumbled toward his car, "What are you trying to do, kill yourself?"

He blurted that he wished that he and his car would crash into a tree on the way home. Then, he slumped into my arms. I clumsily maneuvered him over to a log in the woods just behind where his car was parked. I sat on the log with his head resting on my thighs. As I stroked his hair, we remained silent. My touch let him know how much I cared. I believed that his willingness to remain with me meant that my love for him wasn't for naught. I persuaded him to let me drive him home and once we got to his house, he begged me to spend the night. I kissed him good night on the cheek and told him we'd talk in the morning. Heather, who had followed us in our car, drove me home. The next day I waited for his call. It never came.

A few nights later I was at Keeser Pond, a popular party spot.

If it hadn't been for the fact that Curtis would, undoubtedly, show, I would have never bothered to attend. I waited for hours and then his red Ford Mustang screeched to a halt in front of me, too close to the bonfire. He emerged, open Budweiser can in hand.

The crowd of 50 or so hollered, "Hey, Curtie!"

The crowd moved around him as though magnetized by his infectious smile. I moved to the other side of the bonfire and watched as he opened his trunk and handed out beers. He gave his guy friends high fives and his girl friends flirtatious hugs. The energy of the party increased; everyone's spirits seemed lifted by his presence. Curtis made people feel as though they were somebody; he made them feel alive. This was the Curtis I had fallen in love with the summer before.

A few minutes later, he glanced in my direction and smiled sincerely. After he downed a few more beers, he approached.

He began, "I didn't think you'd be here."

"My sister dragged me here."

We both looked in Heather's direction. She was funneling a beer as the crowd chanted her name.

"Yeah, she loves parties," Curtis laughed.

"So do you."

"I'm glad you're here," he said and then he kissed me. No warning, no asking my permission. I was angry that he assumed that I would want to be kissed.

"Listen, about the other night..." I started to say.

"It was a bad night, okay? Let's just forget about it."

"Curtis, you couldn't walk."

"I had it under control."

"You cried to me. You told me that you wished that you and your car would crash into a tree on the way home. What is going on with you?"

Looking right at me, he whispered, "I've never before felt the way I feel..."

A car approached. A girl with long black hair emerged from the driver's seat.

Curtis glanced in her direction and then looked back at me. "I'm sorry."

He walked toward her. She turned her back to him. He whispered something in her ear. She turned around and screamed at him. My name was mentioned. He yelled back at her. I remained at the other end of the dirt parking lot, wondering if he was the same person who had made me laugh and smile just a year before. He drove off in a rage. Much later, the girl approached me with an almost empty bottle of wine in one hand.

"I've heard a lot about you. I love him, but you know him, a part of him that I have never bothered to notice. You believe in him. We just make each other miserable. If we broke up again, would you pursue him?" she asked.

"I don't know."

"Follow your heart," Mom advised after I told her the story. A week later, they were back together, again.

I am not sure what Curtis thought about this period of our relationship; we rarely spoke about the second summer. We didn't even talk about it the year he was sick. Looking back on it, the summer of 1991 was a very confusing time. Many of my actions and feelings were that of a typical teenager. I was so unsure of myself. And, although I didn't think it at the time, we were just kids. His inability to allow us to continue to develop a relationship coupled with my refusal to give him an ultimatum because I was sure he would choose her if she was available created a seemingly impossible situation. During that period of time, I felt like a fool for loving him but couldn't help myself from feeling as though he was my world and it would end if he weren't a part of it.

# *Belonging*

That next summer, the third summer, the summer I was 17, something inside of me changed. In August, Heather convinced me to accompany her to a party at Curtis'. His parents were out of town and Heather was now dating Curtis' youngest brother. There was a keg of beer in the middle of the living room floor and people were sprawled around it. The TV was on. Curtis wasn't one of the crowd. I wanted to leave. I was afraid that he would come home with her, even though I had heard that she had broken up with him again. I wasn't surprised, but I wasn't thrilled either. Curtis had started coming up to my cottage again the previous few weeks, and we still laughed together, but I was tired of the games. I had been tired of the games for quite a while. In fact, I had met another boy that summer. As much as I loved Curtis, I was afraid that he would hurt me again. It was easier for me to pretend that he wasn't my whole world than to have my world shattered. Instead of waiting around for Curtis to call, I spent time with my cousin who went to parties in St. Johnsbury, eight miles east of Danville, where I met the other boy whose family also had a cottage on Joe's Pond. He had recently had his heart broken and we commiserated over how she and Curtis both were unable to commit. And, then we began to really enjoy one another's company. I felt empowered and free and happy.

But Curtis' red Ford Mustang was parked in the driveway, so I waited, because he made me feel so right, and I couldn't ignore that. A look from his green eyes, a smile, a touch of his hand, and I would fall for the Curtis I remembered from the first summer we met: the Curtis that made me feel as though I was alive, the Curtis who made me feel as though I was somebody and finally belonged somewhere. But then I would recall how alone I felt when he was late or stopped calling and coming around for days or weeks at a time, as had happened so often in the two years that we had known one another, or how annoyed I was when he would show up at my cottage belligerent.

Justin showed up at the party and gave me a hug. "Where's our boy?"

"Haven't seen him."

He went up the stairs and came back down a few minutes later. "Curtis wants to see you. He's in his room."

The crowd hollered and hissed, "Ooooh, Curtis wants to see her. Better run. You don't want to keep him waiting."

No one understood Curtis and me. No one except for Heather. I looked toward her, and she nodded her head. I ventured up the stairs. I knocked gently on his hollow wooden door.

"Yeah?"

I opened the door and saw him lying in his bed. The bedroom was dark except for the light from the television and he looked so sad.

"How long have you been waiting down there?"

"I haven't been waiting. I've been hanging out and having fun."

"You hate crowds."

*How could he always be right about me?*

I stood beside his bed and stared at the TV. I don't remember what show was on although I do recall that there was an empty Budweiser bottle and a tin of wintergreen Skoal on top of the television. The raunchy-yet-sweet smell of a newly opened can made me light headed and caused my knees to buckle.

He took my hand out of my jean's right front pocket and held it in his. Releasing my hand from his hold, I crawled on top of the covers and placed my head on his bare chest. He wrapped his arm around me and rested his hand on the small of my back. His heartbeat was still steady and his breath was still sweet and hot. I held on tighter.

A while later, the banging woke me up. Curtis was snoring softly.

"Come in," I said.

Justin entered Curtis' bedroom with a camcorder to his eye. "Look at the precious sweet couple. We'll save this tape for your grandkids."

"Get out of here, you drunk!" Curtis hollered.

He pulled me closer but I stood up.

As much as I loved being physically comforted by Curtis, I felt ridiculous lying in his bed with him when we couldn't even have a conversation about where, if anywhere, our relationship stood.

"Where are you going?"

I lifted the covers and crawled back in. He snuggled close and held me as though he would never let go. Curtis and I didn't need to communicate with words in order to understand how much we needed one another.

At one point, I woke up again to a persistent knock. "Come in."

"Are you almost ready to go?" Heather asked.

"Just a little while longer. Please?"

As Heather shut the door quietly behind her, Curtis wrapped his arms around my body again. My back was to him. He cupped my breasts. I turned around and faced him. I looked into his eyes, but saw nothing. I wanted something, anything. I wanted us to return to where we had been two years before – in love. So I gave my physical being to him. All of me. He took it, gently. He was grinning when it was over and then he asked me if I was okay. We walked out of his bedroom, hand in hand. The crowd's hooting and hollering greeted us. I wasn't embarrassed, though. I had given myself to the boy that I loved. No one had told me to. He hadn't even asked me this time. I walked over to the freezer, took out a frozen Twix bar, and ate it while I watched Curtis watch me. We were surrounded by a mass of bodies but we were the only ones really there. I had been holding onto Curtis for two years because I had loved him as I had never loved another. And I thought that sex would be the impetus that would propel our lives forward together. Instead, that night made me realize that as much as I may have loved him, it was still not the right time for us. Or the right place. As I turned to walk down the kitchen stairs, out of his life, at least for the time being, he called me back.

I faced him. His hand was to his ear and his mouth moved silently, "Call me."

I smiled and walked away.


The fall of 1992, I began my final year at Loomis Chaffee in Connecticut and Curtis attended a technical college in Vermont. The next spring we both graduated: me with my high school diploma and Curtis with honors and a certification in Building Construction Trade. Throughout this time, and over the next few years, we'd never go more than a few weeks without a phone call, or if it was the summer, a visit. Simultaneously, I pursued my education. I had other romantic interests between 1992-1995; I never allowed myself to get too involved. Curtis was always forefront in my mind and in my heart. Curtis saw other girls during part of this time including his on-again-off-again girlfriend.

Curtis was the one I called when I was accepted to Middlebury College as a February student (one quarter of the incoming freshman class was admitted for February rather than September) and, thus, had to figure out what to do with myself for eight months. I told him about SEA (Sea Education Association). I'd take classes in Woods Hole, Massachusetts, for six weeks and then spend six weeks on a 125-foot schooner in the Caribbean. The students would be responsible for manning the ship and we'd be on a 24-hour watch schedule.

"Have you ever been on an ocean before?" he asked.

"Not for more than an hour or so," I answered.

"Sounds like a great opportunity," he told me.

And so I attended SEA in the fall of 1993 and began my college career that next February. The main reason I chose Middlebury was because it was in Vermont, close to Curtis. He spent the year building and remodeling houses. He loved to work with his hands. He relished in the routine of waking up before dawn, drinking a cup of coffee as he and the boys surveyed the land or project and talked about the day's work ahead. He loved laying concrete, sawing wood, pounding nails, breaking for a half hour (just enough time to eat a bag of chips and drink a few beers), carefully measuring the next step with a tape measure, level and charcoal pencil, cutting more wood, pounding more nails, and then, at 3:30 pm in the winter and 4:30 pm in the summer, finishing off a 24-pack with the boys as they stood in the snow or basked in the sun admiring a hard day's work.

Curtis was the one I called when I decided to hike 239 miles of the Appalachian Trail from Fullhardt Knob in Roanoke, Virginia, to Front Royal, Virginia, with some friends from high school after my freshman year of college.

"Have you ever hiked before?" he asked.

"No," I answered.

"Sounds crazy but better you than me," he said.

As much as Curtis loved to build, he also knew that many young men in the Northeast Kingdom of Vermont wanted to start their own construction business and only a few would succeed, especially because a new business required capital. Curtis applied for a part-time temporary job at a semiconductor plant in Essex Junction, Vermont, and was hired in August of 1994, the summer after my freshman year of college. After a while, he applied for a permanent job at the plant. He was offered a 12-hour night shift with a rotating schedule: two nights on, two nights off, three nights on, three nights off. He accepted. On the morning of his last night shift each period, Curtis would escape the sterile, fluorescent lighted room where he had operated machinery that built computer chips, jump into his green Ford F-150, speed home to Danville and meet the boys at the construction site. Curtis only took every other Sunday off. He was eventually promoted to the day shift at the plant which consisted of 12-hour shifts with a three and four day rotating schedule. Curtis was thrilled to be able to work construction for three or four days in a row rather than just two or three.

In the spring of my sophomore year of college, Curtis was the first person I called after I made the varsity tennis team. It was my third season trying out. "I knew you'd do it," he congratulated me.

I attributed finally making the team to the fact that I had joined the college's varsity squash team that winter. Playing squash increased my foot speed and helped improve my reaction time. I had never played the sport before but the squash coach was looking for more players so he had asked those of us who had gotten cut from the tennis tryouts to give the sport a try.

In the summer of 1995, the summer I was 20 and Curtis was 22, we saw one another when we could on the weekends. I was teaching tennis at a summer camp in Connecticut during the week and he was working at the plant and working construction on his days off. I would drive up north on Friday nights and leave Monday mornings before sunrise for the week. At this point in time, although we weren't officially dating, neither one of us was dating or seeing anyone else.

That fall, the fall of my junior year of college, Curtis called.

"Hey, how's it going?"

"Fine. And you?"

"Good."

Silence.

It was strange for Curtis and me to exchange pleasantries. Our conversations didn't typically mirror those of two people who hadn't spoken in awhile. We usually got right to the point of why one of us was calling or one of us would immediately tell the other a story of what had happened to prompt the phone call. This time was different.

Curtis continued, "So, I was thinking. You remember Ryan and Jill, right?"

"Yes, I know who they are." I felt as though I was in the middle of a conversation with a boy whom I had just met.

"Yeah, right. Of course you know who they are. Well, they are getting married in a few weeks."

"Yes, Curtis. I know."

"Well, I was wondering if you'd like to go to the wedding with me?"

This was the first time Curtis asked me out on a date since that first summer five years beforehand.

"Okay. Sure. It'll be fun."

"Great, so you'll come? Wait, will you have a tennis match? Are you sure you can make it?"

"I'm sure, Curtis. I'll make it work."

After we said goodbye, I hung up the phone, ran into my roommate's room (I shared a quad with three friends) and squealed like a young school girl. She wasn't as excited as I was; she was tired of hearing about the boy who wouldn't commit.

A few weeks later, I accompanied Curtis to the wedding of two of his close friends who had dated since middle school. Curtis had gone to school with both of them since grade school. Curtis and I sat through the ceremony and then we drove to the reception just a few minutes down the road. Throughout the day and early evening, Curtis introduced me as his girlfriend to the few people who I didn't already know. This was new. We danced almost every slow dance together which we had not done since we had gone to barn dances that first summer. I was caught between feeling like I was 15 again and like we were finally grown-ups.

Toward the end of the reception, I planted myself in the back of a crowd of unmarried women. I was wearing my red dress. As the bride threw the bouquet, I glanced toward Curtis and saw his eyes watching me. He smiled. I couldn't stop watching Curtis watch me, and I missed catching the bouquet although it had been thrown right at me; another girl had hurled herself in front of me in order to seize the prize. It was a scene like so many from that first summer and a few from the subsequent summers: as we watched one another everything around us stood still. We were on a different plane than everybody around us.

Curtis walked up to me, placed his hand on the small of my back and whispered in my ear, "Ready to go?"

"Yes," I replied. "Where are we going?"

"It's a surprise."

Curtis drove us up to *The Stagger Inn*, his family's hunting camp in North Danville. As we crossed the threshold into the camp, Curtis stopped. He held my chin in his hands and kissed me. That night, for the first time, I learned how it felt to be really loved physically by another. Although we had been intimate numerous times, I felt his soul that October night. After so many years of false starts with Curtis, I fell in love with him all over again. And, finally, the timing was right.

Over the next 18 months, I focused on school, he focused on work, and we both focused on one another. We spent whatever free time we had together. Two particular moments in time are embedded in my heart.

In February of 1996, I sat enveloped in the big, brown comfortable chair in Curtis' parents' living room in Danville. I looked out the picture window at the barren field, the few scattered houses and the wondrous mountains of the Northeast Kingdom. The mountains were giant and beautiful: gray and black and snow covered, tall and wide at the bottom and steep at the top. I imagined myself running toward the top. I could smell the fresh, moving air. I felt the bright sunshine warming my back. The wind was so gentle, I almost forgot it was there. The air was so pure, one would bask an infant in it.

In the background, I heard the ticking and knew that the minute hand was progressing toward the nine. I ignored it.

Instead, I focused on the awakening sun which peeked out from under the majestic forms, painting brilliant shades of red, oranges and pinks.

Curtis' father calmly suggested, "Eggs? I can make you eggs. Would you like some, sweetheart?"

Curtis, standing to my left, was dressed in his work clothes that I had washed the week before, the clothes he had applied to his tired body earlier that morning as I lay in his bed dreaming it was Sunday. He wore thick black pants that kept him warm on those frigid days, a white turtleneck, concealing the long underwear that only I knew lay closest to his soft upper body, those childish bright yellow suspenders with markings of a tape measure, and durable steel-toed boots that fit snugly over two layers of tube socks and one pair of woolies.

I watched Curtis' eyes but pretended not to understand. We had been through this before: I refuse to acknowledge my responsibility, imploring him to act. As a result of his sadness, though, he can't speak the words. A look is all he can muster and his silence allows me to exist in my fantasy world where I don't have to leave him and drive two hours back to college.

"It's almost 7 am. You have been sitting here for the past 20 minutes. It's time to go," Curtis finally spoke.

I stood up.

"I have to go. I have class at 9:05. I must go."

Curtis' father coaxed me toward the front door, "Sweetheart, we'll see you next weekend. We'll miss you."

Accompanying me to my car, Curtis responded to the look of regret in my eyes by placing one last simple, sweet kiss on my lips.

I hesitated.

*Maybe he will ask me not to leave? Tell me to stay, please?*

He smiled, "I love you. I'll see you soon."

As I drove up Hill Street, the golden sun shone on Curtis' lonely figure in my rear-view mirror.

Eight months later, in the fall of 1996, I rubbed Curtis' feet with his favorite aloe vera lotion as we lay in my twin bed in my dorm room at Middlebury. The scent reminded us of the past summers when I bathed my tanned skin with it every night. Our eyes smiled at one another kindly.

"Are you happy?" I asked confidently.

"Yes," he replied.

Stroking my palm up and down the inside arch of his foot, I noticed his hard, rough heel. "Work must have been busy this week."

He nodded and then said, "Did I tell you about the guy at work that I had dinner with last night?"

"Kind of," I replied as I concentrated on the knotted tendon below his big toe.

"I wore the Dalmatian tie. He asked me if my girlfriend gave it to me and if she was from around here."

"And, what did you say?"

"Yes, she's my girlfriend. No, her family lives in Connecticut. She goes to college here in Vermont. And so he asks me more about you: what year you are; your major; your interests. I told him that you were wonderful and mentioned that you were graduating in the spring.

Smiling, I gently released his foot and applied more lotion to my hands.

"And, then he said, 'Oh, a senior? You know what that means.'"

Silence.

I lifted his other foot preparing to massage it.

"And so then the guy said, 'You know, the big C word.'"

"Oh?" My eyes met his. "Did he ask you when you were buying me my ring?" I asked in a playful tone.

"Yes," Curtis answered seriously.

"Is she still getting married?" I dropped his foot on its heel. We rarely brought up his ex-girlfriend.

"Oh, I didn't tell you? She's married. I ran into some of her friends the other night. They said it was nice."

"I'll never like her. I can't even say her name without getting upset."

"You never even knew her," Curtis replied.

"You're right. I didn't."

"Can't we just forget all of that stuff? It happened so long ago." I smiled at Curtis.

"Well, one good thing came out of all of that," Curtis said as his eyes met mine.

"Oh, yeah, what's that?" I whispered as I snuggled his feet against my warm body.

"I got you."

# Birthday Wishes

Almost two years later, on the morning of August 18th, 1998, Curtis' 25th birthday, a ray of light that peeked through a crack in our bedroom window shade woke me up. As always, Curtis had been awake since before dawn. Turning onto his side, he wrapped his arm around me and enveloped me with his body on our bed that we had shared for more than a year. Two months after my college graduation, we rented a second floor apartment in New Haven, Vermont, from my former college tennis coach. Despite the fact that we owned minimal furniture, our first home had all that we needed: large windows, hardwood floors, and just enough space for the two of us to share.

"I love you," Curtis whispered. I loved to wake up to his sweet voice and warm body. He made me feel safe. Wanted. Loved. Throughout the eight years that I had known Curtis, the last three of which we formally dated, I treasured the moments that he held me, and, yet, I always sensed foreboding that the feelings of security and contentment would not last. I suppose it was natural for this fear to creep in since I often had to leave him to go to school or to pursue other interests of mine. Certainly his unwillingness to commit to a relationship also contributed to my foreboding over the years. And I would suspect that even after we moved in together, I periodically felt this way because Curtis continued to work construction for his friend, Joe, in Danville on his days off from the plant. On those nights he would stay at his parents'. Of course, I hated when he traveled to Danville because he left me alone. I could only go with him every other weekend when I wasn't working at my new job as assistant tennis pro at a local country club. At the beginning of the summer I had left my full-time development job at my alma mater to pursue my love of teaching and coaching tennis.

My back was to him; he pressed himself into me.

I turned toward him, "Happy Birthday, baby."

He smiled as he pulled me closer. I pushed forward as he pulled back. We both wanted to lead; neither of us knew how to follow. Hot and tired, he did what he always did: he rolled on top. I grasped his broad shoulders with my small hands and then slid my hands down, sculpting his baby soft back. He buried his face into the soft of my neck as we moved in silence. We always moved perfectly when he thought he was in control but it was my prompts that led us. Although I wanted to ask him to slow down and relish in the time that we had with one another, I had grown to understand that he considered a moment of desire to be intimacy.

I heard a strange hollow noise escape from him.

I stopped.

"Don't ever leave me again. Please," Curtis whispered.

It was not like Curtis to expel too much emotion verbally, but he had been acting strangely the last few weeks. I figured he was overworked and overtired. Perhaps when one's body is exhausted, it forces the mind to exert itself in order to make up for what it cannot physically illustrate. Selfishly, though, I appreciated this rare moment. Although I knew he loved me, it was nice to hear that he thought he couldn't live without me. I had always thought that I couldn't live without him.

"Never," I whispered.

He jumped out of bed. I watched his dimpled buttocks strut out the bedroom door. "Come on," he pleaded. "We don't want to be late."

Living with Curtis for the past year felt wonderful. It had been a long year for me, though. A few months after we moved in together, I had surgery for an ovarian cyst that had grown very large. The doctor cut open the right ovary, removed the cyst and was able to save the ovary. I worried excessively leading up to the surgery; I feared losing an ovary or that they would find something terrible once they went inside my body. I struggled, too, with Curtis living with me in New Haven half of the time and in Danville the other half. The past few months, though, we spent more time together walking, biking, and playing tennis. And, we planned to spend the day alone, just the two of us, at The Great Escape in New York.

I rolled over and saw the green neon stereo alarm clock illuminating 7:11 am. I crawled out of bed and opened the window blinds. The light blue sky greeted me but I could see the dark clouds in the distance. Just Curtis' luck. I walked out of the bedroom and into the kitchen.

"Should we still go?" I tried to hide my disappointment.

"I don't know. What do you think?" Curtis' sadness shined right through.

"It's your birthday. You decide."

Forty minutes into the trip, we stopped for breakfast. Curtis ordered a ham, cheese, onion, and pepper omelet with bacon, home fries, and wheat toast.

As Curtis shoveled the egg mixture onto the toast and into his mouth, I spewed my thoughts. "The past year has been crazy. Not bad, just different. Bills, jobs – well, my job – you've always had a job. Life isn't so simple anymore. Remember just last year, I'd drive up north every other weekend and we'd spend 48 hours together in a row? I miss that. I miss you."

"Uh huh," Curtis replied as he gulped his coffee and devoured his home fries, which were smothered in ketchup.

"Don't get me wrong," I continued. "The past few months have been great. Even though I have 12-hour days on the courts and you have 12-hour days at the plant, we're figuring it out. It's been a great summer. I am nervous for the fall."

"Yup," Curtis reached over to my plate with his fork and stabbed at my half-eaten chocolate chip pancake.

"Let's get married."

"What?"

"Just checking," I smiled. I doubted sometimes if Curtis really heard me. I was grateful that after so many years I had learned how to share all of my thoughts with him. But even if I spoke the words, there was no guarantee that he interpreted them the way I had intended.

"I know that you're ready," Curtis validated my thoughts of doubt. "I want to marry you. Just not yet."

Although I understood why he wouldn't marry me until he felt as though his career was established, I hated that he wasn't ready. I hated that he was asking me to wait. Even though most of my friends thought that I was rushing things and that I should also establish a career before even thinking about marriage, I had already waited for eight years. I couldn't stand the thought of waiting any longer.

We spent the afternoon of Curtis' birthday walking around The Great Escape, riding amusement rides, watching the shows, eating cheeseburgers, fries, ice cream, and cotton candy, and laughing. Curtis loved to be entertained.

The last ride we encountered promoted itself as the scariest roller coaster in New England. Standing in front of us in the line was a five- or six-year-old boy.

"So, pal, are you up for this one?" Curtis asked.

The young boy smiled at Curtis. "Yes, sir."

I envisioned our child, holding Curtis' hand, begging his father to take him for another ride.

A little after 5 pm, we left the unfamiliar town. Making our way along Route 22A, we witnessed the black clouds swiftly moving over Lake Champlain, towards home. I glanced over at Curtis and watched the dexterity and ease with which he handled a vehicle. With his left forearm guiding the wheel, his left hand held the empty 20 oz Diet Coke bottle at just the right angle so that he could flawlessly spit the tobacco juice. He almost never chewed tobacco in front of me; he didn't think it was right. It didn't bother me. He said he was really tired and needed a pick-me-up for the drive home. Although he wanted a beer, he didn't drink and drive unless he was cruising the back roads of the Northeast Kingdom.

Curtis turned up the volume on the radio music so that it was no longer just background noise. His fingers tapped the steering wheel as he sang out loud to the music.

I smiled as I watched Curtis. I struggled transitioning from college student to full-time employee. I disliked my first real job and chose to take a hiatus to spend the summer where I loved to be, on the tennis courts. I worried every day about what I wanted to be when I grew up. At that moment, though, all was right in the world.

As I reached for the radio controls in order to turn down the volume, I shared my joy.

"Curtis, I wish that we could spend all of our days like this. Just me and you."

"Are you ever going to be satisfied with what you have?" His tone carried a hint of resentment.

"Where'd that come from?" I asked.

He stared straight ahead and answered as though he was annoyed, "You're always going on and on about how you wish this and you want that."

"I just want you, Curtis. That's all I've ever wanted."

I worried that with the change of season would come our old routine, so I continued, "I want you to stop running. Three and four 12-hour shifts and then in between you run back to Danville to work with Joe. And then there's your uncle and the farm. Oh, and the projects for your mom, work for your dad, stuff with your brothers. When are you going to stop, Curtis? When are you going to stop long enough to realize that I'm here, waiting for you to commit, just like I've always been?"

"Why can't you appreciate me for who I am?" Curtis was irritated.

"If I saw you, I would." I was angry.

"You make it sound like I don't even care about you," the volume of his voice increased. Curtis' voice, unlike mine, shouted when he was really upset.

"Curtis, do you ever listen to me?" I said in a whisper. "We live in a town where we don't know anyone. Up until this summer, I would work all day, make you dinner, and you'd come home after eight. We'd eat and be in bed by nine, and you'd be gone by five the next morning. And when you weren't working at the plant, you'd go home to work in Danville and to your family. The little time off together that we did have, we'd spend up north with your family. I don't want to go back to that. These past few months have been so nice. I've loved walking, biking, and playing tennis with you. I've loved introducing you to my friends who still live around here. I've loved just hanging out here in our apartment. I'm ready for us to focus on us. I've spent the last eight years waiting to be done with school so that I could be with you. Half of the time we've shared our apartment, you've been gone. I've loved you being here, with me, for a majority of the time this summer. I want more of that."

At that moment, I blamed Curtis' family and friends for the fact that he spent so much time in Danville. I didn't know then what I later learned. Curtis really loved being in Danville. He was afraid that I would never be satisfied there; he didn't think it had anything to offer me.

"What is it that you want?" Curtis' tone didn't carry even a hint of resignation.

"I want us to figure out how we can be here more often. I want to feel as though you want to be with me and that you need me. I want you to be my family," I said.

Silence.

Feeling rejected, my anger turned into resignation, "You know what, Curtis. Forget me. I'm worried about you. I think that you need to slow down. Take care of you. If you don't, one of these days you're going to get sick."

Silence.

That night I lay awake on my side of the bed. Curtis lay awake on his. Thank God for the thunder and for the fact that he lay with his back toward me; he couldn't hear me gulping for air or see my tear-soaked face. I hated to hurt him, but I was 23, and at the time I thought I was ready for marriage and a family. I inched over to his side, slid my arm between his and his warm upper body and clutched his hand in mine.

"I've been thinking of looking into a part-time building job around here so I don't have to go to Danville on my days off from the plant," Curtis confided. "Burlington maybe. Maybe someday it could earn us enough money and I could build houses full-time. That's what I've always wanted."

I didn't know it at the time but a month prior Curtis had sent an email to a college in Burlington inquiring about their BA and engineering programs. Curtis had been listening to me all along.

"Baby, I don't want you to do this for me."

"I would be doing it for us."

"I just want you to be happy, Curtis. That's all I've ever wanted."

"If you were trying to get rid of me nicely, you failed."

"Happy Birthday, Curtis."

# The Diagnosis

The disease came upon us so suddenly. In September, less than two weeks after our excursion to The Great Escape for Curtis' birthday, he began to complain of sore legs. And then a few days later he could no longer carry a concrete panel up a step. A few weeks later, his right bicep ached. His normal eight-hour-a-day sleep pattern became exaggerated. He started to go to bed at seven and sleep through the night until seven or eight in the morning. He appeared discouraged, and some days I was sure he was slipping into depression. Curtis loved to work. One day, though, he didn't want to get out of bed to go to the plant.

"I don't think I can go to work today," he stated.

"How are you feeling?" I asked.

"Fine," he replied.

He got himself out of bed, showered, and to the plant. That evening, instead of driving to Danville after his shift, he returned to our apartment. He had dark circles under his eyes and his face was pale.

"Why don't you take the day off tomorrow, Curtis?"

"I can't do that."

"Well, then let me help you."

"With what?"

"I don't know. I feel like you need help."

He slept for fourteen hours that night.

I suppose that I knew something wasn't right but I was too busy to be too worried. It was my first month as the Middlebury College men's assistant tennis coach. I spent most of September at practice or traveling with the team. I did urge Curtis to take a daily vitamin, though, and to sleep more, work less, and to drink more water. I figured that he was just overtired, dehydrated, and lacking proper nutrition. He replaced chewing tobacco with sunflower seeds and drank only a few beers on his days off from the grueling 12-hour shifts at the plant.

One night near the end of September, the first time I had really seen Curtis in over a week because of our work schedules, I asked him to get me a gallon of milk from the refrigerator. I watched as he struggled to lift it with his right arm. A half an hour later he asked me to help him get up from the kitchen chair. His legs could not lift the weight of his own body. I was suddenly certain that something was very wrong.

As we lay in our bed that night, I asked, "Curtis, your grandmother, your mom's mom, died at a young age, right? Do you know what she died of?" I thought of his grandmother at that moment because Curtis' youngest aunt, Judy, had recently given each family member an eight-by-ten black and white framed photograph of her, and Curtis had placed her framed silhouette on our bureau. When Judy presented the pictures to everyone I was shocked at how much Curtis looked like her. And I wondered why I had never seen a picture of this woman before or heard her name spoken at the countless family gatherings I had attended over the years. Although I know why I thought of his grandmother that night while we lay in the darkness in our apartment, I am not sure why I asked Curtis how she had died. But I did.

He answered, "No one ever talks about it."

That same week, while Curtis was in Danville, he walked out of *The Danville General Store* with a coffee in hand. As he waved to a friend who drove by, he tripped over his own right foot and landed in a heap on the ground. He didn't mention the incident to anyone at the time; he told me about it a few weeks later.

On the last day of September, he stumbled into his parents' house. His father yelled at him for drinking too much again, but when Curtis announced that he was sober and confided in him what he had been experiencing the past month or so, his father begged him to go to the hospital. Curtis allowed his father to drive him that afternoon. Curtis explained his symptoms. The nurses took blood. Then they took more. Then they told him to go home and wait. Curtis and I returned on October fifth for more tests and again on the seventh for even more. Two days later he returned and they performed a muscle biopsy. They said that this was the easiest way to detect trichinosis. Trichinosis? Curtis and I had been to a pig roast in August. Maybe the pork had been undercooked? While we waited for the results, we spent our nights thinking of the worms that were living in Curtis' body. If only we were that lucky.

Three days later, a doctor called to say it wasn't trichinosis and that they would like us to see a neurologist. We returned on October 14, but our appointments with the neurologist seemed useless. They tested and retested his reflexes, his inability to rise from a chair, his atrophied right bicep and both quadriceps. He underwent an EMG (electromyography), a NVC (nerve conduction velocity) and an MRI but nothing could be concluded.

They asked for clues. "Any family history of neurological problems?"

"No," Curtis answered.

In late October, my former college tennis coach who was also our landlord and my current boss, asked Curtis to fix up another apartment that she owned which was located just a mile from our apartment. I had confided in her that Curtis wasn't feeling well. We thought maybe he just needed to stop running back and forth between our apartment in New Haven and Danville. With his second job just down the road, Curtis remained in New Haven on his days off from the plant. I witnessed his rapid physical decline on a daily basis. I recall that Curtis' father was also worried at this point. My family was worried but not overly so. Although I kept my parents and sisters abreast of our situation, they were all in Connecticut and had not seen Curtis since August, when he looked as though he was in peak physical condition. I don't think anyone who didn't see him could have imagined how a seemingly healthy 25-year-old could have grown so weak in such a short period of time.

In November, Curtis' mother, having recently returned to Danville from an extended business trip in Amish country, called me while Curtis was at work. She told me she had something to tell me and asked me to keep it to myself for now. She told me that she didn't want Curtis to worry.

Her speech was racy, her tone full of panic, "Before my aunt died in the late 60s, she told me that she knew she was dying of what my mother had died of. My aunt told me that it was a family curse. A few years ago, my sisters and I discovered a family member's diary. It confirmed that my mom, Curtis' grandmother, died of progressive bulbar palsy at the age of 40 in 1962, and her sister, our aunt, died of progressive muscular atrophy less than a decade later. She was 49."

Curtis' mom explained that her mom had lost her voice and the use of her arms but could still walk when she died of respiratory distress. Her aunt lost the ability to walk but could still use her arms and eat when she also died of respiratory distress.

My heart was pulsating, my underarms sweating, my hands shaking. I fought back the tears. Three weeks beforehand, after the tests for trichinosis had come back negative, my assumption that something was very wrong increased dramatically. I was determined to find the answer, so I spent my nights in front of the computer searching for an explanation for Curtis' fatigue and loss of strength. I had tried so hard to resist the temptation to assume the worst even after discovering various horrible diseases on the Internet. Progressive bulbar palsy and progressive muscular atrophy. My mind recalled that these were particularly devastating.

I told Curtis' mom that I had to check something and that I'd call her back.

I ran to the computer and searched the Internet. I discovered that Curtis' grandmother and great-aunt had died of motor neuron diseases that are related to ALS, Lou Gehrig's disease. I scanned the hundreds of words on the computer screen to find what I had remembered reading a few nights before:

*"The majority of patients with adult-onset ALS (90 percent) have no family history of ALS, and present as an isolated case. This is called sporadic ALS (SALS), and although there is likely a genetic predisposition involved, SALS is not directly inherited in a family. The remaining ten percent of persons with ALS have a close second family member with ALS, which is referred to as familial ALS (FALS)."*[1]

At that moment, I knew that Curtis was suffering from familial ALS and although I could not recall any specifics of the disease, I remembered reading that it was almost always fatal and that practically every site I had searched the past nights described ALS with these words:

*"At present, there is no known cause or cure."*

I could not hold back the tears. I let them flow freely. As I sat on our blue office chair in our tiny living room, I pulled my knees up to my chest, wrapped myself in my own arms, and rocked gently. I thought of Curtis. For the past two months he had told me that he was sure that whatever he had could be fixed. He told me to stop worrying. He told me that everything would be okay.

Just the other night, Curtis had confided in me, "You know, after the extra sleep, vitamins and better nutrition didn't help, I really did think that something was just wrong with my back and spine and the chiropractor visits really did seem to help. Yesterday my chiropractor told me that he can't fix me."

He needed to know the truth.

Curtis' grandmother and great-aunt had died within ten months of their initial symptoms.

Curtis was in his third month.

If a solution was to be found, I figured that it had to be discovered quickly. I did some more research on the Internet and found a doctor in Boston who specialized in familial ALS. I called Curtis' mother back, told her about ALS and about the doctor. She suggested that if I were going to call him to mention the last name Farr. I called the doctor and spoke to his secretary. I described Curtis' symptoms that I thought were indicative of ALS. She explained there was a six-month wait for an appointment. I dropped the name Farr and she put me on hold for ten minutes. When she returned, she stated that they wanted to meet Curtis as soon as possible. I scheduled a visit for later that month.

That night when Curtis came home from work I shared with him what his mother had told me.

He responded, "I don't have ALS."

And then he went to bed.

The next day Curtis and I drove down to the original hospital in New Hampshire for a scheduled appointment with the neurologist we had been seeing for almost a month. He informed us that none of the tests were conclusive.

He continued. "I am leaning toward a diagnosis of ALS but this doesn't make complete sense to me because the progression of your case is so marked."

This was the first time the neurologist mentioned ALS to us. I told the doctor what Curtis' mom had told me about the family history of ALS.

I watched the expression on his face turn from confusion to empathy. Severe empathy.

"I am going to refer you to an ALS specialist in Burlington," he spoke quietly.

"I already made an appointment with a familial ALS specialist in Boston," I replied.

On the ride home that day, we remained silent until Curtis, staring straight ahead at the open road, asked, "Do you really think I have ALS?"

"Yes," I answered as I stole a glance at him while also trying to drive.

"But they know a lot more about it now, right?" he asked. He still wouldn't look at me.

At that moment I realized that my boyfriend was mortal. He was 25-years-old. We were supposed to be married. Buy a home. Have children. Get a dog. I told him a bit about what I had learned about the disease on the Internet. As I spoke, I watched him more than the road. An ashen color crept from his chin to his forehead until it drowned in his thick, healthy, dark brown hair.

"I'm not going to die, am I?" he asked as he turned to face me.

Darkness clouded his beautiful green eyes.

My eyes searched his eyes for the answer. *A hint? Anything?* I told Curtis that there was one FDA- approved drug to slow down the progression of ALS, but there was still no cure.

Curtis replied, "Yeah, well, it isn't gonna kill me."

On Tuesday, November 24th, two days before Thanksgiving, we traveled to Massachusetts General Hospital (MGH) in Boston from Danville. Up until this point, Curtis and I hadn't spoken much about ALS or his family's history of the disease. Looking back on it, I am sure that we were both in shock and in denial. Curtis' mother and eldest brother, Chad, accompanied us on the three-hour drive. Chad was able to keep Curtis' spirits light by joking with him the entire way. Once we arrived at the hospital, Curtis and I met with a neurologist. More questions. More tests. After a few hours the young doctor impressed upon us that Curtis could have a "marked rapidly progressive lower motor neuron syndrome," but that there was still a chance it was just Lyme's disease or a number of other ailments whose symptoms imitate those of ALS. They took 13 vials of blood in an attempt to rule out even more diseases.

"We don't want you to worry until we know for sure," were the doctor's last words as we left the examination room.

We returned to the waiting room and greeted Curtis' mom, who was gripping a stack of papers. They were only papers. But they revealed that Curtis' maternal great-great-great-great grandfather, Samuel Farr, also suffered from what was later called ALS. He was born in 1804 and died in 1865 after being ill for two years. His disease was referred to as a "creeping paralysis" in Massachusetts General Hospital's medical records and he was one of the first people to have been recorded to have this type of disease at this hospital. Samuel's brother died of ALS when he was 40. Their sister died of ALS when she was 54.

Out of Samuel's eight children, four died of ALS. His daughter was only 27. His three sons, one of whom was Curtis' great-great-great grandfather all died of ALS when they were each 40-something. MGH had medical journals from the 1800s in which the Farr family was recorded; the disease was referred to as Farr's disease before it was labeled Lou Gehrig's disease after the famous New York Yankee died in 1941. Approximately 50 percent of every generation of Curtis' family had suffered from FALS (familial ALS) since Samuel Farr in the 1800s.

With the confirmation that Curtis' family was, indeed, descendents of the Farr family, the doctors were obligated to pursue a diagnosis of familial ALS.

The medical write-up from that visit states, "*This gentleman appears to be suffering from a marked rapidly progressive lower motor neuron syndrome. The only sign of an upper motor neuron affliction is his positive jaw jerk. This, in association with his family history, obligates us to pursue a diagnosis of familial amyotrophic lateral sclerosis as well as of autoimmune and other inheritable motor neuron diseases.*"

While we waited for the definitive genetic test, Curtis and I discovered that Curtis' maternal great-grandmother had researched the disease that had harmed her ancestors. She had written pages of information and had shared much of the information with MGH. Curtis' mother told us that when Curtis' grandmother was afflicted with the disease in 1962, Curtis' great-grandmother was so distressed that she had passed the "family curse" on to her daughter that she literally threw her copies of the facts into the fire; the illness was viewed as a curse on the family, not as a genetic disease. When Curtis' great-aunt started to experience symptoms a few years after Curtis' grandmother's death, she pulled Curtis' mother aside, told her about the curse (which indicates that Curtis' great-grandmother had shared the information with Curtis' great aunt before throwing away the research) and warned her not to have children.

Curtis, his mother, Chad and I were silent throughout the three-hour ride home to Danville that evening of November 24. Once we returned to Curtis' parents' house, Curtis struggled to climb the few stairs to his childhood bedroom and then crawled into bed. He remained silent. Beside him, I stroked his hair. Once Curtis fell asleep I crept downstairs to the walkout basement level where Curtis' father's barbershop was located. Curtis' parents sat across from one another, silent. I saw the look of despair and desperation on both of their faces. I felt devastated. I don't remember what, if anything, the three of us said to one another that night except that I do recall Curtis' father asking me how our boy was doing. I told him that I didn't know. I remember watching him drown in his own tears. I also remember Curtis' mother talking about how she had received a letter some time back, years beforehand, from distant family members concerning the fact that one of her cousins had been diagnosed with a horrible disease but that she didn't know or understand the significance. Looking back, that evening was the first of many moments that would forever bind the three of us: we each realized, independently of one another, that our lives would be forever redefined by what was happening to Curtis.

I don't recall how Curtis and I spent the next day but I do know that we didn't discuss ALS. Curtis didn't bring it up and when I mentioned it, Curtis told me that he didn't want to talk about it. We spent the first half of the following day, Thanksgiving, with his family and then the second half with my family. My parents and Tricia had driven up to my grandmother Bubbles' apartment in St. Johnsbury for the holiday. Heather had a new boyfriend and felt as though she couldn't leave him. My grandfather, PopPop, was born and raised in St. Johnsbury, and after he and my grandmother retired from their jobs in Connecticut, they spent their summers at their cottage on Joe's Pond which they had owned since my mother was a teenager. They spent their winters in the apartment in St. Johnsbury that my grandfather's mother had lived in for many years until her death. After my grandfather died of a heart attack in 1987 at the age of 64, Bubbles continued to spend her summers at the pond and her winters traveling or at the apartment. During Thanksgiving dinner that evening, Curtis told my family that he didn't think he had ALS. He was sure there was another explanation.

The next morning, Curtis' parents, Curtis and I drove up to Montreal, Canada, for a second opinion. My aunt, a doctor in Toronto, had arranged the visit. That doctor told us exactly what we had heard in Boston: Curtis' condition appeared to present itself as ALS because all of the tests for other conditions that had been performed thus far were negative. And the family history of ALS, of course, was compelling.

After that appointment, Curtis spoke about his condition frankly and confidently, "If I do have ALS, I am going to beat it."

A few days after Thanksgiving, I wrote in my journal, *"Two full months of absolute bewilderment, pain, waiting, anticipation, horror, faith. Yes, faith. Please let him be okay. I do not want him to suffer. I do not want him to feel pain. I do not want to live without him. I cannot imagine life without him. We are so happy. We are like one. I finally understand his frustrations and his moods and how important being busy, being with his family and spontaneity are to him. He sees how important exercise is to me and how I need to have everything planned. Bam. ALS came out of nowhere. Miracles can happen. And he is so upbeat and positive. If anyone can fight to survive, it is he. And he has me, my family and his family to support him. I have started taking pictures of Curtis with his family. Not sure if we'll ever need them but something is telling me to do it. I have put my life on hold. I am still teaching tennis which is good but haven't been at the apartment for a week. I can't bear to be away from Curtis. He shaved his beard yesterday. He looks so young. So innocent. Too young to suffer and to be in pain. His upper legs appear so thin. Can't we save him? I haven't cried in a while. I think I got that all out the first month and a half reading all the research and imagining the possibilities. Now, we're waiting some more. For the visit in December. For happy news. Curtis is going to be okay. Curtis is going to be okay and then so will I."*

Over the next 15 days, Curtis and I went to his physical therapy appointments every other day. We also went to the occupational therapy appointment that the doctor had insisted upon. Curtis had not been able to physically work a 12-hour shift since October, and our Boston doctor extended the New Hampshire doctor's original orders by declaring that Curtis could only work at the plant for a maximum of eight hours a day. On December 11th, Curtis went to his work's Christmas party. His co-workers had insisted he go even though it was at 7 pm and he was now usually in bed by that time. They awarded him with the "Employee of the Year Award." He was so proud.

On December 15, Curtis and I returned to Boston for the definitive diagnosis. Before we entered the doctor's office, I was certain that Curtis had ALS. I did not fear the care or comfort he would require. I was afraid of the day he would leave me and wondered how I would continue to work to develop a relationship that could cease to exist in less than a year. Curtis had not mentioned the words ALS to me since the day after Thanksgiving, after our appointment with the doctor in Canada, when he told me, "If I do have ALS, I am going to beat it."

Throughout the two weeks of waiting for this doctor's appointment, I watched him try to conceal his awkward leg and right arm movements from everyone he knew. Those limbs were no longer limber and nimble; they were stiff. I watched him try to ride the stationary bike as his physical therapist encouraged him to do. He was exhausted after just a few minutes. And, then, after I would help him get off the bike, I would stare at his incredibly thin legs. Almost all of his leg muscles appeared to be gone. Just a few months prior we had been biking over ten miles together up and down the hills of New Haven and Danville.

The doctor led us into the stark white room. I stood by as Curtis eased himself into the orange padded chair that was located next to the doctor's desk. After taking off my knapsack, which contained Curtis' vitamins and all of my own research, I sat on a black plastic chair in the corner.

The doctor asked, "Curtis, how are you feeling?"

"Great. But I can't walk without a cane. And I can't lift a gallon of milk with my right arm."

"How are you doing?" the doctor asked me.

"Worried."

Curtis excused my behavior. "She's always worrying."

"Well, as you two know," the doctor stated, "I am prepared to let you know what we believe is happening here with Curtis' body. Let me start by saying that the tests we have received back were negative..."

The only word we heard was negative.

Curtis' head rose and the darkness immediately disappeared from his eyes.

My confused stare met his, and we smiled.

He silently mouthed, "Told you."

In one second, I pictured our future wedding, dog, house, and children.

The doctor continued, "With that in mind, we have concluded that you have ALS. We are still waiting for the genetic test, which is the only test that has not come back yet."

The darkness reappeared as Curtis' gaze turned to the door.

"I am so sorry." The doctor continued to explain that they would do everything they could to help us. Another doctor entered and asked us if we would travel to Vancouver so that other doctors could use Curtis as a model for familial ALS in its early stage. Then, a third doctor rushed in and presented us with an experimental double-blind study that Curtis might be eligible to join. We said we thought we were interested. Instantaneously, a nurse and the study's manager filed through the door and stated that all they needed to do was draw a little blood and test Curtis' breathing to make sure he was still healthy enough to participate. In the middle of this procedure, we were shuffled out of the room and led into another office, where the head neurologist was waiting. He introduced himself, apologized for having to meet us under these circumstances, asked us if we understood the diagnosis, and did we have any questions.

I looked toward Curtis. His eyes searched mine for the answer.

"No, I think we are pretty much set," I replied.

The doctor left the office.

At last, we were alone.

Tears crept into my eyes slowly, at first. Then they flooded my senses. I could not see or hear anything but the letters, ALS, until I heard Curtis ask me to stop.

I saw Curtis' face through my tears.

He said, "Don't worry. Everything is going to be okay. I am not going to let this hurt us."

Somehow, I believed him.

And all I could say was, "I love you."

Amazingly, it seemed to be enough.

Days later it was confirmed that Curtis had familial ALS. He did have the A4V mutated SOD-1 on chromosome 21, which he presumably inherited from his mother. Basically, the gene that codes SOD was misspelled. If you have the mutation, there is an 85 percent chance it will "trigger" at some point in your life, but the doctors have no idea why it triggers when it does and why it doesn't trigger in the other 15 percent of cases.

We had finally discovered why Curtis' body was turning on itself. I wrote emails to my extended family and closest friends in order to inform them of our situation. I also sent Christmas cards to our families and friends and included a picture of Curtis and me: we were seated on our maroon futon couch that we had recently purchased for our small living area. A green, blue, and yellow-flowered down comforter was draped over the futon. I was nestled close to him and his arm was wrapped around me. The photograph captured his thumb stroking my bare upper arm right below the hem of my casual red short-sleeved shirt. I was not flashing my usual bright smile. My half-smile illustrated a hint of apprehension as though I was trying hard to hold it all together even though I couldn't comprehend what we would be facing. Curtis, dressed in his dark green mock turtleneck, wasn't smiling. His slight closed-mouth grin was surrounded by his full goatee. Our eyes, though, shone brightly. Years later, when I looked at this photo again for the first time since we had sent the news that Curtis was facing a terminal illness, I recognized the hope and determination in our eyes.

The note that I sent to accompany the photo stated, in part, "Unfortunately, we don't have very joyful news for the holidays. Curtis was diagnosed with ALS yesterday. It has been a very long fall and now the real battle begins. Curtis is shocked but upbeat and positive. He is still laughing, joking, and smiling. It is certainly overwhelming but he believes that he will combat this disease. I believe in his strength, and we are going to fight it together."

Three days after the diagnosis, Curtis and I met 16 of his family members in Florida for a Caribbean cruise. Curtis' Aunt Judy, who worked for a cruise line, had started to plan the trip in November after it was first thought that ALS could be the culprit. Curtis spent a majority of the time on the ship drinking. On the second to last day, after my daily workout, I was walking back from the steam room and was greeted by Curtis' parents.

"You need to find Curtis," his mother stated. "He's with his brothers and is in tough shape."

I found him at the bar. A small silver-plated cup on a string hung from his neck. They had spent the early afternoon at a wine tasting. But then they had sauntered to the pool to drink daiquiris and now were in the Schooner Bar. They each had a beer in front of them as well as two empty shot glasses. Curtis' face was flushed and he was laughing hysterically. He looked as though he didn't have a care in the world. His speech was slurred. I couldn't understand a word he was saying. I was disgusted. But I had never been able to change him. I certainly wasn't going to try then. I smiled at him, gave him a kiss on the cheek, and walked away.

I returned to the ship's gym and hopped on the treadmill. I ran faster and faster as I envisioned Curtis drinking his way through the disease. Up until that moment, I hadn't thought about what our daily lives would entail as his disease progressed. Now all I could imagine was him drunk all the time. After running for 45 minutes, I switched to the elliptical. Thirty minutes later, exhausted, I wandered around the ship searching for Curtis. I needed to tell him that I wasn't sure I could stand by him if he was going to give up and not even try to live with and possibly conquer ALS. He wasn't in any of the ship's bars or the restaurants. I found his brothers, though, at one of the bars.

"He left here a bit ago. He could barely walk. But, he wouldn't let me help him. He wanted to make his way back to your cabin on his own," one of his brothers informed me.

I returned to our tiny cabin. The stench made me ill. Curtis was passed out on his back on the bed. Vomit covered his shirt, shorts, and his hair. It was all over the sheets, curtains, and on the rug. Opening the small door to the bathroom, I almost hurled myself. There was barely an inch of floor or wall that wasn't covered with Curtis' throw up. I have never felt as disappointed in and sorry for another human being as I did him in that moment. Quietly, I sat beside him. I put my right hand on his chest to be sure that he was still breathing. Then, I scrubbed the bathroom, cleaned off the curtains, mopped up the rug, and stripped the sheet that covered him. I did not want him to remember. Two hours later, when Curtis awoke, I was sitting on the room's only chair crying.

"Please don't be mad," he said.

"We're beyond that, honey. You're lucky you're still alive. Your brothers told me you refused their help making your way back to the cabin. You can barely walk on your own sober. Did you plan on falling overboard?"

"Please don't go into the bathroom. I couldn't even stand up when I was heaving. I guess I'm lucky I didn't pass out in there. I'm done. No more."

# ALS, Lou Gehrig's Disease

Amyotrophic lateral sclerosis (ALS), commonly known as Lou Gehrig's disease, is a horrific disease. Not just because of what it does to the body, but because of what it doesn't do to the mind. As the victim's motor neurons die, the person is paralyzed body part by body part. The brain is spared, though, as are the senses, bowel, bladder, and sexual function. ALS "is an adult-onset, invariably fatal neurodegenerative disorder characterized by the progressive dysfunction and death of both the upper motor neuron (UMN) and the lower motor neuron (LMN) systems."[2] "The progressive degeneration of the motor neurons in ALS eventually leads to their death. When the motor neurons die, the ability of the brain to initiate and control muscle movement is lost. With voluntary muscle action progressively affected, patients in the later stages of the disease may become totally paralyzed. Yet, through it all, for the vast majority of people, their minds remain unaffected."[3]

Barring complications, ALS patients can live indefinitely if they choose to live with invasive life support (feeding tube and ventilator). The question of quality of life is raised and many factors are considered in order for a patient to decide upon his/her quality of life choices. In addition, because of the severely debilitating nature of ALS, most patients require one or more full-time caretakers in order to live throughout their illness.

It is estimated that as many as 30,000 Americans may have the disease at any given time. A little over 5,500 people in the United States are diagnosed with ALS each year. Half of all people affected with ALS live at least three or more years after diagnosis. Twenty percent of people with ALS live five years or more and up to ten percent will survive more than ten years.[4] There are medically documented cases of people in whom ALS "burns out," stops progressing or progresses at a very slow rate.[5]

Ultimately, though, ALS is almost always fatal, and, thus, the question of the patient's quality of life while living with ALS is as important as the medical research of ALS itself. There has been ample research on the social environment of ALS patients.

Two reports regarding ALS, *Correlates of Quality of Life in People with Motor Neuron Disease (MND)* and *Subjective Experience and Coping in ALS*, speak to the fact that social support greatly improves an ALS patient's quality of life and that family members greatly help ALS patients cope with the disease.

*The Quality of Life* report aimed to "examine whether self-generated ratings of QoL correlated with measures of physical impairment and self-reported functional status, psychological wellbeing and self-reported cognitive functioning and with factors such as social support." [6] The study found, interestingly enough, that one's physical strength and ability to perform functions (one's health), social life, mobility, leisure activities, or finances were not the highest rated in terms of an ALS patient's view on their quality of life. [7] Rather, "the degree of confiding/emotional support given by the closest person nominated was found to be positively correlated with global (QoL) ratings."[8] The data suggested "it is the emotional nature of support, rather than the practical nature, that a close person can supply that is important in influencing the perceived QoL of the person."[9]

*The Subjective Experience and Coping in ALS* report aimed to better understand how ALS patients cope with a terminal illness about which there is very little known. This report concluded, "Family members were most helpful in coping with the disease."[10] It was also stated, "The most frequently mentioned benefit for the ALS patients in our study was the family. Most ALS patients in Germany live at home with their families who are the main carers. If the family is the most important benefit for ALS patients, it must follow that family support has a direct impact on the quality of life of the patients."[11]

Although the goals of these two reports varied greatly, they both determined that the role of social support and care played by a person who is genuinely interested in the well-being of the patient has a positive effect on the patient's quality of life and ability to cope with a terminal illness.

These studies raise questions. Because the caretaker plays such a vital, central role in the care and well-being of the ALS patient, one would wonder, what role does the caretaker play in the patient's quality of life decisions? And what impact does the relationship of caretaker to patient have on the quality of life choices? The two studies discussed the patient's social environment and the effects that it has on them as a patient, but little attention has been paid to the caretaker. Caretakers support ALS patients fully; in particular, toward the end of the disease, the caretaker helps the patient perform all of his daily functions and, in essence, becomes the patient's life support. The focus of social studies has been on the patient him/herself rather than on the caretaker's psychological capacities, their understanding of themselves, and cultural notions attributed to them.

What is the self-understanding of the caretaker and how is he/she viewed by society? Like most MS, AIDS and cancer patients, persons battling ALS do not require hospitalization from the onset of the disease. Most patients live at home where a family member, significant other, or a hired person fulfills the role of the patient's caretaker for the duration of the disease. The term "caretaker" is interesting when looked at closely. "Caretaker," in the English language, means one that cares for a person diagnosed with a terminal illness. The term "caretaker" in the English language is also used to describe a person who cares for and prepares a dead person's body for its burial. In addition, what is the difference between the words "caretaker" and "nurse"? What is the difference between "caretaking" and "nursing," and how do these terms relate to the roles and functions when conducted in the patient's home versus a hospital? The term "caretaker" can imply desperate, tragic, and hopeless work; but some caretakers of ALS patients, and the ALS patients themselves, retain hope and faith throughout their terminal illness.

When Curtis was first diagnosed with ALS, I never thought of becoming his caretaker. And then later, when he did require someone to help him function and survive on a daily basis, I didn't think at all. There was no time to decide. Everything happened so quickly. I did the work automatically without realizing the role I had assumed. What I did know was that I loved him, and I couldn't imagine my life without him.

# Living Will

We began the new year, 1999, with a trip to Vancouver. Canadian doctors who were studying SOD-1 patients wanted to perform tests on Curtis, who at the age of 25 was considered a very young ALS patient. Although ALS can occur at any age, symptoms typically begin in persons between the ages of 55 and 75. And, in Curtis' family's documented lineage about which we were aware, only one other relative had developed ALS in their 20's. She was 27.

Curtis and I were grateful for the almost fully paid vacation. Even though we spent a majority of our days with doctors, we were able to see a beautiful city, eat good food, relax in the hotel's pool and the room and spend time together, alone. Curtis was still walking with a cane and we had to use a wheelchair on this trip; he wasn't able to walk long distances. Although it was very difficult for me to wheel Curtis up and down the snowy and icy streets of Vancouver, we were able to see a Canucks hockey game. We sat in the wheelchair-accessible section.

As the month of January came to a close, we realized that Curtis would soon lose the ability to climb the stairs to our second-floor apartment in New Haven. I spoke with our landlord and, with her permission, asked the first floor tenant if she would be willing to switch apartments with us.

"Sure. If you pay my January rent, pay for the cost of switching utilities and pay for the cost of moving my stuff to the second floor," she replied bluntly.

She knew our predicament. I couldn't believe she was asking

us to cover a month's rent. All she had to do was say, "no."

I called my mom in a panic. Where would we live? Perhaps we could move into the house in Danville that Curtis had helped build for his aunt and uncle? This particular aunt was one of Curtis' mother's three sisters and mom to Laurie (who had been my boss when I was a swimmer's aide and had first introduced me to Curtis that summer over eight years prior). They had not moved in, yet, and it was perfect. The first floor not only had an open living space such that the kitchen and living areas were one room, it also had a full bathroom. I called Curtis' mom to talk to her about this option. A few hours later she called back and said "yes." In fact, she said that Curtis' aunt and uncle preferred to remain in the parsonage of the Danville Methodist Church where they had been living while waiting for their retirement home to be constructed. That night I wrote in my journal, *"We're moving into a house that Curtis helped to build. Whoever said that dreams don't come true?"*

The idea to move to Danville came upon us suddenly, just as suddenly as ALS happened upon us, just as suddenly as I fell in love with Curtis that first summer. Looking back upon those events in my life, I acknowledge that all three of them occurred without me really realizing that they had happened. As much as I am a planner, one who thrives on order and routine, I am also a passionate person. And, once I have discovered a passion, the regular rules and regulations, the ideas and laws of what "should be," no longer apply. I push and push and push until I've worked for what I want. I had become who I was as a result of hard work and persistence. I believed that anything was possible.

On one of the last days of January, I gripped the blank living will that was folded in the right pocket of my red winter jacket as Chad drove us in his tan Chevy Tahoe through the snow-covered white mountains of New Hampshire toward Boston. Although petrified to discover Curtis' wishes, I knew that decisions needed to be made because in a few hours he would undergo surgery for an experimental double-blind study (a comparative study in which neither the patient nor the physician knows whether the patient is receiving the treatment of interest or the control treatment)[12]: a pump the size of a hockey puck would be surgically implanted under his skin in his abdominal area and a catheter would be thread under his skin from the pump into his spinal fluid. Two weeks later, we would return to Boston for the first of the monthly visits during which the drug would be injected with a needle into the pump. There was a 33 ⅓ percent chance that 50 mL of the experimental drug, the growth hormone BDNF, would be administered into the pump every month. There was the same chance that 100 mL would be inserted and, as with any double-blind study, an equal chance that he would get a placebo and, therefore, no BDNF at all. Curtis could not understand why they wouldn't just give all of the participants the 100 mL of the growth hormone.

"What do we have to lose?" he had asked.

I had minored in biology in college and learned that this was the way the medical world worked. Before the FDA can allow a drug to be available for the treatment of a disease, a double-blind study has to be performed in order to prove that the drug is effective. BDNF had been proven to slow down the progression of ALS in mice but this was the first time BDNF was being administered to humans for this purpose. Therefore, even if Curtis was to receive 100 mL of the drug, there was no guarantee it would slow down the progression of his disease.

Curtis' mother, seated to the left of me in the back seat, had urged Curtis to take part in this study; Curtis' father, seated to the right of me, had not said much to Curtis about the disease since the month before when he was diagnosed.

With half of his family as witnesses, and potential supporters, I pleaded with Curtis again, "We need to fill out this paperwork."

"What paperwork?" Chad asked from the driver's seat.

"It's nothing." Curtis turned and glared at me from the front passenger seat.

"Sweetheart, what paperwork are you talking about?" Curtis' father questioned and then spoke before I could answer, "He'll sign whatever it is you want him to sign."

"A living will," I declared.

"I told you, I'm not going to fill it out," Curtis mumbled as he stared straight ahead.

We were approaching the Old Man on the Mountain, which had been naturally carved in Cannon Mountain as a result of years of snow, wind, rain and, perhaps, intervention.

*I do not want to be the one to make these decisions. I do not want his family to make these decisions. Please help Curtis to be strong enough to realize his own wishes.*

I began again, "Curtis, if something goes wrong..."

"Nothing is gonna go wrong. I'm going to be fine. Would you stop your badgering?"

I turned and looked at Curtis' mother and then his father.

They both stared straight ahead.

I spoke, "Curtis, as the doctor told us, this surgery is not some minor deal. It's invasive and so it comes with risks. If something should happen, we need to know your wishes."

"I wish that you would shut up," Curtis snapped.

"Curtis Roger Vance, don't you speak to her like that," Curtis' father said sternly.

I continued, "Curtis, you are the only one who can make the decision regarding the quality of your life. None of us in this car knows what you want."

"You are forcing me to do something that is unnecessary and stupid. I won't do it."

Silence.

More silence.

Curtis' mother reached into her jacket pocket for a string of black licorice. Curtis' father rolled his thumbs in his lap. Chad turned on the radio and remained silent along with the others.

I wanted to shout. *Say something! Anything. Don't any of you get it? He's your son, your brother.* I felt my face turn bright red. The tears began to form and almost began to stream when Curtis turned, looked me in the eye, and smiled. "Let's talk about something else, okay? As I've said before, everything is going to be okay. Please don't get all worked up over nothing."

A few hours later, while Curtis was in surgery, Chad and I sat in the neurologist's office. Chad had asked me if I knew if it was possible for one to be tested for the gene; I led him to the head ALS doctor at the hospital. In the four months that Curtis had been sick, this was the first time I was with a doctor without Curtis.

The doctor informed Chad that he could be tested if he wished. We also learned that since Curtis had the gene, his mother presumably had it, for it is a dominant gene, and had not been proven to skip generations. With Curtis' mom likely having the gene, then each of her five children had a 50 percent chance of having it. The doctor also informed us, though, that although one may have the gene, there is "only" an 85 percent chance that the gene will trigger in that person's lifetime. So, Curtis' mother, who presumably has the gene, may never experience ALS, for the gene may never trigger. Would Chad want to know if he had the gene? If he found out he had it, would he spend the rest of his life wondering when and if it would trigger? If he didn't get tested, would he spend the rest of his life wondering if he had the gene? Chad and his wife already had two children. Did they want to know if their children had a chance of having the gene?

"Doctor, from what I've read, Curtis' case, the A4V mutation on the SOD-1 gene, is the worst possible form of ALS because it is the most progressive. Is this true?" I asked.

"Yes," replied the doctor.

"Is it also true, then, that we are talking less than a year?" I asked.

Chad stared at me.

The doctor drew a deep breath.

Curtis had not been given a timeline. He had never asked. When diagnosed the month before, we were told that no known cause or cure exists. We knew that years ago his grandmother and great aunt had died within less than a year of their initial symptoms. Curtis had not asked because he didn't want to know.

But I had to know. My eyes had already witnessed the day he could no longer rise from a chair without the aid of his arms. My ears had heard him swear while he attempted to climb the stairs in our apartment by gripping the handrails with all of his strength in order to pull his body up the flight. I was the one who had sat in the passenger seat of his new Honda Accord and witnessed the fear and disappointment on his face when he no longer had the power in his left leg to push down the clutch. He had only driven the car five times when he had to relinquish it to me. We swapped cars and he drove my automatic, until the other day when he could no longer do that, either. It was I who listened to his breathing once he fell asleep to try to gauge if it was deteriorating, too. While it was still rhythmic and deep now, I knew that someday it would become shallow and slow. I feared the day he could no longer stand on his own two feet.

We hadn't yet even talked about the issue of care. In fact, I hadn't even thought about it until this day in the doctor's office. Curtis was still walking with a cane, feeding and washing himself, speaking and eating. I had become his shadow, standing beside him in his every action, waiting to be needed, but I had not taken over. Would I be able to handle this responsibility?

I had always been responsible. The middle child in a family of three girls, I was the mediator, the person upon whom my sisters and parents depended. I had been a good student over the years, president of the Student Council in high school, captain of Varsity Tennis and Squash in college. I had the work ethic, discipline, and stamina to take over once Curtis' body could no longer do what it needed to do to survive, but would Curtis want me to? The funny thing is that it had nothing to do with a sense of responsibility. It didn't matter if Curtis wanted me to become his caretaker or not. At the time, I never thought about it this way at all. I just knew that I loved him and I wanted to spend every moment possible with him.

The doctor looked at Chad and then at me. "If nothing works, not the Rilutek, not the BDNF, and if he decides not to use any aids to keep him alive, then Curtis almost certainly has much less than a year to live."

Chad dropped his chin to his chest.

"From when the symptoms began or from the date of diagnosis?" I asked.

"His symptoms began in August?" the doctor questioned.

"Yes. Maybe July," I verified.

The doctor declared, "Unless Curtis decides to extend his life with scientific measures, he likely has less than six months."

*It is January. His birthday is in August. Curtis is not going to live to see 26.*

Chad spoke for the first time. "What measures are you referring to?"

"Barring complications, an ALS patient can live a long time on a respirator and feeding tube. With these two aids, there is a possibility that Curtis could survive a long time. We have patients who have been living five, ten, 15 years on mechanical support."

"What can they do? Can they move anything?" Chad asked.

"It depends on the patient. One man, in whom the disease has seemingly run its course, can only move his eyeballs. He cannot swallow, or breathe, or move any muscles in his body on his own. But, he has a computer that speaks for him, in response to his eye movement. He requires 24-hour-a-day care. That is one element to consider when weighing the pros and cons of mechanical support. Another is the financial burden. ALS is an extremely expensive disease. Even if the patient is insured, not all insurance plans cover all of the necessities when it comes to ALS. Costs could run up to $200,000 a year in the later stages. Of course, though, it is up to the patient. The real question is quality of life."

Hope swept through me like a hurricane.

*Curtis could live for a very long time.*

A few minutes later Chad and I walked slowly to the elevator.

Once inside, I whispered, "I knew about the feeding tube and the ventilator, which is why I was adamant about Curtis filling out a living will, but I didn't realize one could be kept alive for five, ten, even 15 years."

"Yes, but only his eyes? Curtis needs to fill out those papers."

We greeted Curtis' parents and my mother, who had driven up from Connecticut, in the waiting room.

Chad relayed the information about the gene to his parents, and then he stated, "Curt has less than a year to live. Most likely much less."

Curtis' father dropped his head to his chest and sobbed. Curtis' mother threw the hand-held poker game that she was playing onto the table, and it skidded onto the floor.

"Unless he chooses a respirator and feeding tube," Chad said, explaining the details of mechanical support.

Curtis' mom rose from her chair, picked up the computer game, and said, "I will not refuse the respirator and I would never take him off of it. My mother didn't have that chance."

Meanwhile, Curtis, who was in the operating room, begged for more Novocaine as the surgeon sliced open his skin and installed the pump, which would hold and transport the BDNF or placebo into his spinal fluid, in his abdominal area. The doctors would not take the chance of using a general anesthetic given the severity of the progression of the disease.

Hours later I greeted an exhausted, pale, and, for the first time, visibly worried man in the recovery area.

"How was it?" I asked as I kissed Curtis gently on the lips.

"Horrible." No smile, no smirk, no sparkle in his eyes. He had no energy to even try to pretend.

I remained beside him until eight in the evening, when he insisted that my mother and I leave to get some food. Curtis was waiting for two of his brothers to stop by. They lived in Boston at the time. Curtis' parents and Chad had already retired to the hotel across the street.

"Okay, but I'll be back," I said, and reluctantly followed my mom out of the hospital room.

Once in the hall, my mother spoke. "Curtis is heavily medicated and the nurses will be able to do more for him than you will. I'll get us a hotel room. We can have a nice dinner, a glass or two of wine, and then we can get some sleep. Please, take this opportunity to get a good night's rest."

"Mom, I can't leave him."

"He will be fine."


A few minutes later, over sun-dried tomato and basil toast, sausage and mushroom pizza, and house white wine, I confided in my mom that I was seriously considering having Curtis' baby.

Mom looked up from her plate and took a long, deep drink of wine, "What does Curtis think?"

"He doesn't know," I answered.

My mom looked directly in my eyes.

"Mom, I won't do anything impulsive. I am still on the pill. It's just that, oh, Mom, I can't imagine life with... I mean, if something should happen... I can't... I'm going to need a part of him, you know? I am going to need something. Why is this happening?"

"What can I do?" my mom asked as she finished the glass of wine.

"That's the thing. There's nothing anyone can do. We're all just here, alive, and there's not a damn thing that we can do to save him. He's dying, Mom. I watch it every day. I see the changes, the deterioration. It's killing me. It's right in front of me and I can't help him. What am I going to do?"

"You're going to do what is right. You've always done what you think is right. Just remember, you've got some time. And, whatever you do, always know your father and I are here to support you."

We returned to Curtis' hospital room at 9:45 pm. He was alone.

"Did your brothers come?"

"Yeah."

"Where are they now?"

"At the hotel." Curtis' six-foot frame looked child-like in the blue and white hospital gown. The colorless room seemed to gobble up his brown hair and green eyes that stood out from his ashen face and body.

"Mom, I'd rather stay here with Curtis."

Mom shot a look at him.

He smiled. "I'd rather you go to the hotel with your mother. Get some sleep. I'll be here in the morning."

I kissed him goodnight on the forehead and walked backward out of the room.

I lay in bed in the dark staring at the fluorescent hotel clock; it was 10:30 pm. My heart raced, my mind was full of guilt for leaving him alone, and my arms ached to hold his body. I tried to relax. I thought of my yellow security blanket that I had held onto for six years when I was a child. I couldn't even bear to leave it long enough to have it washed. I would sit on top of the washing machine to protect it and then once it was transferred to the dryer, I would sit in front of the dryer and massage the warm, white machine with my hand by creating endless circles and cry, "Blankie. Oh, I love you blankie." Eventually, Mom forced me to replace the mangy material with a similar, bed-size yellow blanket. I cried for many nights. And weeks. Months? I couldn't remember.

"Where are you going?" Mom whispered in a half-awake state.

I left the hotel room, went downstairs, and ran on the hotel's treadmill at the highest speed until the janitor asked me to leave because the fitness center was closing. I went back to the room, lay on the bed from midnight until five in the morning, returned to the gym, and ran some more.

I greeted Curtis a minute before the visiting hours officially began. He looked drugged and exhausted but adorable in his hospital gown.

"Where have you been?" he slurred with his eyes half-open.

"Right here," I replied. "How was your night?"

"I am in pain."

"Was the nurse here? Did she help?"

"All night long I called but couldn't find... I needed you."

That was the last night we spent apart.

After the hospital stay, we lived at Curtis' parents' house while we waited for the hardwood floors in Curtis' aunt and uncle's house to be finished. As a result of the experimental drug surgery, Curtis could not sit up for more than a few minutes without getting a spinal headache. He could no longer make it in to work at the plant. He could not even leave the bed, which is where he spent his days and nights. His employer gave him a laptop so that he could work from home and continue to be paid sick time and keep his health benefits, which was a blessing, but at this point he couldn't sit up enough to even do his work.

One evening Curtis' mother invited family and friends over for dinner. Curtis usually loved parties. Curtis' father came upstairs to help Curtis get out of bed and down the stairs.

"I'm not going," Curtis stated.

"Curtis, how about if some of them come up here to the bedroom to say hello?" I asked, knowing that Curtis needed socialization to feel normal.

"I don't want to see anyone. No one wants to see me. Look at me. I am useless. I can't even get out of bed to go to the bathroom."

Curtis' mom entered the bedroom. "There are people here who came to see you. Go downstairs and see them or they will come up here to see you."

Curtis looked at me like a little boy who knew he should do something but really couldn't.

That evening, people came into the bedroom to say hello. Within less than a minute, though, each of them recognized Curtis' physical and emotional pain and left us alone.

I officially quit my job as assistant tennis coach, and once the house was ready, I moved our lives out of our apartment in southern Vermont and into the house that Curtis had helped to build in his hometown of Danville. Curtis' aunt and uncle refused any payment for rent, and although we insisted on paying at least the utility bills, we never once received one.

Two weeks after the experimental study surgery, Curtis and I returned to Boston for the first dose to be injected into the pump; we imagined and hoped that the solution was the largest possible dose of the growth hormone BDNF rather than the placebo. We believed that this was our miracle cure and that he was one of the lucky recipients. There were no physical signs of improvement at first but the doctor had told us that even if it were to work, it would take a while.

At first I kept the conversation that Chad and I had with the doctor from Curtis in terms of the projected timeline of his disease. Even before he was officially diagnosed, Curtis had told me that I could research whatever it was that he had but that he didn't want to know anything.

"I need to concentrate on getting better," he said.

But, I did tell Curtis that, barring complications (pneumonia, choking etc.), a person with ALS could live indefinitely with the aid of a feeding tube and respirator. I also shared with him what his mother had said that day in the hospital about wishing for him to choose life support when the time came to make a decision.

Yet, despite my continued urging, Curtis still would not speak about a living will. I was worried but my mother was terrified.

One night while she and I were on the phone, she shared, "I'm afraid of what will happen if an emergency situation arises and Curtis can't express his wishes. As time has shown, thus far, you are the one who is with Curtis nearly every moment, and the chances are you will be the only one there if and when an immediate decision has to be made. Have you thought about what choice you will make? Have you thought about the possible ramifications of your choice? What if Curtis' family sues you or brings you to court for whatever decision you make? I can't have you going to prison for doing what you feel is right at the time for the boy who you love who refuses to make this decision ahead of time."

I told my mother that she and I both knew that Curtis' family would never bring me to court.

"I know. I know," she agreed. "And, I also know that we don't understand how all of this works and if there would even be a decision that needed to be made other than tell the emergency responders that he doesn't have a living will. This is a very, very complex and difficult situation. You need to figure out how this all works. Curtis could prevent any tension, any stress by making his wishes known."

That next morning I shared both my mother's and my concerns with Curtis, and he called the whole thing asinine. At the time, I didn't have any idea what would happen if we found ourselves in an emergency situation. But I did know that the thought of his last moments being enveloped in a haze of indecisiveness and confusion scared me to death. I needed to know how he felt about extending his life with extraordinary measures.

Four weeks after the surgery for the experimental study, Curtis could finally raise his head without getting a spinal headache but he had become so weak that he had trouble standing on his own. We blamed the surgery and its aftermath for this set back, but, of course, the disease may have been to blame as well. During this same time, I took my mother's advice and met with the minister at the St. Johnsbury hospital to discuss the topic of a living will and medical power of attorney. He verified that no one could make medical decisions on Curtis' behalf without legal appointment, explained the documents to me, asked me if it would be all right if he came to talk with Curtis and also suggested I call a lawyer with regard to legal power of attorney.

When I asked Curtis if he would be open to a visit by the

minister to discuss legalities, he stated that he was appalled and that I was paranoid. At the time, I thought I understood why Curtis wouldn't discuss his wishes. If he did, it would mean that the decisions he made would someday come into play. In order to face each new day, Curtis had to believe that he would never physically get to that point. He had to have faith that the disease's progression would halt. He had to believe in a miracle.

The minister was aware that there was no living will or medical power of attorney and he knew that we were not married. He stated to me, "At this point in time, I am more worried about you than Curtis."

I scheduled the appointment for the first day of March.

"Curtis, he'll be here at ten. Do you want to talk about it before he comes?"

"What's there to talk about?"

"Curtis, please don't make this any more difficult than it already is."

"Me make it difficult? You've invited a stranger into our home so that he can tell me how to live my life."

"Curtis, he is a good friend of Bubbles' and he's known your family for years. He's going to educate us about your options. You need to make a decision or things could get very messy."

Immediately after the minister arrived and sat down on the maroon futon in our living room with unfolded documents on his lap, Curtis began, "I do not want to be kept alive on machines."

The minister looked at me and I stared at Curtis. I had forewarned the minister that Curtis hadn't said a single word to me about anything regarding what he was thinking about in terms of allowing the disease to run its natural course or use extraordinary measures to keep him alive.

The minister responded, "Have you made your decision based on facts?"

Curtis looked at me. "I do not want to be kept alive on machines."

I nodded towards the minister, and he replied, "Curtis, who will be your agent? It should be someone who you trust will keep your interests in mind."

Curtis looked at me.

"And why her?"

"Because she is my friend."

I scowled.

He corrected himself and smirked.

"A very good friend."

The minister asked me, "Should Curtis be unable to speak for himself, would you be able to make decisions based on his wishes?"

"Yes."

"Even if it means standing up to his family?"

I could not believe that Curtis had referred to me as his friend. Before he got sick, we had been talking about our engagement. Since he had gotten sick, I had given up my job, our apartment, essentially my life for him. I looked up at him, prepared to say or do something rash, but was greeted by his smile, the smile that always made me forgive him. It started out as a subtle, innocent, and submissive smirk, which prompted me to forget his domineering tendencies and insisted that I remember that he needed me. The smirk gently broadened into the smile that had stolen my heart years beforehand.

"Yes. I will uphold his wishes under any circumstances."

Curtis' expression turned grave and desperate. It was a look I would witness many times in the following months.

Later, when the minister left, the voices inside my head that were questioning Curtis' decision let themselves be heard. They had to. I did not want to listen to them after his death.

"Honey, are you sure?" I asked.

"If I stop breathing, that's it," he responded. " I am not going to fight it anymore."

"I know. But, I don't want to lose you. What will I do without you?"

He looked at me through the tears in his eyes, "I am here now, aren't I?"

"Yes."

*You need to take this time to be with him. Tell him you love him every day. Touch him and smell him and hold him. Remember that you are so lucky to have him now.*

But then I cried to him for not being his wife and for not having his children already.

"How can you not survive this disease?"

"I made this decision to keep you from worrying, but it will not be needed. We are going to survive together."

I wanted to believe him. But I couldn't. So, instead, I questioned him, hoping our conversation would contradict his false beliefs.

"But what if you die? Where will I go without you? Who will I be without you by my side?"

"You will never be alone."

I understood that he needed to believe that he would not die in order to have any chance of survival. So, instead of trying to make him admit that he would die, which was the only way I could begin to prepare for his death and a life without him, I took his hand in mine and laid my head on his chest. A few weeks later Curtis asked me to contact a lawyer so that he could sign the papers giving me legal power of attorney.

Curtis was still being paid a salary. I was waitressing at Vinny's, a local family-owned restaurant, one night a week, and we didn't have rent or utility bills to pay, but we still could not afford the cost of living as well as all of Curtis' treatments and medical bills. Curtis' health insurance only covered a percentage of the medical costs and it didn't cover any of the alternative treatments. Since the disease progressed so quickly, we found ourselves in immediate need of pieces of equipment that would help make our daily life easier but if we waited for insurance to pay Curtis wouldn't have the capacity to benefit. One example of this was when Curtis started to lose the ability to stand from a sitting position, we heard about a powered reclining chair that could also lift him all the way up to a standing position. When I contacted Curtis' insurance company, they informed me that it would take months to get the chair. There were forms that needed to be filled out and time that needed to lapse before it could be approved and... and... and. I was frustrated and dumbfounded. I wished that we had the money to just go out and buy one for I was pretty sure that once it was approved by insurance Curtis would have already lost the ability to stand upright on his own.

Starting in January, people began to send us money. At first, the checks and cash came sporadically with notes such as, "Just a little something to help with the medical expenses." In March, a group of Danville townspeople joined together and organized a fundraiser for Curtis. Although we were grateful for the gesture,

Curtis was very nervous to attend the event. He was embarrassed to be seen in his wheelchair. He wasn't afraid of what people would say to him; he feared that no one would speak to him because no one would know what to say. He also felt uncomfortable with the fact that now everyone in town was aware of his family's ALS gene and he still didn't know how he felt about it. Up until this point, we hadn't spoken much about the genetic mutation or that this disease had caused so many of his relatives and ancestors such sorrow and death. And, this would be the first social event in a long time that Curtis attended sober; he hadn't spoken about or had any alcohol since that night on the cruise ship.

The event, which was held at a restaurant in St. Johnsbury with food, drinks, dancing, and an auction, was a huge success. Hundreds of people attended. No one stared at Curtis. Some people did cry. The last time most of the people had seen Curtis, just a few months prior, he was walking and well. But people were still drawn to him. People, one by one, two by two, approached Curtis, who remained stationary in his wheelchair on one side of the large function room. Within seconds, he had them smiling and laughing. Curtis' self-effacing and gentle humor made others feel comfortable in his presence.

# *The Healing Circle*

The disease progressed. One day in late March, three months after the official diagnosis, I tried to get Curtis out of bed our normal way: he sat on the edge of the bed with his left arm draped over my shoulder and I pulled up as he used his right arm as leverage to push himself into a standing position. This day he could no longer use his arm as leverage, nor could his legs sustain the weight of his upper body. So we tried another way. I pulled our blue office chair next to the bed and tried to lift him into it. Because my five-foot-three, 125 pound body couldn't hold his six-foot, 185 pound body, the blue chair wheeled away. I attempted to set him back on the bed but instead dropped him onto the floor. He was naked and in desperate need to go to the bathroom. I tried to get him up. I couldn't. A loud groan escaped from him as he screamed at the world for his misfortune. Silent tears streamed down my face.

By April, the disease continued progressing. Quickly. Curtis' legs were extremely weak, and he could not walk or even stand. His right bicep was virtually useless. His breathing was labored. But his left arm still functioned, and he had relearned how to do daily tasks such as feed himself and brush his teeth and hair with his non-dominant side. Despite the fact that we were fighting his rapid physical deterioration and facing an incurable disease that had taken the lives of 50 percent of every generation of his ancestors for hundreds of years, we did not lose hope. In fact, we began to make plans for our future. Curtis sat in his blue recliner in our living room on a Sunday in April and stated, "I want a dog, and I want a black Chinese Shar-Pei. You know, those wrinkly dogs with the squished-in faces?"

We scoured the day's *Burlington Free Press* and found an advertisement for Shar-Peis. Curtis asked me to call and find out if they had any black ones.

I called.

I asked.

Yes, they had one black Chinese Shar-Pei.

They sent us information regarding their dogs, including a description of their only black one: "Wofosi (Reclining Buddha). Wofosi is a great black long brush-coated puppy. He is a fun pup and the class clown of this litter. He just loves to snoop around outside, and that nose doesn't miss a thing. As a little guy he used to fall asleep with all four feet straight up in the air. Now after a hard day he stretches out, and he can even snore. Wofosi is just a love affair waiting to happen."

Curtis appreciated that this little puppy made funny noises when he breathed, too.

Later that month, on our return trip from our monthly doctor's visit to Boston, we stopped in Woodstock, Vermont, to see the dogs. Chad had driven us that month, and when we arrived at the house after five at night Curtis was too tired to attempt to enter the home, so Chad and I went in. Upon our arrival, several Chinese Shar-Pei dogs scrambled to our feet. Some jumped up, others licked my face as I bent down to greet them. But Wofosi sat off to the side. He was black and long-haired and had such a squished-in little face that he made the most ridiculous noises when he breathed. I picked him up and brought him out to meet Curtis.

Curtis asked me to leave the dog in the car while I returned to sign the papers and the check.

We loved the name Wofosi and nicknamed him Woo Woo. As we made our way north that evening, towards home, I wondered how I'd take care of Curtis and a newborn puppy. But the look on Curtis' face those first and subsequent mornings when Woo Woo kissed him good morning was priceless. We watched in awe as our little Woo Woo grew and learned new things every day.

Curtis thought that he would survive because he believed that treatment was there to be found. He didn't care whether it was mainstream or unconventional. And I just wanted the peace of mind that should Curtis not survive we had tried everything possible. Curtis was still participating in the experimental treatment in Boston; he believed that he was receiving 100 mL of BDNF, and he anticipated that the medicine would slow down the progression of the disease while also regenerating the motor neurons that had died. He was taking Rilutek, a medicine proven to slow down the progression of ALS in mice, as well as an assortment of vitamins and nutritional supplements that had been recommended by his doctor in Boston. He religiously took herbals and more vitamins in an attempt to keep his body clean of toxins. Costing about $500 a month, these pills were prescribed by a woman in West Danville who lived in a teepee.

We bought a wet cell battery system over the Internet. We had read that it was designed to help enhance the body's natural healing tendencies by generating a very, very low electrical flow in the body. Curtis saw a network chiropractor who was working on keeping his energy pathways open and clear, a physical therapist who worked his remaining muscles as hard as possible, a masseuse who helped his body to stay comfortable and limber (although its tendency was to stiffen and not do as it was told) and a former Harvard Medical School doctor who had left mainstream medicine to treat people with terminal illnesses by helping them to discover what it was that was keeping them from being able to heal themselves. He believed that Curtis could heal himself by mentally fixing the mutation in his DNA. I think that Curtis believed that he could overcome the effects of the disease if he tried hard enough; we both believed that hard work could and would get you where you wanted to be. I am not sure if he thought he could alter his mutated DNA. I do know that we were both willing to try almost anything. And, I was grateful that Curtis was focusing on something else besides his own deterioration. The few weeks following the surgery for the experimental drug had been very difficult for Curtis. Now, though, he was back to his optimistic self.

When Curtis and I were diagnosed with ALS, I wanted to crawl under a large rock, bury myself deep in the dark and weep, but Curtis told me that everything was going to be okay. I say that we were both diagnosed because although Curtis was the one who had ALS, we took it on together. We were both living with it, wrestling with it, treating it and hoping that it would just go away. We never spoke about our partnership in terms of how we formed a team of two in order to try to survive. We just did it. We somehow knew we had to do this together. We knew that we needed one another to survive.

Curtis possessed an inner strength. At first, I wasn't sure how to label what it was that kept him going. But during the course of the illness, he helped me discover my inner strength, which I can only describe as faith. We had faith that Curtis could heal. We also knew that a kind and generous community surrounded us, and with the urging of the former Harvard Medical School doctor,

Curtis agreed that we should publicly acknowledge the genetic mutation, that we should not be ashamed or fearful of it, that we should embrace it and move forward, that we should call it what it is and ask for help to try to fix it. The doctor believed that our community could be a very important part of the answer in terms of Curtis trying to manipulate his own DNA.

In April, I wrote an article for the local Danville paper to thank our community for all that they had done but also to ask them for more.

*"We, Curtis and I, wrote this article to let you all know the secret. There is a genetic mutation in his family that has caused turmoil and confusion for hundreds of years. Scientists now understand what the mutation is and that it degenerates the human body, but they do not know what triggered it or how to stop it. We have an idea. We have brainstormed the possibility that community energy could heal Curtis. Positive energy sparks a human being, fills them with love and can help them to achieve improbable feats. We have witnessed this in athletics, music, dance, and other arenas for years. We believe that this same energy can also heal. So, we ask that each and every one of you send positive energy to Curtis at any time throughout any day. You can envision sending it to his right bicep, his legs, his diaphragm, or his entire body. And you can also envision Curtis moving as he did before the disease. Picture the energy flowing through his body as it works as a whole. We are going to hold group-healing sessions at our residence in Danville, during which we will practice funneling the energy of an entire group into Curtis' body. The first one will be the evening of April 22, and future sessions will be announced at a later date. We ask you all to join."*

At the time, I am not sure if I believed that others' positive energy and thoughts could help Curtis to heal or if Curtis could heal his own body. The days, weeks, months of his illness just happened. There was so much to do. Taking care of another human being is exhausting. In order to do for Curtis what he could no longer do for himself, I sacrificed caring for myself. I did not eat well. I barely slept. I never stopped moving. The physical exertion was so tremendous that my mind had no energy to really think about what I did or did not believe in. But I was very aware of the fact that Curtis was a social being, and he needed others around him to feel alive. He needed the support of others to make him feel as though living was worthwhile. I needed him to retain hope and remain positive. I needed him to live.

About 20 or so family and friends attended the first session, and the number of attendees grew week by week. Julia, Joe's wife, (Joe was Curtis' boss from when he worked construction in Danville on his days off from the plant) facilitated the circles. By June, over 50 people had joined. Those who came were young and old, poor and rich, townspeople and flatlanders, believers and nonbelievers. The youngest were Curtis' six-year-old niece, Annie, and eight-year-old nephew, Tommy. Some came just to see Curtis as part of a group since they were too uncomfortable to visit him alone or without an apparent reason. Some came to let him know that they, too, had experienced hardship in their lives that they had overcome. Some came to grieve the loss of a loved one of their own.

The healing circles were a time for sharing memories of the past, and of Curtis and me as healthy, happy and fine. They were a time for grief, an opportunity for family members and friends to grieve over the loss of Curtis' healthy body. They were a time for laughter and pure joy, as Curtis realized that he was alive, and although not physically healthy, he was in possession of a thriving mind and soul.

Miraculously, we gave more than we got. People left our home feeling full, blessed and as though they had been given a second chance. At what? At life? At grieving? At the opportunity to use the time they have? Curtis and I knew we were giving, but we weren't sure how we could when we ourselves were exhausted. And, why were we, when we knew we had so little left for ourselves? Love. There was so much love between us, in us, through us, around us, that it flew off into every direction, onto anyone who asked for it, or didn't ask, but needed it just the same. We gave people love, and hope.

Some people whom we loved and who loved us never attended a healing circle in our home. Curtis and I would talk about why. We knew that it must have taken great strength and courage for those who did enter our home to witness the physical deterioration of Curtis' body and we just assumed that those who did not attend were afraid of losing him. Curtis accepted this. I had trouble accepting this because it saddened me to think of the regret people who did not spend as much time with him as they could have might live with if Curtis were to die. I knew that I never wanted to feel that way. How could others? I shared these feelings with Curtis and his reply was always the same.

"Accept people for who they are."

On Curtis' good days, we would beg time to stop. Those days we spent playing with Woo Woo, talking with friends and neighbors, going for walks (with me pushing Curtis in his wheelchair), watching one another, making love. ALS primarily affects the voluntary muscles of the body, those that can be moved at will. So while a person with ALS may lose control of all or most voluntary muscle functions, a different part of the nervous system, the autonomic nervous system, is largely unaffected. Thus, a man with ALS can still perform sexually. And in Curtis' case, his sex drive increased. Perhaps it was because we were with one another 24-hours a day, perhaps it was because we were 20-something year olds, perhaps it was because as a result of Curtis' decreased ability to move we were forced to experiment; perhaps it was because we didn't know what else to do. Whatever the reason, we didn't complain that sex became a major focus of our days. Being together intimately made us feel good and it made us feel normal.

When spring in the Northeast Kingdom finally arrived, Curtis' father bought him a motorized scooter, which made him feel less handicapped and enabled him to ride down to the local hardware store by himself to have coffee with the boys. He even rode the eight miles to North Danville one morning to visit with his uncle on the farm. Of course, I checked on him when he was approaching the fourth mile. I had told him that I had an errand to run in St. Johnsbury; I was just nervous that he would lose the ability to man the controls in the middle of the trip. The scooter gave Curtis the freedom to go outside before dawn and wheel around his aunt and uncle's gardens with Woo Woo following close behind. Curtis would speed up so that Woo Woo would run after him, then he'd slow down and stop so that Woo Woo could jump onto the base of the scooter and sit on Curtis' feet while they looked to the east and witnessed the beginning of a day. Weather permitting, the scooter allowed me, Curtis, and Woo Woo to travel into town daily. Woo Woo and I would walk or run and Curtis would drive down our driveway, up Sugar Ridge Road, down the main street, towards the town green. We would wave to our neighbors and to those who passed us in their cars. We would pick up garbage on the side of the road along the way.

Once we got to the center of town, we would normally cross Route Two to the post office where we would check our box for mail. This was the highlight of our day. Most days we would have three, five, even ten cards waiting for us. The cards were from people we had known all our lives, or people who had read about the fundraisers for Curtis in the local papers, or people who had read the articles I had written. Some of the messages within those cards offered help, some offered inspiration, and many of the cards offered monetary assistance. A dear college friend of mine wrote a note I will always remember. She expressed what, I think, most people feel when they try to reach out to someone who is experiencing the seemingly impossible.

She wrote, "Every time I have sat down to put pen to paper, the words came out awkward at first and then dry. It was as if I felt what I wrote to you had to be a masterpiece, but was time and again insufficient. Now as I am writing, these seem like silly excuses when all I wanted to tell you was that I care."

As time went on, more people, both locally and nationally, learned of our healing circles via word of mouth, local news, and an article written for the *Burlington Free Press*, which the Associated Press distributed around the United States. The number of notes we received in the mail became overwhelming, but they made us realize that we were inspiring others by continuing to live our lives. Just knowing that we were making a difference for others was what kept our spirits high, even on our bad days when Curtis would beg me to find a cure or wonder how much one could handle before it was too much. The pain came in many forms. Sometimes it brewed for days and then crept up behind us and slammed us on our backs; other days it popped up in front of us, and slapped us in the face.

Curtis mourned the loss of his body every time he lost a particular ability. One day he could use his right hand, even if just a little bit; the next day it could do nothing. One night he could walk; the next morning he could not. I often think about how Curtis was able to live through the pain. I can't even imagine the physical hardship or the mental anguish of not being able to move your own body. I still cry just thinking of how horrible it must have been for him.

Curtis experienced cramps, stiff and sore body parts, backaches, and headaches. Watching him deal with and work through the physical pain, though, was easy for me compared to the heartache. It was agonizing for me to watch Curtis limply hold his razor in his hand and try with his whole being to make that hand do what he wanted it to do. Holding him on his tub bench in the shower, lifting his arms to wash under them, spreading his legs to wash between them was not hard for me. Watching his expression turn from thankfulness and admiration to pity for me and to a sense of helplessness was devastating. ALS took away my youth, my innocence. Every night, though, after I got him into bed, undressed him, gave him his last group of vitamins and medicine and kissed him, he would say, "Another good day. Another good day to be thankful for."

The healing circle provided us with an avenue to reach out to others and for others to reach out to us. We needed to know that we weren't alone. We needed courage to sustain ourselves. Curtis and I knew that we wouldn't have been able to do what we did on a daily basis without the love and support of the people who entered our home, or who used the written word to express their sadness, hope, and gratitude. And they wouldn't have been able to experience us if we didn't allow them to. We had created a circle. Of life. Of love. Of hope. Of healing.

# Breathing

Time tricked Curtis. He had signed the living will and medical power of attorney that day in March, saying that he did not wish to be kept alive on machines, which meant that he would refuse a feeding tube and respirator. He had made that decision based on how he had imagined he would feel at a certain point in the future. But his forethoughts did not completely coincide with his feelings, thoughts, and desires once the time came to make the final decisions.

We drove down to Boston in May, five months after the diagnosis, for his monthly check-up.

At this visit the doctor declared what we already knew, "Curtis, your breathing is declining." He continued, "There is a noninvasive option. Would you like to hear about it?"

We were introduced to the BiPAP (Bilevel Positive Air Pressure), a machine that would pump air into Curtis' lungs, allowing him to continue to breathe. It required a mask, one that covered his nose and mouth when used at night and one that only covered his nose if used during the day. A flexible hose connected the mask to the machine.

"What do you think?" the doctor asked.

"I am only struggling at night," Curtis responded.

"You can just wear it at night. It will keep you comfortable."

"Can we have a minute?" Curtis asked the doctor.

The doctor left the room and Curtis looked at me with that look of desperation.

"What do you think?" he asked.

I had researched various breathing aids. I understood that a BiPAP was an intermediate step between no assisted breathing and using a ventilator. If one goes the route of a ventilator or respirator, one has to undergo a tracheotomy, a surgical procedure that creates an opening in the neck to the windpipe through which a tube would be placed, and then the ventilator would deliver air through the tube [13] whereas a BiPAP helps by pushing air into a person via a mask. As ALS progresses, it becomes harder to exhale against the higher pressure. One difference between a BiPAP and a ventilator is that a BiPAP delivers a preset air pressure while a ventilator delivers a preset volume of air.[14]

"You struggle to breathe at night, Curtis. It scares me," I said.

"I can still eat. I can still talk. I will only use it at night."

And so we spent the night in the hospital so that the doctors could monitor him while on the BiPAP. He begged me to not leave him alone this time; he slept in the hospital bed and I slept in the chair beside him.

At first, Curtis did only use the BiPAP at night, but a month later he was using it a few hours during the day as well. By the end of June he depended on it 24-hours a day. Curtis' breathing was not the only thing deteriorating during this time. He was also losing the ability to feed himself. Worse, though, for him, was his difficulty in manning his scooter.

One day in June, we were getting ready to go out to the Danville Inn for breakfast. I cranked him up in the Hoyer, the contraption that allowed me to move him, and he smiled as a result of the relief that came when his buttocks and thighs were no longer supporting the weight of his body. I wheeled him over to the scooter and unscrewed the gadget on the Hoyer, which prompted him to be lowered slowly. I quickly moved behind him and pulled him back. Curtis began to slip.

"Goddammit. I am not on the seat. My hips are not on. Pull me back."

Standing behind Curtis, I grabbed the back of his shorts, wrapped my right arm across his chest and pulled. His upper body flung too far forward, but his hips were all the way back.

"You're going to kill me, you know," Curtis smiled.

"You're far enough back, aren't you?"

I opened the front door of the house all the way and was surprised when Curtis asked me to stand in front of the ramp.

"My fingers sometimes don't work for me in the morning," Curtis acknowledged.

I knew that they barely worked at all.

I stood guard and watched as Curtis used all of his strength in his left arm, which still worked a bit, to pull his right arm, which he couldn't move at all, onto the scooter's controls and wrap his right fingers around the lever.

A second after Curtis started to move forward in the scooter, though, Woo Woo ran in front of him.

"Get him out of the way," Curtis shouted.

I called Woo Woo's name, but he wouldn't leave Curtis' side.

I ran toward Woo Woo and scooped him up.

Curtis didn't wait for me to return to position. He drove down the ramp, his right arm slipped, and the scooter veered left. With Woo Woo in my arms, I slipped in between the doorway and the scooter and grabbed Curtis by the shirt.

"No, the scooter," Curtis yelled.

With Woo Woo still in my arms and my right arm steadying Curtis' upper body, my left hand grabbed the handlebars and corrected the scooter's angle.

We arrived at the Inn an hour late for breakfast. Nine o'clock in the morning was when all the ladies gathered, and it was mainly for them that Curtis wanted to go. Curtis knew that he could make them smile and laugh with his stories. He could still tell his stories.

The Inn's owner met us at the back door. He had built the ramp just for Curtis. Curtis tried to silently get my attention. People who weren't used to handling Curtis' body hurt him unknowingly, and he was getting too weak to be mishandled. I caught Curtis' eye, which told him that I understood that he wanted me, rather than the Inn's owner, to help him, but I ignored his pleading; I was still angry with him for trying to man the controls of the scooter when he knew that he had lost the ability to do so and for yelling at me.

Once inside, Curtis insisted that he drive the scooter through the narrow openings, which would eventually lead us through the kitchen and into the restaurant. I picked up Woo Woo, for he feared entering the restaurant from the kitchen; the floor reminded him of the vet's office. The Inn's owner realized that Curtis was having difficulty maneuvering the scooter and asked if he could help. Curtis insisted that I take over, but the Inn's owner steered him through the kitchen with careful guidance.

We rounded the counter; the ladies cheered. Some had already left, but Curtis' mom and a few others remained. There were other customers in the restaurant but no one stared at Curtis even though a large mask covered his nose and a large clear plastic pipe ran from the top of the mask near his forehead, around the top of his head and back to the BiPAP. Instead, they waved to us or smiled and continued on with their business. The townspeople were used to seeing me, Curtis, and Woo Woo. We ventured outside our home as often as possible.

The Danville Inn was warm and pleasant, and it smelled delicious. I let Woo Woo down, and he began to wander. Curtis glared at me but the Inn's owner insisted, "He is welcome to roam wherever he pleases."

Coldly, Curtis motioned for me to situate his arms and hands and legs and feet.

Curtis' mom asked, "What is wrong with you two?"

"Oh, she's mad at me again, Mother."

"Curtis, you insisted on using the scooter and you are too weak to do so."

"Well, he looks comfortable to me," Curtis' mom replied.

Curtis ordered a pancake. I knew that he preferred eggs, bacon and toast but they would be too hard to handle. I ordered my favorite, a chocolate chip pancake.

Curtis attempted to lift his water with his left hand, but he could not lift it high enough to get the straw into his mouth. The ladies continued to chatter. I raised the glass and placed the straw in his mouth.

"Since when can he not drink himself?" Curtis' mother's tone challenged my reaction to help him.

The ladies continued to chatter.

Curtis did not want others to know how bad it had gotten over the past few days so I replied, "Oh, he can, but I am trying to butter up to him this morning, that's all."

"The more aid you give him, the less he will do," she answered.

The ladies continued to chatter while Curtis struggled to spoon the pieces of pancake into his mouth with his left hand. Their eyes did not glance toward him when he dropped pieces onto his shirt and the floor. I took over feeding Curtis after he dropped the third.

The chatter continued.

An hour later, Curtis' plate was clean; my pancake was half eaten. I had shifted Curtis' weight numerous times by either pulling his right or left leg forward, or adjusting his hips by pulling him back by means of his shorts. Curtis barely said a word; his butt was just too sore. It took all of his energy to concentrate on eating and drinking. It was time to go. The Inn's owner steered Curtis out of the restaurant and down the ramp.

When we were halfway up the main street, the scooter began to veer to the left. I grabbed the controls just in time.

Curtis looked up at me, "I can't do it anymore."

I kissed Curtis on the forehead, placed Woo Woo at Curtis' feet and walked beside them, steering them home.

In the middle of July, seven months since the diagnosis, we sat with our former physical therapist in our home. When we had first started working with her, she spent an hour with Curtis twice a week helping him to move and stretch which allowed him to concentrate on the tangible goal of getting stronger. During that one hour twice a week I would go for a run, take a shower, or hop in the car to run an errand without worrying. We trusted her. Five months after her first visit our insurance decided that a physical therapist's professional services were no longer necessary; Curtis was not getting any stronger. Instead, then, I stretched, moved and massaged all of his extremities that could no longer move on their own in order to keep them from stiffening and causing pain. Even though our physical therapist was no longer getting paid, she still came to see us once a week just to spend time with us. She was one of the only people our age who had known others with ALS and she would talk honestly with us.

"What do you expect will happen this month in Boston?" she asked.

"They'll tell me how great I look," Curtis grinned. "I'll crack some joke. Some of them will get it. The others won't laugh. They'll ask me if I've thought anymore about modeling for a healthcare products magazine. People keep telling me how great I look in a wheelchair."

She and I laughed; Curtis' eyes and complexion were vibrant.

She noticed the tears in my eyes.

"What do you think?"

Darkness overcame Curtis' green eyes as he watched my tears fall.

"She knows that they're going to talk about my breathing," Curtis answered.

"What do you think about your breathing?" she asked.

"It sucks," he answered.

Curtis, still watching me, began to cry. His was a silent mourning. It always was. His eyes would moisten, his face would turn red and his facial muscles would tighten.

Our physical therapist looked at the floor; Curtis and I stared at one another. I saw our past in his eyes: the afternoon we met and that evening when we first kissed by the bonfire; the early summers we fished and laughed and the early winters we called and argued; the night at his family's hunting camp when I fell in love with him again; the countless phone conversations we enjoyed the few years we were maintaining a serious, long-distance relationship; the walks, bike rides, meals, and lounging around time we enjoyed the year that we lived together in our apartment in New Haven; the hours we explored one another and all of the days we spent together since ALS became a part of our lives.

"What do you think?" she asked me again.

"As I've told Curtis since the beginning, I don't want to lose him." Curtis' cautious expression, which illustrated fear, begged me to be honest.

"Curtis, I want you to be happy. As long as you are happy, I will be okay. But I do want to know more about the ventilator. I think that it will be a lot easier to make an informed decision once we know the facts."

From my research, I understood how a ventilator worked. I didn't understand how to care for a person with a ventilator, nor did I comprehend what would happen if, once on a ventilator, Curtis decided he no longer wanted the assistance to breathe.

Our physical therapist took Curtis' right hand as I held his left. We silently allowed our emotions to expel from our beings, each of us crying for one another's pain.

Three days later the doctor in Boston greeted us at our monthly visit.

"We need to discuss the topic of a ventilator," he said.

Our doctor informed us that Curtis would still be able to speak with a ventilator if the disease had not taken his voice already, but it would take a few days to a week after the operation for him to relearn how to speak. He would still be able to eat once he recovered. Having a respirator would require 24-hour care. Curtis' saliva would have to be suctioned constantly to prevent him from choking.

I stood behind Curtis' wheelchair; my fingers wiped his eyes.

"We want to make the right decision," I stated. "If Curtis would remain as he is now, able to eat and speak and move his head, we would consider it. But what if we get one, and then he loses his voice, can no longer eat, and can move nothing but his eyes? How long do we stay on it? Can we decide one day that we've had enough? Or is that suicide? We don't understand how to prolong his quality of life but not get ourselves into something that we won't be able to reverse."

Our doctor spoke to us honestly, "This is one of the hardest things anyone can face. With ALS and medicine today, you have options, but none of the options are great. It is up to you, but from our end, I can say that we can help you with anything you need. If, after the respirator is in, however long, you have had enough, then we can take it out. There are drugs to dull the sensation of not being able to breathe. They will make you feel sleepy. You will go peacefully."

My hand gripped Curtis'. Neither of us could speak. I looked at our doctor. *How can he know that death will be peaceful?*

Curtis broke the silence, "I don't know. Do I have to decide today?"

"No. We just need to plan ahead. I need you to be prepared, keeping in mind the marked progression in your case. In fact, I am going to write a prescription for a suction machine today just in case."

"Will we need it soon?" I questioned.

That morning, while we were making love, I noticed a considerable amount of thick saliva on Curtis' lips.

"I think that you should have it," the doctor answered.

While the nurse measured Curtis' breathing, the doctor asked me to step outside.

"How are you?" he asked. "I mean, really. How are you really?"

"When I go to bed at night and Curtis is sleeping, I hear the

BiPAP going ever so slowly. It sounds as though it is really pushing in the air and forcing Curtis to breathe, and sometimes I think that I am going to lose him right then."

The doctor drew a deep breath and cleared his throat.

"It would be a blessing if things happened that way. The likelihood is slim, but it would be nice."

On the ride back home to Vermont, my mom, our driver this month, asked, "So how was the visit?" My mom, a physical education teacher, spent her summers at our cottage at Joe's Pond. Once school was let out in June she was right up the road in West Danville and able to help us with whatever we needed, until the end of August.

"Oh, you know, same old same old," Curtis answered. "I can't breathe so they want me to get a respirator. They'll cut a hole in my throat, I'll breathe through a tube, have to relearn to speak and eat, and then if I decide I've had enough, I can go back to the hospital where they can take it out, and I'll die."

My mother glanced at me in the rearview mirror.

We had not changed the living will or medical power of attorney since that day in March. In an emergency we would still opt not to have a respirator. But, barring an emergency situation, we were still undecided whether or not we wanted to try it. Our main argument against getting one was that it meant we would have to hire a nurse. I couldn't be awake 24-hours a day. Curtis loathed the thought of sharing our home and our life.

The lull of the tires gliding along the highway, the heat of the sun through the back window of our blue Chevy Blazer, and the fact that I had not had a good night's sleep in months compelled me to close my eyes.

I awoke to Curtis speaking. "Why me? What could He want with me?"

My mother answered. "I believe, Curtis, that if God takes you, then He has a big project in store, and He needs some great people. That's the only reason that I think that He would take you now."

"Yeah, well, I'm not ready to go, so I'll tell you one thing, if He does take me, I'm not gonna do a damn thing for Him when I get there."

It was strange for me to hear my mother and Curtis speaking about God. I did not grow up with religion. I had been baptized Protestant, but had rarely gone to church, except for a few years when my sisters and I were younger and this was only inspired by the fact that one day after school Heather had asked my mom if we were Jewish. A childhood friend of Heather's had told her that she must be Jewish because our last name, Erdmann, sounded Jewish. My parents figured that they should teach us something about our religion. Curtis had been baptized Baptist and attended church as a young boy but religion had not played a major part in his adult life.

A half an hour later we stopped in Derry, New Hampshire, at Curtis' favorite restaurant. The fries were famously delicious. Before ALS, Curtis had watched his waistline. After the diagnosis, he ate whatever he wanted whenever he wanted. While Mom went inside to pick up our food, I reclined Curtis' seat, bent his legs up towards him and rubbed his sore butt.

"Do you think that God has something very great in store for me and that's why He may take me now?"

Ever since I had met Curtis, I knew that he needed constant and consistent reassurance, but today he needed to know that he was worthy to me, to God, to anyone.

"Of course," I answered.

He smiled.

For the second time since the diagnosis, I voiced my feelings of doubt that Curtis would survive, "Curtis, if you were to leave me, I would spend the first months doing everything that you have missed doing and that you dream of doing: hiking mountains, traveling, biking, and playing with Woo Woo. And then I would write my book."

"Don't talk about this, please."

"You need to know that I can make it. I can. I will. I want you here forever. I want to marry you and have your babies and spend the rest of my life with you by my side, but you need to do what is best for you." And, then, I said, "Baby, I want to have your child." Although we had spoken about having children often, this was the first time I blatantly confided in him that I constantly thought about having his child.

"No."

"Why?"

"Because I don't want our child growing up without a father." This was the first time Curtis ever suggested that he thought he would die. "And it would have a 50 percent chance of getting this horrible disease."

"Curtis, the gene has reportedly never triggered before the age of 18. I'd have 18 years to find a cure. I'm going to need someone if you don't make it."

"You have Woo Woo."

And then Mom appeared with our dinner in the greasy brown bags.

For the remainder of the ride home, I rubbed Curtis' head

from the back seat while envisioning his death. The acknowledgment on his part that it could happen spiraled into me imagining it over and over and over again. I saw myself beside him, holding him. It would be peaceful, I hoped, but I knew that it was not time. Then, for the first time, I silently prayed, *Please help Curtis to make a good decision and allow him to be comfortable and happy with his choice.* But then I silently yelled at God, a God who I had never really thought about. *Why would you want to take him now? We have grown and learned already.* I had faith that this being, who I was suddenly calling God, knew but I wished that I could understand. That night, after I had prepared Curtis for bed and lay beside him, I fell asleep to the sound of his BiPAP breathing for him. *Maybe he won't be taken after all. I don't get it because it won't happen.*

Eleven days after our visit to Boston, near the end of July, Curtis and I awoke to find that the stitches in Woo Woo's eyes had opened. He had had surgery a few days earlier for entropion, an eye condition in which the eyelid rolls in towards the eye. The eyelashes or hair on the eyelid can rub against the cornea causing irritation and possibly corneal ulcers, and surgery is required to correct the problem. Overnight, Woo Woo had batted the stitches apart even with the plastic cone-shaped contraption on his head. I called the veterinarian in Manchester, New Hampshire, who had performed the surgery. One of Curtis' cousins who lived in New Hampshire was dating a vet technician who had asked if one of the veterinarians in her practice would perform the surgery at no cost. They had graciously agreed.

The veterinarian insisted I drive Woo Woo down immediately. I was grateful for Tricia who had offered to live with us that summer, the summer after her senior year of high school. Because she was there, I had the option of leaving Curtis in order to take care of Woo Woo. But I had been looking forward to going to the Danville Inn for the Friday lunch buffet and to an afternoon during which we had no scheduled appointments and no knowledge of any visitors. The previous weeks had been hectic, and our restless nights caused irritable days.

Turning right instead of left onto Route Two, I drove Woo Woo to my parents' cottage on Joe's Pond. I reappeared at home 15 minutes later without Woo Woo.

Curtis greeted me. "What's wrong?"

"Mom and Dad are going to bring him. I couldn't leave you, Curtis."

"I wanted you to bring our boy down. He shouldn't have to go through this without you."

"Curtis, I am only one person."

Curtis and I had traveled to and from the Danville Inn numerous times over the past months and now, since Curtis could no longer man the scooter's controls, I pushed him in his wheelchair again. On the walk home from the restaurant this late July day, Curtis yelled at me at least a dozen times, "My ass kills, my feet are sore, can't you go any faster, my arm's falling, I'm slipping, wheel me backwards through the grass, don't let the wheelchair tip back so far, can't you do anything right, are you trying to kill me?"

I felt sorry for Tricia, who tried to calm him, and support me.

Tricia and Curtis developed a very special bond that summer. She offered to live with us because she loved me and wanted to help in some way; as she and I have spoken about in the years since, she was so grateful that she had been given the opportunity to get to know Curtis for who he was rather than just who I told her he was. And, she grew to really love him, like one would love a brother. As she wrote in one of her letters to us that fall after she left us for her freshman year of college, "It is hard to be far away and try to be the front wheel of the tricycle because I'm not there for you guys everyday – but I know you guys are not only surviving but thriving as a bicycle."

Once we got Curtis safely inside the house, Tricia headed up to the cottage. It was a beautiful day, not a cloud in the sky, 80 degrees with no humidity, a slight breeze.

"Go with her," Curtis demanded.

"Curtis, you will have to come too then."

"I'm staying here."

"Who's going to watch you?"

"I am not a baby."

"You can't stay here by yourself, you know that."

"I just want to be alone."

"Curtis, you know you can't be alone. What happens if the electricity goes out, if you have to pee, if your arm slips, if your legs get a cramp, if you have trouble swallowing? You can't even change the channel with the remote control let alone punch the numbers on the phone."

"My mother will watch me."

"I don't want to leave you."

"Go. Have fun."

"Don't you get it? I don't want to have fun without you. I can't. I don't want to play tennis or ski because it will kill me to think of you just sitting here. We can do things that make both of us happy."

"Jesus Christ, don't cry."

"I don't want to go unless you come too."

"Call my mother."

I wanted to tear out of our home and be by myself, but I didn't know what I would do without Curtis. He needed me to move, to breathe, to eat, and to keep him alive. I needed him to keep me from falling, to keep me smiling, to keep me alive. Just as a friend had written in his poem about us, "In him there are the eyes that have the gift to see what must be seen in me to be alive," we had become one body, one mind, and one soul.

"Leave me," Curtis insisted.

I called his mother, drove up to the cottage, took a nap, played tennis, and water-skied. I marveled at how empty I felt, at how useless I regarded myself without Curtis there to need me and how nice it was to be free. I was only 24-years-old. I had a full life ahead of me. On the drive back home, I decided that I would have to create situations in order to allow him to be without me more often. For him. For me. In that moment, I envisioned the day when we would no longer have one another to rely upon. It scared me. If we were to experience life without one another with no preparation, it would be too shocking. I thought that I needed to begin to break away because I imagined that an abrupt separation later might kill me. Once inside, though, after his mother left, his eyes beckoned me to him. I bent down in response to his silent plea.

He kissed my lips and whispered, "I am so sorry. I don't want to do this without you. I can't."

I still think of this moment often. I am grateful that I did not take my own advice and manipulate situations in order to gradually separate us. I also marvel at my premonition that an abrupt separation had the capacity to destroy me.

"Curtis, I just want you to get well," I said.

"I am getting well." His faith calmed me. It was all I really needed.

One morning in early August, I awoke to Curtis' head rubbing mine. I knew that he wished he could wake me with a kiss or a hug, a hint that he was ready for some love. It had been a long while since he was able to hold me.

"You don't have to go to the bathroom right now, do you?"

Curtis shook his head no.

We made love for an hour. Curtis asked me with his eyes to hold his hands on my hips, so that he could feel my flesh and then they asked me to stop moving. Curtis watched me move on top of him. When he was well, the lights had always been off, or we would hide our bodies from one another under the covers. We had loved each other distantly. There was a part of ourselves that we had been afraid to let the other see, and I think that we thought if we hid our physical bodies from one another, our true spirits would remain hidden as well. ALS took his body away from us bit by bit, but prompted our souls to reveal themselves.

As I lay with my head on his chest, I felt Curtis' head brush mine again and I looked up to see his wide-open eyes. He had to go to the bathroom. I pulled off of him, scrambled toward the Hoyer, ran into the bathroom, and flew back toward him with the bucket. I pulled his upper body forward, jammed the Hoyer pad behind him, lifted his left leg, shoved the pad under and did the same with his right side. I slipped the pad's hoops over the bars of the Hoyer and cranked him up. I grabbed the bucket, pulled the Hoyer back, and slipped the bucket under Curtis' butt, forgetting to direct his penis toward the bucket. Curtis' pee squirted all over the floor, the walls and Woo Woo, who had risen from the dog bed in order to witness the commotion.

Curtis' eyes yelled, "Why don't you ever remember?"

I did not reply. I had yelled at Curtis the day before when I had not had the bucket ready, and the second the Hoyer lifted his butt off the bed, he had gone to the bathroom. It had taken me an hour to clean up the poop and pee from the grooves of the wide pine floor. The day before that, Curtis hadn't been able to wait for me to pull him away from the bed, and he had soiled the bed sheets.

Curtis' green eyes turned dark and his facial expression said what he could not with the nighttime mask covering his mouth. He had had enough.

"Curtis, do not give up on me. Please."

Sleep, for me, had become impossible because I feared that the time was coming. I hoped that he would at least make it to his 26th birthday party, which was planned for two and a half weeks from then, but I was also sure that he was getting ready to go. I could no longer comprehend him staying here; he was tired, sad, and sick of not being able to move, to be, to live. That night, after a particularly hard day full of disappointment and frustration, I lay awake listening to his body wanting to stop; I heard his soul wanting to fly away. I wrote in my journal, *"But he is not quite done here. God, I pray to you for a miracle. I pray to you for a child: a healthy, non-SOD1-mutated girl. I see her in my dreams, a beautiful baby girl who looks like him, like me."*

The probability of getting pregnant was almost zero; I was still on birth control. At the time, our rational minds could not justify bringing a human into this life knowing that there was a chance the child could someday suffer through ALS. Curtis said that he could not endure the possibility, and at the time I couldn't imagine watching another person whom I loved with all of my being live with ALS. And, yet, despite our hesitancies, we spoke about having children almost every day.

We also spoke about some of the times over the years when I thought I might have been pregnant. Because of my irregular cycle, there had been more than a few of these instances. We both smiled when we recounted that first time after that first summer; there really had been no reason to worry. I had never shared with Curtis the second occurrence: it took place when I was a senior in college. Even though I loved Curtis and dreamt of having his child, I didn't want to get pregnant before graduation. As I told Curtis about that time, he told me that he wished I had allowed him to carry the burden of worry as well – he was sad that I had carried it all on my own. The third time was a few months before Curtis started to feel ill. At the time, I had confided in Curtis that I was worried. Before I took the test, he told me that he very much hoped it would be negative.

"We're not ready for a baby," he had said.

When we recounted this occurrence, months after the diagnosis, Curtis confided, "Maybe it would've been okay."

Despite Curtis' terminal illness and his adamant stance that he didn't want to chance passing on the gene to his own child, I yearned for his child because I loved him. I also wanted to believe that we could have a family like we had always planned, and a very selfish part of me wanted to get pregnant so that I could hold a piece of Curtis in my life forever.

As I lay in bed that August night, I thought back to a morning years beforehand when I had been in Curtis' bedroom at his parents' house. He had gotten up early for work and I could not fall back asleep. Turning over in his bed, I glanced at a class picture that lay on his carpet. First, second, third grade, or was it kindergarten? I didn't know, but his beauty and innocence made me cry. Recalling that moment, I was not sure if I had cried that morning out of joy for what I had thought was to come someday, or for what would never be. Could I have foreseen the fact that he would never live to have a child of his own? I wrote in my journal, *"Curtis is breathing better at this moment, so I shall go to bed for he will wake up early. I will try my hardest to be kind and not get annoyed at the time of day that he wakes me. I am so tired, and yet afraid to sleep, exhausted and yet wired. I don't know what to do but love him."*

The next day Curtis told me that he had decided that under no circumstances did he want a respirator. He asked me if I would help him tell the others, so I called a meeting that afternoon. Curtis and I sat in our living room as I informed those who would ever be alone with him that his living will, the same one that he had declared in March, was in the cubby of our oak desk.

"Curtis has decided that when he stops breathing, that's it. No CPR. No ventilation. Do not call the ambulance for they will be obligated to administer CPR. It's their job. You must call the police, explain that you have a Do Not Resuscitate patient, and they will come and declare his death."

Curtis said nothing as I declared this to his parents, my sisters, our neighbor who visited often and helped us tremendously on a daily basis, and his friend Joe.

Later, when we were alone, Curtis asked, "Heather seemed relieved, didn't she?"

"She's been anxious the last few times I have left for a walk.

She is afraid to make a mistake. We all are. Now she knows what to do."

Heather, who was also a teacher in Connecticut, spent as much time as she could with us in Vermont that summer, too. Ever since that first summer Curtis and I had met, she and he had enjoyed a special relationship. Curtis was very protective of Heather. So much so that when Heather called me one day a few years prior to let me know that she had decided to leave her husband, Curtis insisted that we drive down to North Carolina immediately so we could get her and all of her belongings.

"My parents were shocked and not pleased," Curtis continued.

"Baby, they don't want to lose you. Although we cannot even begin to imagine how you feel, we do feel our own pain."

"I have had enough. I am ready to get better."

"You will, baby."

A week later, at our August appointment at MGH, we told our doctor that we had decided that we did not want a respirator.

"Okay, but I will give you the numbers of some doctors in Burlington just in case you change your mind and we need someone in the area to perform the procedure."

Throughout the visit all of the doctors and nurses commented how wonderful Curtis looked. Many of them asked him if they thought he might have hit a plateau.

"Not quite," Curtis answered. "My neck is a little weaker and so is my breathing and my left arm."

"Oh, but you look as though you are doing so well," they all said.

Curtis attributed his great looks to his new hot tub. He had been so tired of sitting and was aware that his range of motion was decreasing and so one night a few weeks beforehand he had said, "I need to buy a hot tub." I stayed awake all night calculating the weeks of groceries we could buy for the price of the hot tub and tried to figure if we would have enough money for the nursing care I imagined we would need for the final months or weeks if Curtis should get his wish and die at home.

"If we don't live for today, then what are we living for?" Curtis asked me.

A few days later I wrote out a $5,000 check. We still had money left from the numerous fundraisers that the townspeople had held for us when Curtis was first diagnosed. And Curtis was still being paid his full time salary from the plant. We understood that their policy was that they would pay him sick time for up to a year. The expression on Curtis' face the first time he was lowered into the hot tub was priceless, and the next morning he awoke with a smile, "I am happy, again. I am free."

On the ride home from Boston in August, Mom, our driver again that month, asked Curtis what his plans were once he got better. Curtis loved to speak about what things would be like once he got better.

"I will start and own our business." He strained to look back at me from the front seat. "We will work together, until you have our babies. This way, we can be together all day just like we are now, and we can have our Woo Woo with us."

His dreams made him so happy. They inspired me, too, but then, later, they made me so sad. That night, I questioned the fairness of our situation as I put Curtis to bed, "Why now, when we are finally realizing all that we are? Why now when we are so aware of one another and our needs and wants? Why now when we both know that we want to spend the rest of our lives together?"

We celebrated Curtis' 26th birthday in mid-August with a grand party at *The Stagger Inn* in North Danville. It was an outdoor party with food, drink, and many people. It was a celebration of Curtis' birth and of his life. We celebrated the fact that he had lived with ALS for over a year (in hindsight we figured that he had started to experience symptoms in July or so of 1998) thus surpassing the six to 12 month prognosis, albeit with the aid of the BiPAP. And he wasn't just alive. He was living.

Like the weekly healing circles, the birthday party became an opportunity for others to express to Curtis what he meant to them. Many people came up to him and shared a few words; others stood beside him for what seemed like a very long time telling story after story having to do with something they did together in the past; still others wrote cards and shared their feelings through the written word. Curtis' co-worker who hadn't seen Curtis since he had physically worked at the plant, over eight months beforehand, wasn't able to come to his birthday party.

Instead she wrote to him in part, "I don't know if you realize just how special you are to me. You were so patient with me when we first started working together. Your jokes, I didn't know how to take at first. The more I worked with you, I saw how vibrant and full of life and energy and how positive you are and you didn't let things or people get to you. And keeping two jobs going and keeping up your relationship with your girlfriend and how special and compatible (and competitive!) you two were. I had nothing but admiration and respect for you. I really miss working with you and just listening to you. Just your outlook on everything gives me this inner strength. I miss you so much and I love you dearly. You are a great friend. Don't lose your faith. There are a lot of us praying for you. I am keeping your chair warm."

The day after Curtis turned 26, we received the papers in the mail that we had requested in order to verify the beneficiary of his life insurance through his place of work. We had taken this step because we had started to talk about his funeral and burial. Curtis had no idea how much his life insurance was worth but had said that he was sure that it would cover the funeral and related expenses.

"How much are funerals?" I asked.

"I have no idea," he replied.

As legal power of attorney, I signed the documents designating me as the beneficiary like Curtis had asked me to do.

All that was left to do was to prepare a document declaring his burial wishes.

That same day I wrote in my journal, "*Every time I hold his hand in mine, or intertwine our fingers, or look into his eyes, I concentrate on memorizing the lines, their shape, and their beauty. Today, while I held him in our hot tub, and yesterday, while we sat with his hand lying upon mine, all I could wonder was how strange and wonderful the physical is. And yet, what is it? What is it exactly that separates those who are 'alive,' the earthly humans, from the spiritual passers, or those we call the 'dead'? What is it that Curtis is now that he won't be if he dies?*"

There were now fasciculations, muscle twitches, under the skin in Curtis' chin. This was a telltale sign that the motor neurons that control his facial muscles were dying.

At the healing circle that evening, with everyone silent and waiting to hear what he had to say that week, instead of speaking to the crowd, he looked directly at me and declared, "I love you." Although he recited the words to me daily, he did not normally express his emotion in public. I lived to hear those words. I loved his voice.

After I put him to bed around nine, I turned off all of the lights.

He whimpered, "Turn a light on. I am so scared."

After I turned one on, he asked if I could buy a few night-lights.

As I lay awake beside him, I thought, *of course he is scared in the dark. He can't move. He can hardly be heard. How scary and horrible. How does he go on? Will he be ready for more? Losing his voice? Not being able to swallow?* I wanted to hold onto him forever, but I did not know how much longer he wanted to be here. He still said that he was so sure that he would reverse it. I wanted to believe that he would survive and someday be healthy and fine, but I did not know if we could handle the steps in between. We had made it this far, so I supposed that we could keep going. But I was so tired.

A week later Curtis complained of constipation. And he had strained his back while being transferred. He was so uncomfortable that we didn't even go in the hot tub for two days. Instead, I massaged his back and his butt while he lay on his side, and then I turned him over and gave him his medicine. After I had gotten him ready for bed, and was in the process of preparing for the next day, Curtis motioned with his eyes and head for me to drop what I was doing and rub him.

With his legs pushed up towards his chest, and my hands under his butt, he said through the nighttime mask, "This isn't so fun anymore."

For the third time since the official diagnosis, eight months beforehand, I was certain that he would die. Time stopped, I panicked silently, and yet he lay next to me.

"Are you sad?" I asked.

"I am not happy."

My hands slipped out from under him, I took off my Tevas, climbed next to him, and lay beside him. I held him with all of my soul and then I cried. I hadn't meant to.

When he noticed my tears he said, "I'm okay."

"You are not okay, Curtis, and it's okay not to be okay. Are you really sad?"

"It is hard to be happy now."

The weight that I had been carrying on my shoulders since the day I had decided that I had to be strong for him crashed down through my bones, ran through my blood, rushed out of me as quickly as it had appeared so many months earlier. "Curtis, I am so tired. Are you?"

"Yes."

"But I don't want to lose you." The tears rushed down as fervently as the weight had just a few moments before.

"I am ready to go to bed now," he declared.

The tiredness that I had allowed to sweep over me could not just vanish. The weight reappeared, and its heaviness made me feel as though I were drowning. *Help me, somebody please, help me.* But Curtis couldn't hold me or touch me in order to attempt to make me feel better. He could only wait out his own pain.

I got up, turned on the kitchen light so that Curtis would not be enveloped in darkness, turned off all the others, sat down at my desk, and turned on my computer.

"What are you doing?"

"Writing."

"Why?"

"I don't know what else to do."

"I think that I will feel better when I poop."

Curtis knew that he could not let me think he had given up.

The next day Curtis told me that he wanted to be embalmed, have an open wake, and be buried in his own plot in Danville that Woo Woo and I would choose. The following day Woo Woo and I walked through the cemetery and found the spot immediately. High on the hill, looking out at the White Mountains, I felt at home.

# Learning to Live
# While Preparing to Die

After surviving beyond the twelve month prognosis from the onset of symptoms (with the aid of the BiPap) and thus surpassing the hurdle of false pretenses, we believed that we would be together for Woo Woo's eighth month birthday in September, which we were. We imagined harvesting our pumpkin patch together, which we did. Every day we made new plans and goals. We looked forward to going down to Middlebury College on Saturdays in the fall to watch Tricia play her tennis matches. We planned on setting up *The Stagger Inn* so that Curtis could enjoy hunting season and hang out at camp, his favorite place. We had visions of watching Woo Woo play in the snow for the first time. Curtis and I had faith that we would see these events take place.

We also had dreams. We envisioned Curtis walking with a cane by Christmas, which is where he had been physically the Christmas before. We were invited to speak to the local Rotary club and during that speech, I told them about our vision of Curtis walking with a cane by Christmas and afterwards many of them came to us and said, "We are sure that it will come true."

We imagined Curtis and me and Woo Woo hiking that next spring, and running and playing ball that next summer. And, we pictured our wedding day: Curtis and I standing side-by-side in front of our friends and family outdoors at Joe's Pond.

"It'll be a beautiful day," Curtis assured me. "Not too hot. Not too cold. Just a slight breeze."

"Do you think it'll happen, Curtis?"

"Yes. Next spring or summer. I have no doubt."

Looking back upon the late summer/early fall of that year that Curtis was sick, I marvel at how optimistic and, I suppose some would say, unrealistic we were in believing that Curtis would ever walk again or that we would celebrate our wedding. I can only explain it, again, with the fact that at that point in time we loved one another so deeply, so truly, so remarkably that neither one of us could imagine being without the other. The only practical solution, the only answer that at the time we could comprehend, was that Curtis would have to survive.

But, just as we simultaneously traveled mainstream and alternative medical paths in our search for a cure, we confronted the idea of death at the same time that we imagined that Curtis' ALS would stop destroying his motor neurons and that he would regain strength. We were straddling two worlds, two streams of thought – a balancing act that we would both experience again.

One person in particular who pushed Curtis to explore the idea of death was Cathy, a minister at one of the local churches. She helped us to contemplate the worst possible scenario and, as a result, Curtis and I learned of yet another miracle, the miracle of death. Curtis and I grew to understand that death is a miracle, for in the process of preparing for death, we were learning to live. She helped us to accept that the only certainty in life was that we would die and that that rule applied to everyone but that we were the lucky ones because we were given time to live while we prepared to die.

In August, our community urged us to hold a healing circle at the annual Danville Fair. About 150 people attended this healing circle, during which many people commented to us, "I want to help," and "I want to be a part of your project." The green ribbon campaign was born out of this healing circle during which we explained that we were learning to live while preparing to die. We asked those who supported Curtis and me in this idea to wear a green ribbon, or adorn their car or house or other things with green ribbon. Within a few days, the color green surrounded us: people wrapped green ribbons around their trees, placed them on their cars and doors and displayed them on their lapels. Once again our families, friends and community members showed their support in amazing fashion.

As the Vermont summer drew to a close, we also experimented with hypnosis. Cathy believed strongly in the power of one's mind and had extensive experience using hypnosis to dull her own pain from a chronic health condition from which she had suffered for over 30 years. Cathy hypothesized that Curtis, while under hypnosis, could try to manage and work through his own physical and emotional pain. As had been the case since almost the beginning of our journey, Curtis was willing to try almost anything.

Once Curtis, who was seated in his blue recliner in our home, was in a hypnotic state, Cathy tried to guide him toward figuring out how to manage the pain that accompanied not being able to move his body. Curtis began to speak and he told Cathy that he found himself in an old abandoned house and that there was a large man present. She prodded Curtis in order to learn where he was, who he was, how he got there and the identity of the large man.

After a few minutes of silence, Curtis answered, "I am in my late teens in battle with an old machine gun in a different country crawling through long grass. I have been shot in the shoulder as well as in the back. Other men are protecting me. We are all going into this old house for shelter against the enemy and then suddenly there's an explosion. I can't see anything. It's all blank."

Silence.

Cathy questioned, "Do you see anything now?"

"The large figure, the man, is beside me, still. He's been with me the whole time. I think that it is God. And, now, there's an angel taking me 'home' to heaven," Curtis explained as a few tears ran down his face.

I cried. At the time, I believed that I was tearing because Curtis' experiences while under hypnosis forced me to consider altered states of existence. As I write about this moment in time, though, I realize that I may have physically expelled my emotion because this was the first time that Curtis spoke about angels and going "home."

While he was still under hypnosis, Cathy asked Curtis how he could apply what he learned from this experience to his current situation with ALS, and he answered, "That I did all I could do but that I also have to keep trying. Persist. Never give up. I can win the battle."

Cathy then asked him to go to a place where he was happiest.

"I am here. At the back farm. I see all of the apple trees. Now I am on a ladder, picking the apples from the trees." Curtis continued, "Now, I am in a cabin. It's not *The Stagger Inn* but it's by the orchard. We are slow dancing. We have always loved to dance."

Again, I cried although I was confused. There weren't any apple trees at the back farm. And, there was no other cabin. I had no idea how significant this experience would come to be years later.

Despite our spiritual and emotional growth, though, the disease progressed. Yet even as his body continued to turn on itself, Curtis continued to appreciate life and his faith seldom faltered. At a healing circle one August night, he commented, "There are a lot of different ways of approaching this. It's not that bad. I could have gotten hit by a car but here I've got all this time. And like I always say, who knows?" That same night he also said, "We've got these beautiful mountains. I've lived here my whole life, and I saw them, but I really never noticed them and their beauty. Now I do all the time."

One day he sat for hours in his blue recliner that I had dragged outside onto our newly poured square of concrete, which we called our patio. It allowed him to feel stable as he watched his garden grow. This particular day, he was waiting for a hummingbird. He marveled at how it could move its wings at incredible speed and yet stay in one place.

"This bird reminds me of me before ALS. I was always running. But not really going anywhere," Curtis marveled.

Yes, he had accomplished things of which he was proud, but what did these things really mean, he wondered. Right before ALS, he held two great jobs, was financially secure, lived with me, and ran himself ragged trying to please me, his family, his bosses, his co-workers, and his friends.

"ALS has given me time. Funny, isn't it? Time to live," Curtis said. "Time to notice the little things. Time to discover who I am, and what I want to be. Time to wonder what this life is all about, and why it is I am here."

"And why are you here?" I questioned.

"To learn how to love. To help my family understand this disease. To make a difference. To bring us all together. We're doing it. You and me," he answered and then continued, "Why aren't I getting better, then? Why isn't the BDNF working? Why can't they find a cure? Why did it trigger in the first place?"

In the beginning, we had hoped that the diagnosis was wrong. Then we had prayed for a cure, a miracle, a new, alternative treatment that would not only stop the progression of the disease, but also reverse the symptoms. Later, we wished for more good days than bad, for more quality time, rather than just time. Quality time, in our minds, was time spent with one another when Curtis wasn't extremely uncomfortable, in pain, or consumed with the fear of dying as a result of an accident or a mistake. The disturbing memories from the year that Curtis was sick grow more vivid as time moves forward because I blame myself for him having had to experience the pain. I wonder if I hadn't pushed so hard to encourage him at the beginning, would he have tried so hard to get better? Would it have been easier on him if he had just given up? And, was it my fault that he had gotten sick in the first place - I was the one who had told him in August of 1998 that if he didn't slow down, he'd get sick.

The progression of Curtis' familial ALS was so marked that there wasn't time for us to be proactive; we always found ourselves reacting to the disease. We were able to laugh about some of the accidents; others, though, never made us laugh.

One morning in September, I wanted to go for a bike ride. We had to leave for Boston for our monthly doctor's visit by 10 am and I desperately needed some exercise. I typically only left Curtis with one of my sisters, a few others, or our home health aide. It was a Tuesday. Our home health aide only came on Mondays, Wednesdays, and Fridays for an hour.

"Ask my mom," Curtis offered.

After she arrived and before I left, I whispered to Curtis, "I will be gone for less than a half an hour. I love you."

He blinked his eyes and went back to sleep. At the ten-minute mark in my ride, my stomach began to ache and my head swirled. I increased my speed on the return journey. Curtis' mother greeted me at the green kitchen door. Her face was ashen white and tears were in her eyes.

"I tried, but I didn't know what to do. I couldn't understand him. He..."

I pushed past her and saw Curtis. He was sitting straight up in bed, with the breathing machine's tube stuck in his mouth. His eyes were wide open as he struggled to keep his lips tight around the hose.

His color was good.

"Are you okay?"

He nodded "yes."

Curtis' mom was still talking, "... woke up and was trying to tell me something. I couldn't understand him. I put the head of the bed up. I saw that the mask had slipped. I grabbed it, pulled it down, and it came apart. I held the..."

I gathered the pieces of the nighttime mask, and tried to fit them together, but realized we didn't have too much time.

"You are going to be fine," I told Curtis. "Just give me a minute. I am going to run into the bathroom to get your daytime mask."

I returned. He was struggling. It took too much energy for him to take the air only through his mouth and to exhale it through his nose.

It took me one minute to put together the daytime mask.

"Now, on the count of three I will remove the hose from your mouth and then I will switch the hoses that go into the machine, just like we do at night and in the morning, okay?"

A second later, the transfer was complete.

His mother sobbed, "I didn't know what to do. After I pulled down the nighttime mask, he was lying there, and he couldn't breathe. The mask was broken. He was shaking his head and then I realized he was telling me to stick the hose in his mouth. I wasn't sure it would work. And then I waited for you to come home. I just waited."

From that day forward, I always had a daytime mask ready beside the bed. We also purchased an ambu bag, a plastic contraption with which someone could manually push air into him should the mask not work for one reason or another.

A second occurrence that we never laughed about happened just a few days after the BiPAP incident. There was a terrible windstorm that evening. As I crawled into bed, the electricity flickered. I sat up.

"If the power goes off, so will the BiPAP," I said to Curtis.

We realized that night that there wasn't an automatic backup battery for the system or an alarm. If the power went off and I was not awake, I would not know to plug the BiPAP into the battery pack.

"Can you stay awake and watch over me?" Curtis asked.

I knew that I was too tired to guarantee that I wouldn't fall asleep. Curtis suggested that I call his mother and his friend Joe. The three of us took shifts that night watching Curtis, with the ambu bag, battery pack and adaptor beside him, ready to be used. The power did go off three different times for a few minutes but each time we simply connected the BiPAP to the battery pack. The next day Joe bought Curtis a UPS (uninterrupted power system), so if we ever lost electricity again, an alarm would sound, and the BiPAP would keep going for at least ten minutes, giving me time to connect the BiPAP to our battery system.

A third incident that was particularly troubling happened one Sunday in September. I turned my back to Curtis while he sat in the driveway in his reclining wheelchair. The wheelie bars, which would normally protect the chair from tipping backwards, were up since I had just dragged the wheelchair backwards across the lawn home from church. I wasn't strong enough to push him when the grass was long. I turned around in time to watch him tip backwards. He did not lose his air, and he did not bang his head, but he was on the ground and his body was contorted into a shape that no one would put oneself in willingly. He writhed in pain while I called Joe and continued to whimper for the five minutes it took Joe to come to the house in order to help me pick Curtis up off the ground.

The next day, the hose that connected his daytime mask to the larger air hose started to "pop" off randomly. We bought a replacement, but after a few days it followed in the first hose's footsteps. We tried tape, which worked for a while, but as a result I could never leave Curtis alone even for a split second. I questioned our medical supplier about this faulty piece of equipment.

She reiterated, "The BiPAP isn't supposed to be used as life support. It is simply an aid. That's why it doesn't have a built-in battery or an alarm system."

We had originally agreed to use the BiPAP so that Curtis would sleep better at night but over a few months' time it had become life support. By the end of September, Curtis and I realized that he would die without the BiPAP. We also realized that we could turn it off if we chose to do so.

# The Feeding Tube

One morning in late September I awoke to Curtis' head rubbing mine just as it did every morning.

The phone rang.

I held the phone to Curtis' ear.

After a few seconds of listening he nodded, "Yes."

"Yes," I voiced into the speaker of the phone.

Curtis' words were now difficult to understand.

Curtis motioned for me to hang up the phone.

"What did we agree to?" I asked.

"Breakfast at the Inn at nine."

"It is already eight. I still have to brush your teeth, wash your face, give you your medicine, and get you dressed."

Curtis' body was no longer his. I did for it what it could not do itself which was practically everything.

"Let's get going, then."

Curtis hated to brush his teeth when we weren't able to get into the bathroom because he hated to spit into a cup. But the Hoyer didn't fit in the bathroom. We both loved it when our home health aide came for an hour to help me get Curtis into the shower; he loved to be doused with hot water from the showerhead while he sat on the tub bench. He also loved to have his teeth brushed in the shower because it was there that he could spit freely although the spit was now more like a drool. I could shower only if someone watched Curtis. I often didn't brush my own teeth, for I would forget that it was already night, or already morning, or already the next day. I didn't floss for over a year. This particular day was a Thursday, a day without our aide, so I brushed his teeth while he sat in his blue recliner and washed his arms, legs, and face with a baby washcloth and baby soap.

I brought him his 20 pills that needed to be swallowed before breakfast. Curtis always complained that his belly was too full to eat after the pills and it was especially bad now because they took so long to swallow. I demanded that he eat three meals a day and warned him to keep the weight on. We both knew that he would soon have trouble eating, but I was the one who would voice the concern.

"Why do you always have to state what will happen?" Curtis asked.

"Having knowledge of the future is my way of dealing," I explained. "I am the one caring for you and I need to know what to expect." This particular morning I couldn't leave it at that, though. I continued, "I don't see anyone else here, do you?"

Curtis' insurance didn't cover respite care, but more importantly, I didn't want anyone else to care for Curtis, just as he would have refused anyone else's help besides a handful of our friends and family who helped out for a few hours or for an evening a week while I waitressed. Curtis knew, though, why the tone of my voice carried bitterness. Since Curtis' diagnosis, my sisters lived with us whenever their lives allowed it. My mother helped throughout the summer while she was at the cottage. I had been spoiled all summer with my family around to help so now that I had been without them for a bit, I was in a state. Still, though, our neighbor was available for anything anytime. She cleaned, cooked, and visited almost daily. Joe was always willing to help; he came by the house often. A friend of ours who was a nurse offered her services as well. But most of Curtis' family, who lived in the same town, rarely helped with his daily physical care or the housework.

"You need to ask them," Curtis answered.

Asking for help did not come naturally to me.

"Please, just let it be," Curtis continued.

I did let it be. I let it be because I felt terrible for saying what I had said. I imagined, like I often did that year that Curtis was sick, that it was just too difficult for some members of his family to see the daily struggles that Curtis was forced to endure as a result of the disease because they knew that there was a chance that someday they, too, may experience ALS. I couldn't then and I still can't begin to comprehend how that fear would feel. I also imagined that, perhaps, they felt as though their constant presence would be viewed as an intrusion into our lives.

With Curtis ready to go, I walked toward the wheelchair.

Suddenly, I felt faint.

"Are you okay?" Curtis asked.

I made my way to our beds, my twin and his hospital bed which were pushed together in the corner of our living room, and sat down. I didn't feel well and hadn't been feeling well for a while. A few weeks beforehand I had begun to have coughing fits, which would escalate into me not being able to breathe, and then I would feel as though I had to throw up. One day, after running with Woo Woo in the fields of North Danville while Curtis sat in the front seat of the blue Chevy Blazer watching us, and me keeping my eyes on him the entire time to be sure that the hose on his BiPAP didn't pop off, I threw up. Then, I began to throw up almost daily. I went to the doctor. He asked me questions, one of which was, "Do you cough upon laughing?" I couldn't answer him because I couldn't remember the last time I had laughed. I mean, really,

really laughed.

As I wheeled Curtis down the main street that September day toward the Danville Inn, he said, "I think that we'd make great parents."

This was the first time that Curtis mentioned children without my urging.

"And I was thinking. We should buy a house. It's time to have our own house," Curtis continued.

Curtis' ability to continue to see our lives progressing forward as though ALS didn't exist allowed me to continue to imagine that he just might survive.

As amazing as it was that the progression of the disease seemed to level off in September because there didn't seem to be any apparent, significant loss of abilities, more mind-boggling was the fact that in just the first week of October, Curtis' ability to swallow and speak declined rapidly. He began to choke frequently whenever he drank, ate, or took his medicine. The choking spells were horrific. While he struggled to breathe, I was convinced he was going to die a horrible death. If he was able to use his voice at all during these episodes, he would try to yell at me. If he couldn't, then he would try to yell at me afterwards. He grew angrier each subsequent time he struggled. I began to pray for a peaceful death. I didn't want our last moments together to be marked by anger or defined by guilt or the thought that if only I had done this or done that.

Around this time we received a note in the mail from Curtis' ex-girlfriend. When I first saw her married last name on the return address on the red envelope my heart raced and my palms pooled with sweat. I felt like a jealous young girl.

I read the note to Curtis which in part said, "I'm so sorry. I don't want to interfere with your life but I do want you to know that I'm thinking of you. I am here if you would like a friend."

My gut reaction was to tell Curtis that there was no way he was going to see her. The old feelings of jealousy and spite only lasted a split second.

Instead, I said to Curtis, "We should invite her up to the house to visit."

"Are you sure?" he asked.

"Yes. You should see her. She needs to see you."

I called her because she wouldn't have understood Curtis' speech.

I invited her up to visit.

A few days later, she came with her parents and we all visited together; I had to remain in order to help interpret Curtis' words for them. We surrounded Curtis who sat in his blue reclining chair. I am grateful for that visit that allowed me to see her for who she really was: a kind, compassionate woman who loved Curtis.

A few days later after her visit she wrote me a note that read in part, "Thank you so much for inviting me up to see Curtis. That meant so much to me. You are a wonderful, caring person. You and Curtis are lucky to have each other. Two very special people. If you ever want someone to talk to – I'm around a lot. If you would like to go for a walk or do something – I would like that."

Twenty-two years later, she and I keep in touch via social media. We have never gone for that walk, though. I look forward to sitting down with her over a glass or two of wine and talking about Curtis someday. I am ready to hear their story - one of the only parts of Curtis' life about which I don't know.

One afternoon in the first half of October, the turkey wrap Curtis was eating for lunch slipped down his airway causing him to choke because he lacked the strength to cough it up. I called an ambulance to take Curtis to the local hospital in St. Johnsbury. X-rays revealed that while the sandwich had dislodged itself, he did have fluid in his lungs and a good chance of developing pneumonia. I had read that many ALS patients die of pneumonia. The doctors gave him an antibiotic and sent us home.

For the next two days, Curtis was mean. He tried to yell at me constantly, and when his voice grew too tired, he ignored me. Finally, I encouraged him to get into the hot tub. Here, I held him and told him that I could deal with the disease taking his body, and even his life, but I would not stand for it to destroy us.

"Curtis, you have been so good about not blaming and being angry at others. You have done an incredible job with keeping positive and believing in yourself."

"Lot a good it's done," he slowly responded. "Look at me."

"But, as you've told me, you've been healing. Spiritually and emotionally, you're better. We just have to focus on the physical, now."

"I've been focusing. It's not working. It's not going to work."

"Maybe it won't. We have to face that. But anger is a cop-out. I refuse to stand by and watch you be angry. Not now. Not after all that we've done. This disease is taking your physical abilities away from us, and I can deal with that. But if you let this disease take you away from me before your body fails on us then that is when I will leave. I will walk away, Curtis. I cannot bear to watch you let this disease get the best of you."

And, then, I begged, "Please don't take away the little time we have left together."

"Aren't you sick of me, yet?" he whispered. "Why are you still here? Since the beginning, I have told you that we have to take people for who they are. We cannot expect them to change just because I am sick. We both know that so many others have had to be reminded to visit me; and when they are here they comment that they wished they could visit longer or more often but that they are just so busy. There are exceptions, yes, but no one has sacrificed their life. Why have you?"

"You are my life, Curtis. Don't you know that by now? You are all that I have."

I cupped the base of his head with my hand, so that it would not bang against the side of the hot tub, held his back with my arm, and allowed him to slip inside of me. Making love in our hot tub had become routine ever since the fall. The hot tub allowed Curtis' body to experience freedom from pain so his mind could concentrate on us.

A while later, I began, "Our beings have been coming closer to one another's since the day we met. And now, we are..."

"One," we both finished.

Because Curtis had brought up the topic of children and a house numerous times over the last few days, I asked him, again, if he wanted to get married. His usual answer was, "I don't want to marry you and then die on you." This day his answer was the same.

But he continued, "How about we get engaged?" he asked.

"Yes," I replied. The prospect of being engaged felt exciting for a brief moment.

There was no time, though, to think, talk, or act upon this

new development. The next day we went to Boston for our monthly trip. Our doctor spoke to us about a feeding tube. We didn't know what to do so we asked him for his opinion.

"It may be better to die by respiratory distress peacefully with morphine than starve to death, waste away, lose your body totally and be incredibly susceptible to infection," he said.

We appreciated his honesty and professional view.

Curtis and I decided to opt for a feeding tube. Our doctor didn't think that it needed to be done right away so he sent us home to Vermont.

The next day Curtis suffered from dehydration. We returned to the emergency room in St. Johnsbury and spent the night in the hospital. The following day, our doctor in Boston asked the staff in St. Johnsbury to keep us through the weekend so that Curtis could stay hydrated via IVs through Monday, which would be the earliest they could schedule the surgery for the feeding tube. And so we did. Over the weekend, there were 15 people in our hospital room at any given time. Many of these people were those who had not visited or spent quality time with us in months. Curtis' favorite visitor, though, was Woo Woo; I sneaked him into the hospital room. Although we missed being at our house, it was nice for me to be able to sit in one place. I still took care of all of Curtis' needs; he wouldn't allow the nurses to do anything.

On our third day in the St. Johnsbury hospital, while Curtis was in the room with his many visitors, a minister from another local church, with whom Curtis and I had spent a lot of time, spoke with me alone in the hallway.

I confided in her about how frustrated I was when his anger took over, "I've told him, though, that his greatest gift to me would be for him to be able to continue to separate himself and his actions from this learned behavior."

Our minister listened to my concerns and then asked about the next steps in terms of Curtis' health.

"We will go down to Boston to get a feeding tube. We have to, again, decide whether or not to have a ventilator. I am pretty sure that Curtis will not choose it. He can only move his head and his eyes. He can barely be heard and only I can understand his speech. He's had enough. But we've got it all planned. He would like to die at home. And he wants only Woo Woo and me there in the end."

"Have you thought about marriage?" she asked.

"We talk about it often. Actually, we've agreed to get engaged. There hasn't been any time to think about when or how. He just doesn't want to marry me and then die on me."

"I hear what you are saying and what you are feeling," she replied, "But, I imagine that it would be a lot easier for a wife to ask to be alone with her husband than for a girlfriend to kick a family out."

She asked if I would mind if she spoke to Curtis and me alone. She encouraged me to practice my assertiveness by asking those in the hospital room to leave.

We walked into the hospital room.

"Would you excuse us, please? We need a few minutes alone," I asked.

Some family members looked at me and others at Curtis.

Curtis nodded his head toward me.

Once alone, the minister asked Curtis, "Have you thought about getting married?"

Curtis spoke and I interpreted his words, "It's the one thing I still want to do. I just don't want to marry her and then die on her."

She explained to Curtis what she had said to me about the

difficulty I might face in the near future if we were not married.

"I want to get married," Curtis agreed. "It's time to acknowledge our eternal love in front of God and it's about time we displayed our affection in public for all of society to witness."

Curtis, the one who had often struggled to express his true feelings verbally, recited these words perfectly at a time when it meant the most.

We returned to our home the next day and waited for the phone call from our doctor in Boston. He had let us know that he would call us immediately once a bed opened up. After he called, I told Curtis' family that we would drive down alone. I knew that we could still opt for the ventilator and that the doctors would encourage us to have both surgeries at the same time. We needed the time alone to make a final decision.

Others helped me get him into the blue Chevy Blazer. We weren't sure how I'd get him out once we got to the hospital. Curtis had become so weak and paralyzed that it took more than one person to transfer him from place to place even with the Hoyer lift but we really wanted to make this trip alone. We figured it would work out. We barely spoke during the three-hour drive except while we sat in traffic ten miles outside of the city.

Curtis looked out his window at the other cars, "I wish we were going to the Red Sox game like all of these other people, don't you?"

Curtis and I spoke for the last bit of the trip about how abnormal we had become. In our minds, our lives were suddenly defined by sickness and restriction although we had been knowingly living with ALS for ten months.

"Everything else up until this point has been pretty

manageable," I said, "Except, of course, those weeks last winter when you had the spinal headaches."

"That was awful," Curtis agreed. "The past months have been pretty good. This past summer reminded me of the summer before when we spent so much time together and with friends and family. Kind of the same. But different."

"It's been better and worse than I could have ever imagined," I replied.

"Yes," he said. "Better. And worse."

We reminisced about our trip to Vancouver in January and our trip to Amish country that we took in the spring. Curtis' mother had been in Ohio for business and we decided to drive out to spend Easter with her. We also went deep-sea fishing in March with two of Curtis' buddies with whom he went fishing almost every year. Curtis had recently gone to a Nascar race with his brothers and met his favorite driver, Tony Stuart, in person. Most importantly, though, we spent every day together.

"I feel as though I've lived a lifetime with you," Curtis said.

We were now only a few miles from the hospital but traffic was at a standstill. I turned my attention from the road to Curtis.

"I feel like we're 80 years old," he continued. "And, I would do it all again with you. This part, though, is hard."

Almost literally overnight, we had crossed the threshold from living our lives to waiting. Waiting for the pain, exhaustion, and anxiety to end.

That night I slept beside Curtis in the hospital bed. The nurses allowed it because he was not capable of pushing the call button for help. And, then, the next day we were granted most of the day to decide whether or not to have the ventilator. If we chose it, we figured that unless he developed pneumonia or something like that, he could live indefinitely. It wouldn't be too long, though, before he was fully paralyzed. Unable to move. Unable to eat. Unable to speak. If we didn't choose a ventilator, we really didn't know how much longer he'd be alive.

Curtis was unable to make a decision until I asked him, "What do you need in order to be happy?"

"What do you need?" he asked me.

"I would like to be married, have children, and have time to write," I answered.

"I would need to be married, have children, a nice house, and be able to walk."

I saw defeat in his eyes. Given the deterioration of Curtis' body, at that moment we couldn't envision him walking in this lifetime. We chose to forego the tracheotomy. But like so many other moments throughout the time we had lived with ALS, we fought to maintain normalcy. We needed to feel like 20-something year olds. And so we spent the remainder of our day planning our wedding and talking of the children about whom we dreamed. Curtis spoke to the nurses and me about his desire to have me with him during the feeding tube surgery.

"She has to be in there," he said. "I can't do this without her."

The next day I was in the room with Curtis for the surgery. I watched on the screen as they put a tube down his throat that had a camera at the end. Soon after, I heard piercing beeping noises.

"Get her out," a doctor said.

"You need to come with me, honey," a nurse put her hands on my shoulders and pushed me toward the door.

The nurse left me right outside the room and rushed back inside. I put my ear to the door but couldn't hear anything. I stood there for what seemed like a half a day but was most likely around a half an hour.

Then, the nurse came out and hugged me, "He made it. His breathing became very compromised. We almost lost him several times. He's a fighter."

That night I asked him why and how he continued to have the strength and determination to live.

"I told you I'd marry you, and I will," Curtis answered.

Curtis' parents arrived at the hospital the day after the surgery. They spent time with us in the hospital room. They were there when the occupational therapist taught us how to use an alphabet letter spelling board so that others beside me could communicate directly with him and in preparation for when he couldn't even mumble to me. They were there when the nurses came in to teach me how to use the feeding tube although they explained that someone would come to our home and go over it again. They were there when all of the doctors visited each day. Curtis' doctors genuinely liked him and it was a teaching hospital so many medical students would come in to meet the 26-year-old ALS patient who had become almost fully paralyzed in less than a year since diagnosis.

I appreciated Curtis' parents being there, especially because their presence allowed me to attend a reception in my father's honor in Connecticut. He had been elected "1999 person of the year," by the Wethersfield Business and Civic Association. My aunt and uncle who lived in New Hampshire offered to pick me up and drop me back off at the hospital on their way to and from the event.

On the third day after the surgery, though, once I returned

from my six-hour-long trip to and from Connecticut, I told Curtis' parents that they could go. We'd be fine alone, I had said. They stayed. The next day, the day that we were being released, they arrived at the room at 7:30 am even though I had asked them to not arrive before nine. And then Curtis' mother stated that she would drive herself back to Vermont and that his father would drive us back.

"We would really like the time to be by ourselves, again. Once we get home we'll be inundated with visitors," I stated.

"He will drive you," she said and then left.

My heart began to race. I felt as though I had lost control of my life. But I didn't say anything to her as she flew out of the hospital room without waiting for a reaction to her statement.

But later, I cried to Curtis, "We are fighting so hard to stay alive but why live when we can't even control the time that we have left?"

We arrived home after six days to discover that in our absence Woo Woo had developed a terribly high fever, had refused to eat, barely drank, and turned jaundice. The whites of his eyes as well as the skin under his fur were bright yellow. As I bent down to pick him up, his burning frail body collapsed into my arms. Curtis kissed him and insisted that he get better. I begged him to get better. Immediately upon our return, he resumed eating and drinking and recovered.

Curtis suffered from diarrhea for the first week back at home as a result of the feedings via the feeding tube. He had numerous accidents. We looked forward to getting the drip machine (once the insurance company signed off on it) because then he could be fed slowly all night long and, hopefully, regain control over his bowel movements. With Curtis' physical condition so deteriorated, others began taking over our lives more and more each day. After Curtis' mom told us that we should no longer host the healing circles in our home and that she had asked the Inn's owner if he would host them at the Inn, we attempted to take back control by holding a meeting, again, with Curtis' parents as well as others who spent the most time with Curtis and me.

With Curtis' urging, I spoke to them about the importance of us continuing to make our own decisions, "We chose the feeding tube so that we could continue to live, but without independence and control over our own lives, it's not a life worth living."

We also informed them that when the time came, we wanted to spend the last moments together, alone: Curtis, Woo Woo, and I.

# The Engagement

I had asked my parents not to come to the hospital in Boston for the feeding tube surgery because there wasn't much that they could help us with there. But, I encouraged them to visit us up in Vermont once we returned home. They drove up that next weekend, Halloween weekend. That Saturday night, Curtis insisted that he was comfortable enough to go out to dinner, so we went out. Curtis watched us while we ate. Upon our return to the house, my mom lit the 34 pumpkins that we had carved during our pumpkin carving party that past week. Over 20 people had come over to help us carve the pumpkins that Curtis and I had harvested on his aunt and uncle's land that past summer. He had sat in his blue recliner and watched with delight while we laughed, talked, ate, drank, and carved ghoulish scenes in our pumpkins. People and parties still brightened Curtis' mood.

Immediately upon returning home from dinner, I transferred Curtis into bed. He could only sit in his wheelchair for a short amount of time now before he could no longer stand the pain brought on by the weight of his body combined with the inability to move. I was about to ask my parents to leave; I knew Curtis was tired. He asked me to tell my dad that he wanted to ask him something.

On the night before Halloween, Curtis sat in his bed, with my standing father beside him. It was ten months after the diagnosis. Curtis was sitting at a 90-degree angle with his daytime mask on. He said something to my dad.

"I love your daughter very much and I want to spend the rest of my life with her."

My father remained where he was, silent.

"Dad, did you understand him?" I asked.

"No."

"I am asking if I can marry her," Curtis clarified.

My father did not say anything.

"Dad, did you understand him?" I asked.

"No."

Curtis' speech was almost always completely unintelligible when Curtis was tired.

"Dad, he asked you if he could marry me," I interpreted the words.

My father answered, "Wow," as my mother walked in from outside.

"What's going on?" my mom asked.

My father replied, "We have both thought of you as a son for a long time. Marriage now would just be a formality as far as we are concerned. You have our blessing, and we hope that things will turn in your favor in terms of Curtis' health."

The next morning, Sunday morning, Halloween morning, Curtis and I designed our gravestone along with our friend who worked for a granite company. He would carve some of the stone himself.

"How many plots? This needs to be determined in order to figure out how large the stone will be," our friend asked.

"Two." Curtis did not hesitate.

I looked at Curtis. He smiled. We had never spoken about this. I did not question his statement; it felt right.

That night I wrote in my journal, "*If he does not make it I will* have a whole life ahead of me. It may sound crazy that we are to be buried together. But I do believe that Curtis will continue to live, and if he does not, Curtis and I are eternally involved, soul mates. We will meet in heaven. And if he is to go now, I want him to go with the knowledge that someday I will join him in the earth at the same time we join in heaven. He will forever own my heart. I will forever be his girl. Although I may someday fall in love again, Curtis and I will someday rest in peace side by side in this town that has been magical for it has transformed me and illustrated love, compassion, and generosity, and given Curtis and me the opportunity to love one another effortlessly. I have experienced a lifetime of love with Curtis. He will stay here with me. He must. Perhaps our wedding will be the beginning. It is a testament of our desire and commitment to live. As Curtis said again today, he is not marrying me so that he can die."

On the front of the stone, the side facing the White Mountains of New Hampshire, a scene would be engraved of a sun and its rays rising above a lake with the green mountains as a backdrop. The engraving would also show the trees' reflection in the water. This represented Joe's Pond without which we would have never met. Underneath the water, the phrase, "Nothing in the world is single. All things by a law divine in one spirit mix and mingle," would be etched. Curtis' cousin Laurie had included this quotation from Percy Bysshe Shelley's poem *Love's Philosophy* in a letter she had written to us at one point during the year that he was sick. To Curtis and me, these words represented our love which we believed would transcend our earthly existence. On the back of the stone, the side facing the green mountains of Vermont, would be our names as well as our dates of birth. A space would be left vacant for the dates of death. Our names would be inscribed in the outline of a book, my promise to Curtis that I would someday document our story. For my senior thesis, I wrote a non-fiction creative writing essay about our early years together intertwined with stories about my family. Curtis had read that book. He knew that I loved to write. We spoke often about the memoir I planned to write about our love and our life with ALS. Two intertwining rings would be engraved in the center of the book on the bottom with the date of our wedding. And on opposite corners of the book would be roses, etched in such fine detail that they would appear to be real.

On November third, we set our wedding day for November 27, although Curtis had not yet formally asked me to marry him.

"The time will come," he had said. "When the time is right."

Since the day he had asked my father for my hand in marriage, he appeared to slowly gain strength. We surmised that perhaps he was receiving the 100 mL of BDNF and perhaps it was beginning to really work. We decided that although we'd marry right away, we would also have an outside celebration in the spring like we had both always dreamed. I signed my journal that night, "Mrs. Curtis Roger Vance."

We spent the next two weeks of November planning our wedding. We created a guest list of over 200 people but also placed an advertisement in *The Caledonian Record*, inviting any and everyone to the ceremony. So many in our community had supported us for the past year, and we wanted to include them in our special day. We drove down to the local jeweler and designed an engagement ring together. Seven days later, Curtis wasn't feeling up to a drive so I drove by myself to pick it up, brought it into the house with it still in the box, thanked our neighbor who had stayed with Curtis, sat on the edge of Curtis' blue recliner and greeted him with a kiss. I had only been away for 45 minutes but it seemed like an eternity.

Curtis looked at me.

He continued to look at me for many minutes.

"I have thought of this moment for so many years," he said slowly. "I had it all planned out. This is not at all like I had imagined it would be. I really wanted to get down on one knee. That is just how I always saw me asking you. Up until this past summer, I really thought I could figure out a way to do it. If only I hadn't waited so long."

Tears streamed down my face.

Curtis asked me to open the box and so I did. We both stared at a diamond solitaire, simply and beautifully set, in a band of white gold. Curtis asked me to take the ring out of its box and so I did. As I took the ring out of the box, I watched Curtis.

"So, will you marry me?" Curtis asked with a slight smile. He could still smile just a bit.

"Yes," I said. "Yes. Yes. Yes."

Within that same week, for our November visit to Massachusetts General, my mom drove Curtis and me in the handicapped-accessible van that members of one of the local churches had recently donated to us. The van allowed Curtis to travel in his wheelchair and made it so he didn't have to be transferred, which caused him agony and discomfort, more so than sitting in the wheelchair for hours. But the van did not have any powerpoints into which I could plug the battery that charged the BiPAP. We thought that our adaptor would fit into the cigarette lighter, but an hour into the trip we realized that it did not. We weren't too worried, though, because we knew that the battery could last a few hours. We recharged the battery while in the doctor's office and felt confident that there was plenty of battery life to get us back to Vermont.

On the way home, though, we came upon traffic and after we passed the last possible stop, the Vermont Welcome Center, my mom, Curtis and I could hear the air that was forced from the machine grow increasingly weaker. As my mother drove as fast as possible, I stood in the back beside Curtis in the wheelchair with the ambu bag ready. Curtis and I did not take our eyes off one another for 20 minutes. We thought about pulling over and flagging down another car but there was nothing that anyone could do except call an ambulance. It was 1999 and cell phones were not commonplace; none of us owned one. We envisioned his death in each other's eyes, and neither one of us wanted it to end this way. Luckily, the BiPAP kept working. As the van chugged up our long, steep driveway, the BiPAP began to heat up. We made it into the house just in time to plug in the battery.

On Thanksgiving night, two nights before our wedding, Curtis returned exhausted from his bachelor party, which his brothers and close friends had insisted on throwing for him at the Stagger Inn. As I undressed him for bed, a dollar bill fell from his sweatshirt.

"Really?" I smiled.

"Two of them. It was horrible. I felt so stupid. The boys enjoyed them, though."

That night Curtis experienced difficulty breathing. He couldn't relax. He couldn't calm himself. He was panicked. I had no idea what to do so I just held him and talked to him. Finally, at three am, I convinced him to allow me to administer the morphine that we had in the cabinet. Our doctor had prescribed it. He knew that Curtis' wish was to die at home, and morphine would dull the sensation of not being able to breathe. We had no idea if the time had come but Curtis was scared. We had decided that, at the very least, the morphine would relax him and, perhaps, allow him to sleep. He begged me to stay close to him, to touch him and hold him. After one dose of morphine, the paranoia dissipated. He finally slept after I read to him what I had written while he was at his bachelor party that night – what I would read to him and to the congregation on our wedding day:

*Dear Curtis,*

*I have dreamed of you since I was a little girl. When I was five, I pictured my husband-to-be as a boy sitting with me on my bed, protecting me from the monsters that would grasp at my ankles as I leapt into bed night after night. A few years later, I imagined my husband-to-be as a young playmate, with whom I could laugh and play for hours. A few months after I turned 12, and my grandfather passed away, I fancied my husband-to-be holding me and telling me that life is wonderful and that death is okay, too. On July 20, 1990, my 15-year-old eyes spotted you, and a second glance turned into a stare and has never been broken since.*

*I have dreamed of our wedding day for nine years. I envisioned us outside on a clear, cool summer day, surrounded by our families and closest friends. I saw us standing up together, promising to be faithful and pledging our lives to one another.*

*Today is our wedding day, and in a few moments you will become my husband. But as we have learned over the past year, our lives are affected by time and circumstance, and, thus, the* events of today are not as I had planned for so many years. Today is so much more special than I had ever dreamed possible.

Curtis, I thank you for making my life better than my dreams ever were. You are my protector, my playmate, my inner strength. I love you."

# Alive

Our wedding day began when the alarm sang at five o'clock in the morning. Curtis had slept through the night. I was afforded the luxury of waking to music rather than to his head brushing against mine. I walked across the living room and into the kitchen. After placing the blue kettle on the stove, I picked up the Ziploc bag full of Curtis' crushed medicine and emptied it into a blue plastic cup. In the beginning, right after the diagnosis, we lugged around a grocery bag full of herbs, vitamins, and one prescription medicine. After each meal, with the aid of a cheat sheet so as to not skip or add any pills, I would take the pills out of the bottles and lay them in front of Curtis and watch as he swallowed one after another. Curtis averaged 60 or more pills a day, more than 20 at every meal. A few months later, Curtis had thought of setting aside the pills in baggies for a whole day, decreasing the times I had to sort through and open all of the bottles. As spring turned into summer, we thought to save even more time by sorting the pills every three or four days. I would sit on our living room floor and fill quart-size Ziplocs with pills and mark them, Monday am, Tuesday am, Wednesday am, Monday lunch, Tuesday lunch, and so on. With the approach of autumn, Curtis lost his ability to swallow the pills whole and so it became necessary to crush and mix the pills with his food or drink. After sorting the pills into their respective Ziploc bags, I crushed them with a hammer, until we got a pill crusher. Once Curtis got the feeding tube, I had to dissolve the pills in boiling water.

The water in the blue kettle still had not boiled. I filled a pink hospital basin with scalding water and a few squirts of baby wash with aloe and then filled an identical basin with hot water. I tossed a yellow baby washcloth into each. After I placed one basin on the blue office chair, and the other on the floor, the kettle began to whistle, hurrying me into the kitchen. I poured the boiled water into the blue plastic cup full of crushed medicine and filled another blue plastic cup with cold water. There was a clean syringe in the drainer. Good. Some nights I remembered to clean them, some nights I didn't. Carrying the cups in my hands and the syringe in my teeth, I could only nod at Woo Woo as he raised his head in acknowledgment as I crossed the wide pine board floor. Once I released the utensils onto the light oak dinner tray, which was home to Curtis' breathing machine, I whispered, "Good morning, Woosel." Woo Woo responded to my routine acts with a grunt. Seconds later, he was snoring. I turned off the feeding machine which was suspended midair on a metal pole to the left of Curtis. I cautiously lifted the sides of the white sheet and green blanket and unhooked the feeding machine's tube from Curtis' feeding tube. Curtis was fed a 12-hour drip of Jevity every night. Jevity is similar to Ensure, but easier to digest, and it doesn't clog the feeding machine. Although Curtis and I appreciated that his body received all the nutrients it needed to sustain life by the time dawn arrived, we both knew that his hunger was never appeased.

Using the syringe, I pushed water into Curtis' tube, a vital step the nurse had told me. You must check that the tube is free of leftover food before attempting to push the medicine through. "No matter how diluted the solution, the dense medicine is likely to create a dam within the tube and then you'd have a mess," one of the nurses had told Curtis and me. Curtis always insisted that I clean his tube with at least two doses of water before anything else. I filled the syringe halfway with the hot dense medicine and halfway with the cool clear water and released the mixture into Curtis' tube. The liquid poured into his stomach. When he was awake, Curtis could feel the substances enter his innards. He liked warm things the best. He shivered when the medicine, water, or Jevity was too cold, and he cringed when it was too hot. He got gassy if I squirted too fast or if I left bubbles of air in the long skinny tube that connected the feeding machine's bag of Jevity to his tube. My hands repeated the injections of medicine until the blue plastic cups were empty. I topped off the morning dose of his medicine with two water injections. Curtis was still asleep. Good.

It was 5:30 am. Curtis' head, raised to a 45-degree angle, was stationed on the king-sized pillow. Moments of peace were rare for Curtis and me. The events of the past year had taught me to take advantage of any calm flashes of time. Normally, a peaceful moment would inspire me to slide under the covers and wrap my body on top of his, but this particular morning we didn't have time to spare. After nine years of waiting, I was finally marrying Curtis.

Woo Woo's snores increased in volume. He looked as though all was right in the world. *What will Woo Woo do if his father...? Oh, there is no time for this, now. No time at all. Get on with your work.* The water in the pink hospital basins was still hot. Curtis hated sponge baths; he loved to sit on his tub bench in the bathtub and feel the hot water pour over his body by means of me standing in front of him holding the retractable handheld shower-head. In the early fall, Curtis had lost the ability to sit on the tub bench. It depressed him that he would never again experience the joy of being doused with hot water. We bought an inflatable tub that we could set up in the living room. It worked well but required two hours from start to finish. So, this morning he had to be okay with just a sponge bath.

My hands found the yellow baby washcloth in the water. We had stopped using adult washcloths months ago. Although Curtis had always had soft, baby-like skin, it used to be able to endure anything; now most anything irritated his increasingly sensitive skin. I pulled the cotton sheet away from his chest. His shoulder bones stuck out from under his skin. His once robust chest was now concave; it appeared as though there were pockets of air between his chest and shoulders on either side. I rubbed his hairless chest with precision, careful not to pull the feeding tube, which stuck out of his skin in between and just under his nipples. The foreign-looking tube was keeping him alive, and over time, like all of his medical equipment and gadgets, it had become a part of him. With every added piece of equipment, Curtis had lost a little more freedom.

But as he said many times a day, "I am still alive. That is freedom enough."

I glanced up at his face every other second to check if he was awake as I washed his upper body. He could no longer move any part of his body except for his head and his eyes, and with his nighttime mask covering his mouth, it was impossible to know if he was asleep or awake unless I saw his head move or his green eyes talk to me. My touch would not startle him awake; he only panicked when he could not sense my presence. After rinsing his chest, I pulled the sheet further down to wash his belly. Curtis used to pride himself on his manliness, a result of the physical labor he performed, which, as he used to say, made him feel useful. "Like I am somebody." Now, his belly was big and round. "Mostly full of air," Curtis would joke. His body resembled that of a baby: a large head and a full belly, surrounded by floppy appendages. But unlike a baby, Curtis' bones were long and slender. And, unlike a baby who is cared for and nourished so that he can grow and thrive, Curtis was being cared for and nourished so that his last days would be as comfortable as possible.

I washed around Curtis' right side. I felt the outline of the pump. "Look, I swallowed a hockey puck," was his favorite explanation for this bulge. It was hard to believe that the pump had been surgically implanted under his skin ten months prior. We had wished that he would be the recipient of 100 mL of BDNF and hoped that it would be our miracle cure. Goosebumps speckled Curtis' torso, prompting me to pull the sheet over his belly and chest. As I raised his left arm, I glanced up and saw that his eyes were open. I smiled. His eyes blinked slowly, saying, "Good morning, baby." *What I would give to be able to awaken to those words, again. No use getting sad now, you've got work to do.* He shook his head, indicating that he wanted his daytime mask that only covered his nose, as opposed to the night mask which covered his mouth and nose.

"Okay," I said, "Just give me a minute."

I threw the washcloth into the basin, hurried into the bathroom, grabbed the hose, which hung over the shower rod, and the tubes and mask that had been placed on the dryer the night before. *Shit.* My mind always temporarily lapsed with the masks; I could never recall which way the straps went; if they were assembled the wrong way the Velcro would not be in the right direction and the mask would not stay on Curtis without my aid. I ran back to the bed, fitted the tubes and straps to the mask properly, raised the head of the bed to a 90-degree angle, and lowered the legs, catching Curtis' upper body before it fell to one side. His eyes smiled. At the beginning, Curtis hid the fact that he was losing the ability to perform a certain function until the day it was completely gone, which created many mishaps along the way. One of the days that he had flopped over to his left when I had raised the head of the bed, his torso looked as though it had been disconnected from his hips. He looked like a puppet whose one string had snapped. He cursed me until his anger and frustration were released, and then he cried. Curtis' tears did not fall often, but their appearance often indicated that he was admitting that he had lost the ability to perform a function, in this case the ability to hold himself upright. The tears also represented the knowledge that he was one step closer to death.

I placed the daytime mask on his thighs and the end of the tube beside the BiPAP, which lay on the wooden dinner tray. "You ready, baby?"

He shook his head from side to side.

As I gave him time to prepare for the air to be taken away, I watched his bare chest rise toward his neck and fall back down. His deep breaths could not be called deep anymore, but they were all he could do. When he was ready for the transfer of masks, I had to be ready; any significant lapse in time could result in a major struggle. The ambu bag lay beside us just in case a tube split or popped off, or a strap tore.

A minute later, Curtis nodded his head, widened his eyes, and then shut them tight just as a child would do before bobbing his head under water. I tore the Velcro on both sides of the nighttime mask, slipped it over his head, took the end of the tube out of the BiPAP, plugged in the end of the tube that was connected to the daytime mask, and put that mask to his nose. He could no longer wait for me to put the contraption over his head; I had to give him a dose of air in between. He nodded again. I took away his air, slipped the strapped mask over his head, fit the mask over his nose, and fastened the Velcro on all four sides until the straps were not too tight, not too loose. Just right. He smiled and whispered, "Good morning, baby."

Who is sick? Who is dying? His smile and his words wiped away reality. I cared for him, catered to him and kept him alive for moments like these. His love was worth everything to me.

When I told him it was already six, he sighed, "We have to hurry. It's my wedding day. We can't be late."

"You're getting married? Who's the lucky lady?"

"Oh, no one. Just my best friend, my lover, my baby Woo Woo's mother."

The words, although slow, quiet and slurred, seemed perfect to me. I could still comprehend the sarcasm and the sincerity.

"I need my medicine."

"You already had it."

"I need to have a bath."

"You're getting one."

"I need a shave and my teeth brushed and my hair and nails done."

"Yes, baby. That is all going to happen."

His needs and demands seemed to progress at the same speed as the disease and this irritated me. Many times, I wanted to kick and scream and tell him that I was tired of caring for him. But then I thought about it. He could not do the simple things; he could not physically perform his daily routine that used to be just that, a daily routine. Of course, he is going to want it to happen when he wants it to happen, and he's going to want it done his way.

I lowered the head of the bed, raised his left arm, washed

under and around it, gently lowered his arm and repeated the routine on the other side.

"When is she coming?" Curtis was referring to Mandy, a childhood friend of Heather's, and she and her boyfriend had become our close friends.

"6:30."

"I'd better go to the bathroom."

As I reached for the Hoyer pad, the Hoyer lift moved slightly. Woo Woo woke up. The Hoyer was the only way that I could move Curtis. Woo Woo knew that when the Hoyer moved his father was awake. Woo Woo lifted his body from his bed, stretched, and walked slowly over to our bed. I placed Curtis' hand on Woo Woo's head. He ducked under the hand, sniffed it and looked up at his father.

"Good morning, Woosel Doosel. It's your parents' wedding day. Finally, you will be legitimate," Curtis whispered.

Woo Woo walked over to the door and scratched. I opened the door to the sight of a downpour. Since Woo Woo refused to go outside in the rain, he lay down, keeping the door propped open with his black, long-haired body.

I raised the head of Curtis' bed with the push of a button, pulled his torso forward, slipped the Hoyer pad behind his back, replaced and straightened his torso against the pad and lifted his thigh individually in order to pull the leg straps through.

"It's time."

"Shit."

I ran into the bathroom, grabbed the Clorox-filled bucket, poured the solution into the bathtub, ran back to Curtis, grabbed the Hoyer's handles, wheeled it toward Curtis, lowered the bar until it was above his tummy, hooked the four straps onto the hooks of the bar, and began to crank the lift.

"It's coming."

Just in time, I shoved the bucket under his butt.

"Isn't your husband-to-be the most seductive?"

Squatting on the floor, I held the bucket until he was done. I wiped him, and then washed him with the cool water in the pink hospital basins. After placing him back into bed, I got new water, and a new washcloth in order to complete his bath.

Then it was time to place him in his blue recliner. Curtis never wanted to stay in bed longer than necessary. "Only sick people lay in bed beyond the time they need to sleep," he often said. Transferring him from place to place had become much easier since Joe had bought us the uninterrupted power service (UPS) device after the storm a few months beforehand. The UPS could run on battery for a short period of time, ensuring that Curtis would never be without the air from the BiPAP. I cranked him off the bed with the Hoyer, picked the UPS device up from the floor, and placed it on top of the BiPAP. I pulled Curtis away from the bed and, inch by inch, wheeled him forward toward the recliner, which sat about ten feet away. The process took longer now because I also had to move the wooden tray that held the BiPAP and UPS inch by inch and be careful not to pull his mask off, or the tube out of the BiPAP, separating him from his life support. Eventually, once Curtis was above and the tray was to the left of the recliner, I plugged the UPS back into the wall socket, lined Curtis' butt up over his chair, turned the lever on the Hoyer just a tad, rushed behind him, pulled him back with my right hand so that his butt was lined up with the very back edge of the chair, wrapped my arm around his chest to steady his torso and held the top of his head with my chin to keep his head from falling too far forward or backward. With Curtis seated, I rushed back toward the Hoyer, turned the lever back again so that the bars didn't crush him and wheeled the Hoyer back to its resting place. One by one, I lifted his legs, pulled the Hoyer straps out, leaned him forward against my chest, and pulled the Hoyer pad out. I placed his arms on the sides of the chair, made sure his legs were close together and slowly reclined the chair. I grabbed the four pillows, two for his elbows, two for his legs, and adjusted them under his elbows and calves to ensure that his elbows didn't dig into the upholstery and that his calves didn't get sores.

It was a few minutes past 6:30 am. Curtis' eyes brightened when Mandy walked through the door. Visitors verified Curtis' existence. She leaned over Curtis and gave him a kiss on the cheek, "Happy Wedding Day, you big stud."

Curtis blushed and smiled, "Don't you wish you were the lucky lady?"

She bent closer to Curtis and asked him to repeat himself. The moment was gone. Curtis knew that his humor was not the same when it had to be repeated.

I interpreted. "He said, 'Don't you wish you were the lucky lady?'"

The moment was saved.

Mandy pretended to jab Curtis' shoulder, "You better believe it."

Curtis smiled.

With Mandy watching Curtis, I could go into the bathroom and dump Curtis' excretions, clean the bucket and two hospital basins, throw the washcloths into the hamper and fetch his toothbrush, razor, shaving cream, and a clean pink basin. I then walked to the kitchen to get two cups, one full of water and one to use as a spitter. As I brushed Curtis' teeth and shaved him, she made our bed and went upstairs to get the tuxedo and to wake up my sisters. She knew that we were going to need everyone's help to get Curtis dressed that morning.

Curtis was fed, bathed, shaved, and dressed by 7:30 am. Mandy, a hairdresser, was manicuring his nails and planned to gel his hair. It was funny to watch Curtis find ways to keep himself entertained throughout his illness; having his nails manicured became one of his favorite activities. I had 20 minutes before I had to leave for my grandmother's to dress myself and get my hair and make-up done, so I decided to take Woo Woo for a run, since that was the only way he'd go out in the rain. With my sisters and Mandy in charge of Curtis, I ran down our driveway, up our hill and toward town with Woo Woo in tow. The air rushed into my lungs and the sweat began to accumulate, fighting for space on my face with the rain. My arms pumped. My legs stretched. I wished I could fly. I envisioned Curtis, in our home, sitting in his chair, trapped inside a body that couldn't move. My arms pumped faster and my legs stretched further until I was out of breath. *Is this what it feels like? Is this what it will be like when Curtis suffocates? Stop it. There is no time for this, now.* Woo Woo and I reached the cemetery, a mile from our home, and as always, we stopped for a second, looked at one another, and then ran home faster than we had run before. I ran into the house, kissed Curtis on the forehead, jumped into the shower, put on a pair of old sweats and a button-down shirt, grabbed my bag and told my sisters to hurry.

Taking Curtis' face into my hands, I begged, "I'll see you in a few hours?"

"The next time I see you, you'll be walking down the aisle."

"You going to be okay? I can stay here if you want me to. I can get dressed here."

"You left instructions for my brothers and the others. You have gone over them a million times. I will be okay."

"I'm going to miss you."

"Me too, baby. Get going. We can't be late for our own wedding."

Like the few other times I had left Curtis alone for more than a few minutes in the past year, I feared never seeing him again. "You promise you won't leave me?"

"I'm here, aren't I? I'm here and I'm alive."

# *Saturday, November 27th*

There are moments in my life that I wish were frozen in time so that I could return to them and witness the same sights, smell the same aromas, and feel the same touches. My wedding day is one of only a few days in my life of which I have barely any memory. I wish that I could revisit the moments, all 100 minutes to be exact, of my wedding day, November 27, 1999, that blended together to create a celebration of marriage that was full of warmth, joy, and hope. I had to watch our wedding video in order to recollect what had happened and to witness the parts that many brides do not notice because they are caught up in the grandeur of the day or do not see because they are the last one to enter and the first to leave. When I watched our wedding day video for the first time, over nine years after the event, I was amazed that I only smiled a few times throughout the ceremony. It was overwhelming to see how reserved I appeared, how I barely moved, how for most of the time I sat still as if in a trance. I only released my emotions out into the open for everyone to see a few times; this was uncharacteristic. I rarely hid my happiness from anyone. Curtis, too, did not move. He couldn't. He could still smile, though, a little bit. We were both still, then, for most of the time, absorbing the words that were spoken and sung by those who loved us. Yes, our wedding day is a day I would return to if I could.

My heart, though, has always, and will always, recall the emotions I experienced that day. Beginning at 10:30 am, Curtis sat reclined in his blue chair, which had been covered with a green sheet so as to blend into the color scheme of the day, on the altar of the St. Johnsbury North Congregational Church. The BiPAP machine was hidden behind the chair but, of course, Curtis wore his mask. Joe sat beside Curtis in the chair that would soon be occupied by Chad once the ceremony began; they surveyed the over 500 participants in the congregation. Many people arrived an hour early in order to get a seat. A few people approached the altar to say hello to Curtis before the ceremony. During this time I was in the side room getting ready. Mandy had already put my long, dark brown hair in an updo and teased it such that it created an illusion of volume which my straight hair didn't typically contain. She pinned the satin headpiece that my mother had sewn to the back of my head to which my mother and Heather attached the long train which was also sewn by my mom and made of tulle with satin edging and teeny, plastic fake jewels that created a subtle sparkle. Mandy had already applied my make-up which concealed the dark circles from not having slept through the night in months. She reapplied my lipstick as I tried to say hello to relatives and family friends who had traveled a long way and snuck in to give me a hug before the ceremony.

It had been over a year since I had seen so many members of my extended family and friends in one place at one time. Curtis and I had last traveled to Connecticut in June, six months beforehand, for Tricia's high school graduation. That had been our last overnight trip anywhere, except for hospital visits. We had to spend the night in a handicapped hotel room so that Curtis could shower, and Curtis had trouble breathing as a result of not being able to sleep upright like he could in his hospital bed in our home.

When my father declared that it was a few minutes before 11, I pushed everyone out the door except for the wedding party. I was anxious to see Curtis. With my father, mother, sisters, and Woo Woo surrounding me, I made my way from the side room to the waiting area by the entrance. I heard the music change after the last guest was seated, signaling the seating of the family members. As Curtis' brothers walked members of my and Curtis' immediate family down the aisle, Joe helped Curtis sit up straight by raising the chair from its semi-reclined position. With my father beside me, I stood still in the entrance of the church behind the large wooden doors that hid me from view.

"Is my train bunched up?" I recall asking Heather and Tricia.

Heather and Tricia handed me and my dad their bouquets of white roses and each took a side of my train with their hands and snapped their wrists such that the tulle rose into the air and fell back down to the ground evenly. Heather touched my shoulder lightly as *Jesu, Joy of Man's Desiring* began, prompting the procession of the wedding party. She had helped me choose the music for the ceremony.

We heard laughter arise from the congregation as our nephew Tommy pulled Woo Woo, sitting in a red Ryder wagon covered with green velvet material, down one side of the double-aisled church. At the end of the aisle, in front of the altar, Tommy took the wedding bands out of the green velvet bag tied around Woo Woo's neck and handed them to one of the ministers. As he dragged the wagon across the front of the church, Curtis' eyes beamed with pride. Tommy wheeled Woo Woo up the other aisle; Woo Woo lay still, his head propped up on the edge of the wagon. He did not move. He, too, was taking it all in. Curtis and I had wanted Woo Woo present throughout the ceremony but, given its length, we had reluctantly agreed to have a friend dogsit him in the church's basement.

Next to come down the aisle were my sisters who wore full-length green velvet dresses that my mom had made for them. Our niece Annie followed next with one arm looped around Tommy's, who was proud to walk down the aisle twice, and the other hand throwing red rose petals onto the white runner. She also wore a green velvet dress that my mom made as well as a ring of white flowers in her hair. She took her place in front of my sisters; her brother stood in front of their father, Curtis, and their other three uncles. Behind them were oversized bouquets of white and red roses placed on stands. Christmas garland was roped throughout the back of the altar. Immediately after the wedding party processional ended, a drum sounded and silence followed for a moment before the organ resumed. Curtis and I had planned this because we learned to relish silence for it calmed us. In the absence of noise comes peace.

After that one minute of silence, though, I didn't feel peace; for the first time in nine years I doubted whether or not I should marry Curtis. Before ALS, Curtis and I had had several conversations about marriage. We both believed in its power and in commitment. We viewed it as an institution that under almost all circumstances should be upheld. We believed it to be a sacred covenant that should be undertaken with only extreme seriousness. In that one brief moment, though, I panicked. I realized that I was only 24-years-old and that what I was about to undertake was for a lifetime. I recalled all of those times in our early history when we grew apart for a while because our lives didn't align. *What if that happened again? What if we changed? What if we grew apart? Would we have the strength to sustain, the courage to uphold our vows?* I was thinking like a normal nervous bride.

As the organ started *Pachelbel's Canon in D*, I glanced up at my dad; he gently squeezed my arm and smiled reassuringly at me. The large wooden doors opened; my dad took the first step. I heard quiet gasps from the crowd as my dad escorted me past the first few back pews. I looked down. I wasn't ready to receive people's admiration. I heard our family friend whisper, "I love your dress," as we walked past her. During my bridal shower a few weeks beforehand, I had tried on several dresses: my mother's wedding dress which was too big, my grandmother's which wasn't quite right, my sister's which was too long, and then my aunt's which was perfect. Hers was an off-white, simple, straight, spaghetti-strapped dress with a long-sleeved tulle jacket with lace flowers sewn along the top and ten buttons down the front that began at a solid, satin quarter collar. I glanced up and saw my uncle and aunt smiling at me and my cousins who were beaming. My closest childhood friend waved at me and winked; I recalled the countless sleepovers through the years during which we had laid awake at night dreaming about our wedding days.

I looked toward the altar and saw Heather and Tricia. They were both crying. I felt my train, which was as long as several pew lengths, dragging behind me and weighing me down. *Help me, please, somebody! Help me!* And then I saw Curtis. I did not see his blue recliner that was covered with green material. I did not see the BiPAP. I did not see his mask or the flexible tubing. I did not see how frail he had become. I did not see how he could barely smile. I did not see how thin his legs were under the black tuxedo pants. I did not see that he was sick. I did not see that he was struggling to breathe. I did not see that he was dying. I saw the boy who I had loved ever since I was a teenager. I saw the boy who taught me how to not take myself so seriously, who taught me how to laugh and how to live. I saw the boy who taught me how to love.

I saw the man who protected me, who always made everything okay, who promised me that he'd never leave me, who promised me that he'd love me forever.

When we reached the altar, my father kissed me on the cheek, walked up the step, and placed his hand on Curtis' which lay motionless on the arm of the recliner to acknowledge that he was presenting me to him. After my father turned around, I glanced at him and saw the tears in his eyes. I smiled at my father as I passed by him to walk up the step, sat down on my chair that was stationed beside Curtis', transferred my trailing arm bouquet of red roses from one arm to the other so that I could lay my hand gently on top of Curtis' hand, and looked at him. I stared at his whole face. I noticed even the smallest details. I wanted to remember this moment forever. Mostly, I noticed his eyes, his eyes that came alive and burned with desire. I saw my future. Our future.

"I love you," my lips moved with no noise.

"I love you," his lips spoke as well.

We watched one another for what seemed like many minutes and then looked out at the crowd and took them all in, too. We were experiencing a moment that we would never want to forget. Curtis bobbed his head, and Chad and I adjusted his body. His shoulders were slouching. He wanted to sit up straighter.

The congregation sang "Come My Way My Truth My Life", and we continued to watch one another as I sang and Curtis mouthed the words. During the ceremony, friends spoke personal wishes and read poems, Bible verses and meditations, and some sang songs including "The Gift of Love." Everyone used a microphone to ensure that their words resonated throughout the congregation. All throughout, Curtis and I experienced joy, sadness, gratitude, discomfort, love, and humor.

Curtis' favorite was the humor. One of the original poems was titled, "This Candle Burning," and as our friend read it, I started to smell something burning. I looked behind me and saw numerous candelabras all of which held very tall, too thin green and white candles.

I leaned over and whispered in Curtis' ear, "The candles are burning too fast. The wax is dripping all over the altar."

The irony of the poem's title was not lost on Curtis as he replied, "It's very fitting, honey."

I experienced sadness as Joe walked his seven-year-old daughter up to a framed picture of a rainbow with Curtis and me underneath it that she drew that sat on an easel on the altar. Our names were written in green marker and there were two deep green ribbons drawn. Joe spoke, "[This picture] reminds us of when Curtis didn't have ALS and we feel that it will be like this again."

At that moment, I envisioned Curtis when he was physically well, one summer day just a year and a half before our wedding day. Curtis and I had been riding in Chad's speedboat on Joe's Pond with Chad, his wife, and the children. Curtis and Chad, with beers in their hands, had been standing, and Chad's wife and I had been sitting in the back of the boat, laughing with Tommy and Annie. I remember looking up at Curtis; the sun was behind him and I had to squint. I watched him talking with Chad. Their bodies were huddled, as though they were talking about something serious, something that they didn't want us to hear. Later that night, Curtis confided in me that his brother had been asking him when he was going to propose. Chad told him not to wait too long. Sitting on the altar, thinking back to that summer day, I reminisced about how tall Curtis had appeared when he stood. He had been a formidable presence. I had forgotten how it felt to touch his lean and muscular body. At that moment, I could not imagine Curtis physically well again.

We felt so much love when Chad, accompanied by Curtis' aunt on the piano, sang, "Suddenly." Curtis and I watched one another as he sang.

I experienced discomfort when a dear friend explained how our love had changed the way she looked at and lived her life. I smiled but felt drained. I had not sat still for this long in almost a year. I had never endured the outpouring of such emotion and gratitude. I watched Curtis as he, too, was struggling to cope with such admiration. It was not like us to take; we preferred to give.

We experienced joy when Julia, who facilitated our healing circles, shared in her thoughtful and patient voice, "In my mind, you already have a true marriage – a union of your souls...stay true to your relationship as much as possible because it's not just for here and now that you join in marriage but for eternity."

Curtis cried.

Chad checked on Curtis, adjusted his shoulders, moved a leg, and wiped his eyes.

Over the past months, Curtis and I had become close with the ministers of the West Danville Congregational Church, the Danville Congregational Church, and of the church in which we were being married. All three conduits of faith participated in our ceremony. Cathy, the minister from the West Danville church, spoke the meditation, referencing that in the *Corinthians*, Paul had written that the greatest gift of all is the gift of love and all of the other gifts are meaningless without love. Cathy stated that what Paul was describing was grace: "Unconditional. Unmerited.

Unending love. Which we know as God's grace. It is a mystery. And when we are asked, why do we love? The very best answer we can come up with is because. Just because."

Curtis and I experienced immense joy and gratitude when I read him my story, the love story that I had written two nights before and had already shared with him when I was afraid that he would not live to hear it on our wedding day.

"...Today is our wedding day, and in a few moments you will become my husband. But as we have learned over the past year," my amplified voice quivered, "Our lives are affected by time and circumstance, and, thus, the events of today are not as I had planned for so many years. Today is so much more special than I had ever dreamed possible..." Immediately following, I turned to our family and friends, "Today, Curtis and I are formally stating our commitment to one another, which we already know is so strong. And we are displaying our love to one another, which has already been tested by events that most couples never face. We are here to be united as one, although we have existed in harmony for almost a year. Today is our day. It is our day to share our love with all of you. We have decided to be married in order to appear before our families, our friends and, most importantly, before God, and ask that we be united in mind, body, and spirit for all eternity. Your presence does make our celebration of love complete."

After this, we stated our vows. We had known that Curtis would not be able to recite the words, so we had written our vows together. With me holding the microphone, we declared in part, in unison,

All that I am I give to you,
and all that I have I share with you.
Whatever the future holds,

I will love you and stand by you.
We will be united for all eternity.
This is my solemn vow.

Chad wiped Curtis' eyes with a Kleenex. I took a deep breath. Heather and Tricia, huddled close with their backs to the congregation, wiped their eyes. They had been so angry with me that I had asked that their duet follow my story and our vows. They had been so afraid that they wouldn't be able to keep their emotions in check. And they couldn't. But after they faced the crowd and the piano music began, they released their feelings into their voices, and as their sounds blended as they sang, "The Rose," I closed my eyes.

Curtis and I had spent the past summer basking in the beauty of Curtis' aunt and uncle's flower gardens which in part contained aster (patience), delphinium (heavenly), gladiolus (strength of character), heather (admiration), hydrangea (heartfelt), snapdragon (desire), sweet pea (delicate pleasure), and many rose plants. Roses mean love. I spent hours deadheading the rose bushes. I would remove the blossoms just after they were spent with the intention of forcing the plant to bloom again. By removing the blossom before it had the chance to fully develop a fruit, the plant sent out growth hormones again, producing a new bloom. Our roses were continuously blooming. They never appeared to die.

Heather and Tricia continued singing in harmony as two sisters whose hearts both rejoiced and ached for me and for Curtis, who they loved as a brother. Curtis bobbed his head up and down, an indication that something was not right. I saw that he was fighting for air. I stroked his hand, and we looked at one another. We were ready for the ceremony to end. We were tired.

Cathy blessed the rings. To exchange rings, I took Curtis' left hand with my left hand and placed the ring on his finger and, while continuing to hold his hand in mine to feign that he could put the ring on my finger, I slipped the ring on myself. Cathy made the declaration of marriage. Curtis' other older brother approached the podium, clearing his throat before he began reciting a poem he wrote, "One." Again, Chad wiped Curtis' eyes. The congregation punctuated the poem with the Lord's Prayer. Our ceremony closed with a dear friend singing, *Through the Eyes of Love* and Cathy declaring us husband and wife. We kissed, and the crowd cheered. I wiped my lipstick from Curtis' lips.

Back in the handicapped van, Curtis and I said to one another, "We did it."

And then Curtis said, "My ass is killing me."

# Sunday, December 19th

For almost two weeks after the ceremony, Curtis and I basked in the glory that we had experienced on our wedding day. Marriage made us believe, once again, that Curtis would survive the disease. We really assumed that we were beginning a new life together. Normalcy was very important to us; if we couldn't act like newlyweds then what was the point of living? We spent more time in the hot tub again, which lifted Curtis' spirits. His speech seemed to be a little clearer. Marriage prompted us to speak seriously about having children. Curtis asked me to wait just a little while longer.

"Let's see if I continue to feel better," he said.

I spent my nights dreaming of our child. I imagined a baby girl with curly, brown locks, and wide dark eyes.

Curtis' visit to Boston on December ninth, 12 days after our wedding, was upbeat and positive. The doctors and nurses commented on how great he looked.

"Marriage is good for you," they all smiled.

Our doctor was amazed that we had not had to increase the pressure on his BiPAP in two months. Perhaps after all this time we had finally hit a plateau? Maybe he was getting the 100 mL of BDNF and maybe it would be our cure after all? Curtis and I felt ecstatic during our car ride home that evening.

That night we returned to Danville and learned that Sam, a long-time resident and our good friend, had dropped dead from a heart attack earlier in the day. His death affected the whole community, and it hit Curtis particularly hard. Curtis could not grasp the fact that Sam had been beside us at the Danville Inn for our rehearsal dinner, apparently healthy and happy and fine. And then he was dead, leaving his wife, Sandra, a widow, his children fatherless and his grandchildren without a grandfather. I silently thought that perhaps Sam would be Curtis' angel, his guide to show him the way to heaven; Curtis and I had recently spoken about how he didn't know who would greet him. Sam's death made us question the fairness of life and whether it was better to die suddenly, without much pain, but leaving everyone around you wondering if they had told you they loved you, or to suffer like Curtis, have a prolonged near-death experience, and give people the opportunity to express their feelings. The irony, though, is that even with the time Curtis was given, some had not yet told Curtis how they felt and Curtis had not told everyone how he felt. I did, though. Every day I told Curtis how much I loved him.

From the moment Curtis learned of Sam's death, he began to pull away. He spent more and more time watching television. The frequency of the UPS truck delivering wedding presents and the presence of wedding cards in our mail waned. We spent less time admiring our new things and more time reading the Bible, a pastime that seemed to comfort us although neither one of us really knew enough about the Book to understand the stories in context. Curtis started to ask for Percocet. He took one during the day and one at night. He complained of discomfort most of the day and slept all night. One day two of his brothers visited, and Curtis listened to them talk about how great the stock market was doing and they cited the analysts who were saying that the next year would be another fantastic financial year. Curtis didn't say a word.

Later, when his brothers left, Curtis complained, "What did

any of that have to do with me? Will I live to see it? Who cares about money? Why can't someone just find a cure for me?"

We increased the pressure on his BiPAP to 16 just three days after our doctor's visit in Boston. No, Curtis had not hit a plateau. But he had been allowed time in November so that we could plan a wedding and be married.

On Sunday, December 19th, 22 days after our wedding day, Curtis woke up at 3:45 am in a panic. His nose and throat felt clogged. He asked me to pick his nose.

"Dig deeper, please," he slurred.

"There's nothing in there," I answered.

Curtis cried. I wiped the tears.

"Get the inexsufflator and the suction machine," he begged.

The machines were no longer stored in the closet. They sat plugged in beside Curtis, charged and always ready to go. We'd been using them off and on since Friday afternoon. I suctioned his nose. We watched the clear tubing to see if anything got pulled out of his nose. Nothing. Curtis' eyes begged me to try again.

Curtis nodded slightly, the only way he could. I turned off the suction machine. My shoulders relaxed a little.

"The inexsufflator, please," he begged.

"I hate this machine. It makes your skin turn pale. It exhausts you. Curtis, it makes it seem as though there is no time left."

His eyes, again, pleaded with me.

I grabbed the mask and silently motioned to Curtis one, two, and three. I pulled the mask away that he wore all the time, taking away the air that he breathed, and replaced it with the mask attached to the inexsullflator, which pushed air into his lungs and then just as quickly sucked the air back out in an attempt to extract any phlegm blocking his airway. One, two, three, four, and five. I switched the masks again. The BiPAP forced little short breaths of air into his lungs, and then his eyes begged me again to try the inexsullflator. Again. Again. Again. No phlegm. No liquid. There was nothing blocking the passageway.

"Again. Do it again," Curtis nodded and whispered. "I can't breathe, and I am not ready to go. Get it out. Save me, Goddammit. Keep me alive."

In. Out. In. Out. I switched masks this time after just two seconds.

"You were turning white," I was scared.

With his eyes, he told me that this was it.

And then, he spoke.

Slowly.

And carefully.

"I'm sorry."

I held him. "Do not be sorry. This has been the best year of my life. No, these have been the best nine years of my life. It's okay, Curtis. We have both tried everything we could. It's okay, baby. There is nothing in your nose. There is nothing in your throat." The tears streamed down my face. "You are suffocating."

We both nodded. He begged for more morphine that earlier he had refused. I grabbed the needle, filled it with fluid, and shot it into his arm.

"I love you," he said.

"Curtis, remember our promise?"

One night, about a year beforehand, after I had learned that he had likely less than a year to live, I had made him promise that if he were to die we would let one other know when we were okay. At that point in time, I had not thought a lot about life after death but I did believe that one's soul does not die when its body can no longer harbor it. Even back then, before our journey with ALS, I had known that if he were to die I would need him to let me know when and if he had traveled to another place or time. And I had known that he would need to know the moment I realized that I could survive without him.

"Yes, I remember." His eyes consoled me.

"Curtis, it's okay. Close your eyes and rest. You will either wake up here in my arms or in the arms of God, and either way it will be okay, right?"

He nodded. He closed his eyes.

I read parts of Deuteronomy 30 as I had read to him so many times over the past year:

[1] When all these blessings and curses I have set before you come upon you and you take them to heart wherever the LORD your God disperses you among the nations, [2] and when you and your children return to the LORD your God and obey him with all your heart and with all your soul according to everything I command you today, [3] then the LORD your God will restore your fortunes and have compassion on you and gather you again from all the nations where he scattered you. [4] Even if you have been banished to the most distant land under the heavens, from there the LORD your God will gather you and bring you back. [5] He will bring you to the land that belonged to your fathers, and you will take possession of it. He will make you more prosperous and numerous than your fathers. [6] The LORD your God will circumcise your hearts and the hearts of your descendants, so that you may love him with all your heart and with all your soul, and live. [7]

[11] Now what I am commanding you today is not too difficult for you or beyond your reach. [12] It is not up in heaven, so that you

have to ask, "Who will ascend into heaven to get it and proclaim it to us so we may obey it?" [13] Nor is it beyond the sea, so that you have to ask, "Who will cross the sea to get it and proclaim it to us so we may obey it?" [14] No, the word is very near you; it is in your mouth and in your heart so you may obey it. [15] See, I set before you today life and prosperity, death and destruction.

[19] This day I call heaven and earth as witnesses against you that I have set before you life and death, blessings and curses. Now choose life, so that you and your children may live [20] and that you may love the LORD your God, listen to his voice, and hold fast to him.[15]

Then I asked him if he wanted me to pray with him. He said "yes." We prayed for peace and comfort as I held him. And I kept falling asleep. My baby was dying and I was so tired.

By 7:15 am, three and a half hours after he awoke feeling like his airways were clogged, he appeared to be asleep but was still in distress. He shook his head as though he was arguing with someone. Then he opened his eyes and looked surprised as though he was shocked that he was still there, with me. I called our local physician and our doctor in Boston. They both told me that they thought it was a matter of days. On Friday, they had told me that it was a matter of weeks. So we called some people. And then he started to turn purple. I noticed it on his neck first, and then on his chest. So, we called more people. As he had wished, I made arrangements so that we could donate his brain and spinal cord for ALS research. I sat with him and rubbed him and told him that I loved him and reminded him of our promise to let one another know when we were okay.

Our family and friends arrived one by one. It was perfect. Everyone was able to say hello and goodbye. Mandy, who was sitting on a chair to Curtis' left, announced to Curtis, who was no longer alert thanks to the morphine and valium, every time someone walked through the front door so that he would know who was there. With our family and friends surrounding us, and with Woo Woo lying in between Curtis' legs, Curtis' mother read the story out loud that she had read to Curtis a day before. A love story that told him that it was okay for him to go. While she read, I held him. In the middle of the story I knew that it was time to be alone with him, and I thought that after the story ended I would ask everyone to leave so that Woo Woo and I could have him to ourselves one last time. Instead, I crawled on top of him and wrapped my body around his and closed my eyes and cried. I cried without inhibition, I cried hysterically, I cried louder and deeper than I have ever cried before. I told him that I loved him over and over and over again. And, then, I told him that I loved him but that it was okay to go. With my hand on his heart, I felt it stop beating. It was 11:30 am on Sunday, December 19th. Curtis was dead.

# Dying

One morning I wake up and my throat is sore. I can't control my saliva, but I'm not choking on my own spit like the doctors said might happen. My nose feels full of snot; I beg my wife to pick it.

"Dig deeper, please," I try to yell at her but can only slur a whisper.

"There's nothing in there, Curtis."

I try to grit my teeth. I can't. I try to scream. I can't. I cry. Thank God I can still cry. But I can't wipe the tears. She wipes them for me as she looks at me carefully, lovingly, but with pity now. I look into her eyes; she is dying right in front of me. It is killing her that she can no longer help me. I close my eyes but the darkness scares me. I have to stay with the light.

I open my eyes and use them to plead with her.

"Get the inexsufflator and the suction machine."

She knows this look, now. The machines are no longer stored in the closet; they are plugged in and beside me. They are charged and ready to be used; we've been using them off and on since Friday afternoon. It's now early Sunday morning. She suctions my nose. Its loud noise comforts me, for this machine, too, is alive. I watch the clear tubing to see if anything gets pulled out of my nose. Nothing. My eyes beg her to try again.

The circles under her eyes are so black and so deep, but her smile is still bright. Her high cheekbones show through pale, taut skin. Her black eyes beg me to tell her what to do to make me feel better, to get me to relax, to bring us back to the good times when our biggest worry was the day rent was due or whose family we would be with for Thanksgiving.

I nod slightly, the only way I can. She turns off the suction machine. Her shoulders relax a little. I am so scared to leave her. My eyes beg her.

"The inexsufflator, please."

"I hate this machine, Curtis. It makes your skin turn pale. It exhausts *you. It makes it seem as though there is no time left."*

*My eyes, again, plead with her.*

*She grabs the mask and silently motions to me one, two, and three. She pulls away the mask that I wear all the time, taking away the air that I breathe, and replaces it with the mask attached to the inexsullflator, which pushes air into my lungs and then just as quickly sucks the air back out in an attempt to extract any phlegm blocking my airway. One, two, three, four, and five. She switches the masks again. The BiPAP forces little short breaths of air into my lungs and then my eyes beg her again to try the inexsullflator. Again. Again. Again. No phlegm. No liquid. There is nothing blocking the passageway.*

*I nod and want to yell but can only whisper.*

*"Again. Do it again. I can't breathe and I am not ready to go. Get it out. Save me, Goddammit. Keep me alive."*

*In. Out. In. Out. She switches masks this time after just two seconds.*

*"You were turning white, Curtis." I know that she is scared. I am terrified.*

*With my eyes I tell her that this is it.*

*And then, I speak slowly and carefully so that she will understand.*

*"I'm sorry."*

*She knows now.*

*She grabs me and holds me.*

*"Do not be sorry. This has been the best year of my life. No, these have been the best nine years of my life. It's okay, Curtis. We have both tried everything we could. It's okay, baby. There is nothing in your nose. There is nothing in your throat. You are suffocating." The tears stream down her face.*

*We both nod. I pray that this will not last long. I beg for more morphine. She grabs the needle, fills it with fluid and shoots it into my arm. I relax, a little.*

*"I love you." I need her to know.*

*"Curtis, remember our promise?" One night, about a year beforehand, she had made me promise that if I were to die, we would let one other know when we were okay. She does not cry now like she did a year ago; she is still acting the role of the caregiver.*

*"Yes, I remember." My eyes console her.*

*"Curtis, it's okay. Close your eyes and rest. You will either wake up here in my arms or in the arms of God and either way it will be okay, right?"*

*I nod. I close my eyes.*

*Some time later I open them and am surprised that she is still beside me. I had not been here for a while, I had thought. I close my eyes again. Later, I can't hear her. I can't feel her. We had promised to be together. I scream her name. I scream again. Can anyone hear me? They are all talking. Some are whispering. I need her.*

*I wanted to shout her name but I could only mumble.*

*"I am right here, baby." She holds my hand and touches me. She tells me that she loves me and that she is going to be okay. She repeats, "Go. I will be alright. I love you. Go. I will be alright. I love you."*

*I feel her gripping my shoulder and rubbing my face. Her tears fall on my bare chest. She begs me to stay with her, but I know that I am no longer living a life that I wish to live and I know that she can no longer bear the pain.*

*"Go. Go. I love you." She knows that it is time. She lays her hand on my heart. I beg her to come with me. She crawls on top of me and tries to get in. I ask them to take her, too. I see the light. I see the beauty. I would give anything to allow her to see it also, to travel alongside me.*

*I try to whisper.*

*"It's okay. Everything is going to be okay." But I can't speak.*

*She feels me drawing away, going home. She sobs with her face buried in the neck of my old body. She is shaking. No one is holding her. No one is telling her that it's going to be okay.*

*I do. My new arms hold her steady and close to me as I now lay on top of her. She feels me. She knows that I am here.*

*Yes, I am with her. But I can also see the other side. It's wonderful. Beautiful. I keep trying to tell her, to show her. My fear is that she will not understand. That she will never know.*

*She stares at my old body and marvels at its beauty. By looking at me, she sees heaven. I am as radiant as light. She stays with the light until my dead body is taken away in a big black body bag. Then she enters the darkness.*

Throughout the year that Curtis was sick, I wrote about many of our experiences within days or weeks of when they happened. I trust my memory in terms of recounting our conversations and actions with accuracy in terms of how I experienced them from my perspective, through the lens of my mind and my heart. But I didn't write about the particulars of the day that Curtis died for a very long time. I didn't talk about that day with anyone after the funeral, except my sisters, and all we had shared about that day was them both telling me how they had never seen me so distraught, so vulnerable, so lost as I seemed to be while practically laying on top of him, trying to keep him from physically leaving me.

One night, a little after the one-year anniversary of his passing, I was writing at our oak desk in my room in my parents' basement in Connecticut. This was not unusual. But, then, I began writing and couldn't stop. My fingers were typing and yet I didn't feel in control of them. Words were being spewed out and I wasn't aware of their meaning until my fingers stopped and I read what I had written. And, then, I cried. I cried just as loudly and as deeply as I had the day that I held onto Curtis, begging him to stay with me while at the same time telling him that it was okay for him to go.

I had written the exact italicized words as they are written above and it was just as it is now: from his perspective. I don't know what I believe is the reason for this. I have thought that the detailed events of those last hours were and are still too painful for me to remember through my own lens. Perhaps my mind protected my soul by allowing me to recall the particulars as Curtis may have experienced the events. I have also fancied that Curtis spoke through me that night so that I could relive the details through his lens because I was obsessed over the thought that I didn't know how dying had felt for him and this was devastating for me because throughout the year that he had been sick there had been nothing that we didn't share. Absolutely nothing.

# The Will to Live

My right arm was wrapped around his chest; my right leg was draped over both of his. My body fit perfectly halfway beside and halfway on top of his. I lifted my face that was buried in the crook of his neck and saw that he was no longer purple, but not skin-white either. It was a grayish color. My hand was where it had been for the past hour. His heart was still warm. With my head no longer supporting his head, it flopped forward and to the right.

"He'll get a cramp," I heard myself say.

I slid my fingers under his chin, lifted it, and pushed his head back. Blood trickled out of his mouth and nose. His head flopped forward again. Seeing Curtis' blood shocked me. Although the few days and hours leading up to his death had been full of panic and pain, both mental and physical, his actual death was almost a non-event. It was the first time I had witnessed someone's death and it was nothing at all like I had imagined, nothing like what I had seen on television or in the movies. His body did not jerk, his eyes did not roll to the back of his head. His eyelids were closed, and he was not screaming in anguish. He had called my name at around 9 am, closed his eyes for the last time, and, seemingly, slept for two and a half more hours, and then he was dead. The doctors must have been right. The drugs must have dulled the sensation so he was not in pain.

Curtis had been dead for about five minutes or so, I think. I did not want to take my eyes off of him because I feared that God would take away the body, too, and I knew that Curtis was still in there. I reached over him and found the bed control. Gently, I allowed him to lay back.

My eyes followed the tubing that peeked out from under the sheets. *He's still eating.* I leaned over his body, shut off the feeding machine, took the tube out and shut his valve. No more, Curtis. No more Jevity (the liquid nutrient that had kept him from starvation the past month and a half). No more all-night feedings. No more bolus (quick squirts of Jevity into his feeding tube when he was really hungry) feedings and syringes. No more crushed-up pills. I gently peeled the fentanyl patch from his skin, as well as the seasickness patch, which was behind his left ear. No more medicine.

I undid the Velcro on both sides and slipped the mask off his head. He had not allowed me to shave him on Friday for he had been so afraid to lose his air, even for a second. The hair was thick under the blood and his three-day-old beard prickly. Staring at my baby, I realized that I had not seen his face without the mask in over six months. His lips were still chapped, cracked, and sore. The indentation on his forehead from the mask was red and swollen. His eyes were closed.

*Curtis, open your eyes, please. I need to see you, baby.*

"I'm right here," I heard Curtis say to me.

My body began to shake and my eyes filled with tears.

"Please don't. Be happy for me. It's beautiful."

My body felt a gentle tingle as its temperature rose. *You're free, baby. Fly. Fly away.*

My eyes caught sight of Tommy standing on the other side of the bed, staring at us.

"Please don't let them forget."

Hopping over Curtis, I took Tommy into my arms. "If you ever start to forget your Uncle Curtie, just come to me. I'll remind you, okay?" I held Tommy tighter. "You see, he is happy. Look at him."

I turned and saw that Curtis' skin changed to the most beautiful color: a soft, silken white. His forehead was no longer swollen and red. His lips were a pale pink. All of his scars were gone. All signs of illness and fear and torment were wiped away. I swore I saw Curtis smile.

"Remember when we used to talk about the morning that we'd wake up and I would be better? Here I am," Curtis assured me.

Curtis was perfect in mind, body, and soul. The sun shone through the window directly above him; his body appeared to glow.

"I love you, you know. I need you to know."

I sat next to my husband, on the side where Tommy had been. I took Curtis' hand in mine, rubbed his wedding ring and looked out at the room full of people. The forms were crying, hugging, sitting, standing, and looking at me.

"Look at him. He's beautiful," I said to the crowd.

One by one, two by two, they came forward and witnessed yet another miracle.

"I am going to shave him," I announced.

"They'll do it," someone in the crowd said.

"They won't do it the way he likes. Heather, will you get the water in the basin, the washcloth, shaving cream, and razor?" I instructed my sister to not let the water be too hot or too cold. Just right.

Heather and Tricia approached me and whispered, "Are you sure you want to do this?"

"He'd be so embarrassed to leave this house not shaven." My

left hand held Curtis' head while I shaved his right side. Water dripped down his neck. "Sorry, baby," I said out loud. I dragged the razor up towards his forehead and laughed.

"What's so funny?" Heather asked.

"Oh, it's just Curtis. He's telling me to go the right way, not against the grain of his skin, but I'm telling him that I can't get a spot but not to worry, I won't knick him. He's got to look good for the wake."

"What's she laughing at?" a voice from the crowd asked.

"Oh, just another one of their private jokes."

Nervous laughter abounded.

"Okay, baby, now tilt your head this way and look up a bit. I'll be careful, honey. This is so much easier without the mask."

I wiped the excess water and cream off his face and neck and took him in with my eyes, my breath, my whole being.

"Remember me this way today, tomorrow, the next day," Curtis implored.

I turned and grabbed my camera.

I could feel the stares around me.

"He was so mad that we hadn't taken a picture of him without the mask at our wedding," I said.

The dried flowers from our wedding that a friend had brought just a few hours beforehand were placed on one side of him. I snapped a picture from his right, from his left, while I was standing on the bed, looking down, and head-on. I prayed that they would reveal what I knew. There was still a bit of him in there.

Some people left, some new people came to say goodbye. Many of the people spoke to him and rubbed his feet and his legs. Yes, he was still there.

I only left Curtis once. I walked a few feet to our Christmas tree, lifted a present out from under it, and then sat next to him as I ripped the wrapping away. I looked at every page of our completed wedding album for the first time with Curtis by my side.

I am so grateful for those three hours that Curtis' body remained in our home while we waited for the undertaker to arrive. It did not seem strange to me that I acted as though Curtis was still alive and listening to me. His presence was so strong and real. I could hear his voice in my head. I could feel his thoughts in my heart.

And then our friend and funeral director greeted me with a hug that lasted too long. "Are you ready?" he asked.

"You're taking him to Boston, and he'll be back to Vermont by tonight? I agreed to donate his brain and spinal cord for ALS research, but only if he would not have to be there overnight."

"Yes, he'll be back before dark."

"Good. He can't spend the night down there, alone, okay? It's been so long since he's had to spend the night alone."

The men in their dark suits stood still.

The funeral director crept toward me. "You may want to turn around or step outside."

"Why?"

"Some people don't like to see this."

"I'll stay right here, thank you. I'll be fine. It's Curtis we should all be worried about."

The room cleared, except for a few bodies.

The men huddled around the bed, and using the sheet like we did in the hospitals, they transferred him onto the black bag that lay on top of the metal folding table. I watched them fit his body into the bag smoothly at first until they had to tug at the sides when they got to his shoulders.

"Do you need to say goodbye?" the funeral director asked.

"No. I'll see him again."

They zipped the bag completely and wheeled Curtis away from me.

Through the window, I watched as they opened the doors to the hearse, but then their motion stopped. Perhaps he had changed his mind?

The funeral director walked back toward the house, and I met him outside on the ramp. He embraced me, again.

"You going to be okay?" he asked.

"Everything's going to be okay," Curtis reassured me.

"Yes. Thank you."

They picked up Curtis and walked the big black body bag into the car.

I watched the funeral director drive away with Curtis in the big black body bag and I felt nothing. Emptiness of the heart. I turned back into the house and saw everything. Clutter of the mind. The Hoyer lift was stationary in front of the fireplace. Curtis' empty hospital bed remained alongside my twin bed, both of which were pushed together in a corner of the living room. I looked above the beds and saw the framed painting of a lakeside cabin with smoke rising from its stone chimney that his mother had bought for him while she was in Amish country. The serene and cozy cabin was surrounded by trees, water, birds, ducks, deer, green mountains, and the light of a rising or setting sun. Thank God I had lowered the head of the bed in order to shave him and take a picture before they walked away with him; to have looked again and seen the head of the bed raised and empty could have killed me. The BiPAP lay on the wooden tray table next to the hospital bed, Curtis' mask suspended in the air, dangling from the hose. *When had I taken the mask off? Had his body stopped breathing with the BiPAP still pushing air into him? How could that be?* "Pressurized air will not sustain you forever. You need volumized air to keep you alive. How about a volumizer? Can you convince him to try a volumizer," the doctors had suggested to us a few times. Yes, his body had stopped breathing with the mask still on, the air invading his peace. The metal pole and machine stood erect, next to the tray table. A half-full bag of food hung from the pole. The tubing, which had been inserted into Curtis' feeding tube, was wrapped around the arm of the pole two, three, maybe four times in loops of equal diameter. He had told me he was hungry. He had been eating. Lucky him. The inexsufflator and suction machine protruded into the walkway between our beds and the bathroom; the walkway was just wide enough for the Hoyer lift to fit through. Their hoses, gadgets, and mask were out of order and strewn about as if their last operator had been in a panic. The wee hours of the morning, during which I had tried to clear his passageways, seemed so long ago.

I glanced at the blue clock on the mantel. Curtis had been so happy when I had received it as a bridal shower present; we had lived in our home for ten months and for ten months Curtis would sit in his blue recliner, with no clock in front of him telling him the time. The only clock in that room sat on the wall above and behind him. At least the clock was in his view for his final morning, during which he had asked me every 15 minutes if the hour was up. He had begged for more morphine. Was he aware that he was on Valium, too, and that there was a fentanyl patch pressed against the upper right-hand part of his chest, just below his neck cavity? Did he know that he still had the seasickness patch behind his ear, the patch that the doctors had prescribed to decrease his saliva in order to lower the risk of him choking on his own spit?

It was 3:30 pm. I had been awake for almost 12 hours, during which I had felt panic, frustration, anger, sadness, fear, peace, and now, nothing. My body shook. The minister would be over in a while to help me plan the wake and funeral because everyone seemed to think we needed to hold the services before Christmas which was six days away. I needed to run.

I ran into the bathroom. His tub bench still sat in the tub. Baby washcloths wet with his saliva lined the top of the hamper. Baby shampoo, conditioner, body wash, lotion, and powder sat atop the dryer. He had refused a bath Friday morning, but I had been ready. *See? Curtis, I was ready, honey. Always.* His sweatshirt and pants and T-shirt and socks that he had worn to his family's Christmas party the night before were folded neatly, also on the dryer. Someone else must have folded them. Last night? This morning? Shit. I'm late. Opening the medicine cabinet, I grabbed my birth control pills, pushed the little green Micronor pill out of its plastic, popped it in my mouth and watched my face in the mirror as I realized that I no longer needed birth control. And I would never have Curtis' baby. My face showed no emotion. I felt nothing. As I placed the packet of pills back into the cabinet, I eyed the Tucks pads that I had used to wipe his butt, the canker sore medicine that I had dabbed in his mouth, the thermometer I had placed under his tongue, the Vaseline I had applied to his cracked lips, the Preparation H I had smeared in his crack, the medicated facial scrub pads I had used to scrub his face. All of the things that were his. Mine and his.

"I have to do it now," I heard my voice say.

I opened the door to the cabinet under the sink, prepared to throw it all away, but just stared at layer upon layer of medicines, ointments, baby products, leftover hospital gratuities, shaving creams, and razor blades. I guessed that the home health aide nurse had forgotten to look under there. While I had been showing Curtis our wedding album, she, who had only been in our home a handful of times since our insurance had just recently given the green light for nursing care, had scoured our cabinets for his medicine. She had flushed the morphine, Valium, codeine, percocet, and Tylenol PM down the toilet and had shredded the fentanyl and seasick patches with scissors. She had gotten rid of his 800 dollar bottle of Rilutek, the only FDA-approved drug to slow down the progression of Curtis' disease, as well as his Neurontin, a drug normally used to treat seizures, but helpful to ALS patients.

"I'm doing this for you," she had explained.

I stood up, turned around, and saw the pink hospital basin on top of the washing machine, his razor still lying in the cold water. *Help me.* His hairs were still stuck in the blade. The smell of his shaving lotion, Gillette gel for sensitive skin, made me feel weak, sad, and nauseous. *Yes, Curtis, I know, I should have cleaned it up right away, but I couldn't leave you.* I flushed the hairy water down the toilet, rinsed out the razor and placed it where it belonged, in our cabinet under our sink, in our bathroom, where we had shared some of our most intimate moments. It was in the bathroom, the only room on the first floor of our home that was truly its own room because it had a door, that we were always alone. No phone calls, no visitors, just the two of us and our hopes and fears and dreams.

My clothes were still in the dryer: black and green running

pants, red turtleneck, white underwear, red socks, black jog bra. Reentering the living room, I realized that I was not alone.

My family was there: Mom, Dad, Heather and Tricia.

They looked at me as though someone had just died.

"Me and Woo Woo are going to go for a run. It's a beautiful afternoon. We'll be back."

"Where? Be careful. Don't go too far."

Woo Woo and Curtis led me down the main street, past Chad's house on the right, past Curtis' parents' house on the left, Curtis' grandparents' home on the right, the dairy farm, the old sunken brick house and the farm where a widow lived with her three dogs. It was a warm day for late December. There was no snow on the ground. Random patches of green grass made the fields look as though they had been given a careless haircut. I didn't speak out loud to Curtis; I knew he was beside me. I felt his hand in mine, leading me to where I needed to go: the Lookout. The mountains. Home.

Once we reached the base of the mountain, I unclipped Woo Woo's leash and we began to run. My arms pumped, my legs carried me swiftly toward the top. I ran until I couldn't breathe. *Is this what it felt like, Curtis, right before you died?*

Facing the north, I viewed a mountain range that expanded across the horizon. Turning to the right, I faced east, where the mountain range stood as a backdrop to the red farmhouse. The scent of fall still lingered; the smell of manure seeped into my nostrils. I closed my eyes and felt Curtis standing behind me, his strength protecting me from the wind that threatened to blow over my fragile frame. His arms were wrapped across my chest. I breathed him in. I could have stayed there forever.

My eyes opened and discovered that my body had turned toward the south. I looked down upon the village of Danville, Curtis' home.

"This is where we would go, Curtis, while you sat in your blue recliner watching TV. Woo Woo and I have climbed this mountain time and time again over the past year, telling you in our hearts how much we wished you could walk and run with us. I often wondered if you could hear us, feel us, see us in your mind's eye while you waited at home for us to return. When we did come home, I could see by the look in your eyes that you had tried to imagine the air pushing past your face as you ran, the sun on your bare shoulders as you sat atop the mountain, looking down at the homes of your parents, grandparents, and brothers. We were going to build our home next to Chad's, remember? Our children would only have to run across the field to play with their cousins and race down the field to visit their grandparents. They would sled all winter, play tennis all summer, pick apples in the fall, and help us plant the garden in the spring. We finally had it all figured out, Curtis. We finally saw eye to eye. This is where I used to lay in the grass, look up to the sky and wish that you could be next to me. And now, you are here beside me. Finally. Forever."

Curtis no longer held me in his arms but I could sense him in the air, the breeze, the birds, the clouds, and the sun. He enveloped me and refused to let go.

An hour later, I sat cross-legged on the floor with the minister facing me from the couch. Joe, who had been at our beck and call over the past year, offered me a spot on the couch next to him; my father insisted that I sit in a chair.

"The floor is fine," I said. I wanted to remain in the pocket of shadowed light so that they couldn't see that I was shaking.

Joe, my parents, and my sisters were trying to think of hymns and Bible verses for the service.

"When should it be?" I asked.

"I think in four days," the minister answered. "That's the earliest it can be if there are going to be two wakes."

"What's the date?"

"December 23."

"He had said that he'd be walking with a cane by Christmas," I stated.

Silence.

"Do you want to continue with this later?"

"No. There is no time to wait. What were we saying?"

"You had just said that you will definitely be speaking," the minister confirmed.

"Yes."

"Are you sure?" The question came from my mom.

"I promised him that I would speak at his funeral."

The minister interjected, "When would you like to speak?"

"Sometime in the middle?"

The minister continued in a soft, slow voice. "I think that you should speak near the beginning. You have taken care of all of us for so long. It is your turn to grieve. You need to allow yourself the opportunity. This funeral is for you. Curtis has already been taken care of."

I knew that I wouldn't cry at the wakes or the funeral. I was not in the same space and time as everyone else. I was still with Curtis. But I could sense that my family and closest friends were worried about, even frightened for, me. I suppose that they knew what was to come.

# A Final Goodbye

Curtis was frugal in terms of not spending his money on senseless, unnecessary items, but once he made up his mind to buy something that he needed, he only bought the best. The best to Curtis meant the most expensive. The day after Curtis died, I entered the funeral home in St. Johnsbury. I do not remember if I went alone or if someone accompanied me. I do not recall if I stood or sat upon arriving. What I do know is that I handed the funeral director the clothes in which I wished Curtis to be dressed for the two wakes and his burial. I also remember being led down to the basement of the funeral home where the caskets were displayed. Overwhelmed by the options, I glanced over the rows of caskets as the funeral director explained the various choices. His words are garbled in my memory but my mind's eye can still see the ornamental boxes lined up one by one: white with gold detail, black with silver detail, warm oak, dark maple, deep red mahogany, and countless other variations. I envisioned Curtis being laid to rest under the ground in one of these dressed-up boxes. I could see him lying on his back, his legs straight and long, his heels almost reaching the soft satin casket lining, his arms beside him as though in a straight jacket, his face expressionless.

He would be dressed in the clothes that I had brought with me that day: his favorite ocean blue button-down dress shirt, the silver cufflinks that we had purchased for our wedding day which were engraved with his initials, CRV, the red Christmas tie with Santa and the reindeer in the hot tub drinking cocktails that we had purchased for our Caribbean cruise the month he was diagnosed with ALS, his gray striped suit, his black and fluorescent orange Halloween BOO boxers that glowed in the dark which I had bought for him for the first Halloween that we had celebrated as an official couple, his navy blue dress socks and of course, the black slippers that he had worn every day except during those humid summer months since he had lost the ability to stand on his own four months after the diagnosis.

His Masonic ring would be on his right pinkie finger and his wedding ring would be on his left ring finger. The funeral director had insisted that I remove our wedding ring from his hand that Sunday afternoon before they placed him in the big black bag because of the chance that it would be lost during the journey to Boston for the brain and spinal cord retrieval. I was grateful that Curtis would once again covet it. I had contemplated keeping it for myself but I knew that he needed it with him. And I would always have his high school ring, the ring he had given to me that summer when we had first met.

"I'll take that one."

The Batesville casket – a warm barkley oak – was perfect for Curtis. Simple but handsome. Strong and yet supple. Understated and yet the most grand.

"Are you interested in knowing the price?" the funeral director questioned with respect.

"No."

"It's one of the most expensive options." He had been a fishing buddy of Curtis'. He and Curtis' good friend (who owned Vinny's and who had given me my waitressing job) had invited Curtis on a fishing trip to Lake Ontario in Oswego, New York four months after the diagnosis, right before Curtis lost the ability to stand on his own. Curtis accepted the offer. They told me that they figured it would be their last fishing trip all together. They insisted on paying Curtis' third of the trip, including meals, hotel room, and the cost of chartering the boat. Although uncertain of our financial future, Curtis did not accept that offer. They told Curtis that they would be more than happy to have me come along; they were aware that Curtis needed me in order to perform many daily tasks. Curtis accepted and we were able to enjoy a day of deep-sea fishing.

"Thank you. I'll take it."

That day at the funeral home, I also decided to have the casket enveloped in a secure sentinel vault for the burial rather than just a plain wooden box at an additional cost of almost 900 dollars. As the funeral director had explained to me, a vault as a burial container protects the casket from water and other elements as a result of an air seal. "Imagine turning a glass upside down," he had said, "then submerge it into water. The air trapped inside the glass keeps the water from rising more than a fraction of an inch. Similarly, the air trapped inside the dome between the casket and the vault prevents outside water from reaching the casket."

Curtis had requested to be embalmed rather than cremated. Although the funeral director had not mentioned that the vault would protect against anything besides water, the vision of worms, bugs, ants, spiders, snakes, and any other insect or critter that lives in the earth slithering into and through Curtis' remains made me physically ill. I was going to take any and all precautions necessary to ensure that his body would be kept as preserved as possible.

I arrived at the Danville Congregational Church at 4 pm on a Tuesday, two days after Curtis' death. The wake was not scheduled to begin until five but the funeral director had asked that the family arrive early in order to witness the casket being carried to the altar and to pay our respects before the crowd arrived. He had suggested holding the wakes at the church rather than at the funeral home because he didn't think that the funeral home would provide a large enough space for the number of attendees he expected. I had struggled with whom to ask to be the pallbearers. Of course, Curtis' father and four brothers would be asked. Justin was a logical choice as was Joe. And I could not forget Curtis' most recent friend who was Mandy's boyfriend whom Curtis had met only six months earlier but with whom he had spent many hours and to whom he confided the few thoughts that he could not share with me. If I had been able to ask only four men, like I had thought was the case, I would have not known whom to choose. Thankfully, though, I learned that there were numerous opportunities for carrying the casket: into the Danville Congregational church for the Tuesday night wake, out of the church after the Wednesday night wake, into the St. Johnsbury North Congregational church for the funeral on Thursday, out of the church after the service. And then, of course, the casket would need to be carried to the burial site that next spring. I asked all eight men to be the pallbearers.

I do not recall which of the eight men carried Curtis to the altar for the Tuesday night wake. I do remember the funeral director asking me if I'd like to be the first to see Curtis. He asked to be given a moment in order to prepare the body, just in case it had become contorted during the eight-mile trip from the funeral home to the church. I waited eagerly at the back of the church. It had been over 48 hours since I had seen Curtis. I had asked the funeral director if I could accompany Curtis to the autopsy and brain and spinal cord retrieval procedure in Boston on Sunday night; I could not bear the thought of Curtis making that journey alone. He had convinced me that he would look after Curtis and reminded me that I had too much to do. "Besides," he had said. "Who will take care of Woo Woo?"

The funeral director motioned with his head for me to come forward. From afar, I could see Curtis' deep blue shirt and dark brown hair. I walked quickly. As I got closer, I noticed the pin-stripes on his gray suit. I wanted to run to Curtis; I couldn't wait to see and touch him again. Once I was within arm's length, though, I saw that the scars on his forehead and the blisters on his lips which had become so prominent his last few days, but which had disappeared after he had died and were still not present when he was taken away in the big black bag, were back. I could not wait to develop the photographs I had taken of Curtis after I had shaven him that Sunday morning; I needed to know that I had not imagined what I had seen, or rather that I had not imagined what I had not seen. The peacefulness that had enveloped Curtis after 11:30 am on Sunday was gone. He no longer looked healthy in mind, body, and soul. In fact, he looked very tired. And old. In an attempt to make him look more like himself, I pinned his Nascar pin to his tie and the angel with its green ribbon that Sandra had given to him to his right lapel.

I took Curtis' limp right hand in mine. It was cold. The temperature did not bother me. I could not believe how soft his hands had become after a full year of not using them to build, hammer, staple, screw, paint, fix, design, hang sheetrock, and spread concrete. Just as Curtis had been forced to reinvent himself in terms of expressing himself verbally rather than commun-icating through his physical movement, his hands had been transformed from those of a hard-working skilled laborer into those of a man who spent his time thinking and being.

I let go of his hand and placed my hand on his heart. I felt no heartbeat. "There's still a bit of you here, my dear. Go. Fly away," I whispered.

Wakes are curious events. I used to believe that they were designed to be a designated period of time during which the family could be comforted by those who either also loved the deceased or whose lives were touched by the deceased. In my experience, though, Curtis' wakes consisted of hours standing in line, my head held high, my feet aching and my heart breaking for the 750 souls that stood in line to tell me how much they would miss Curtis and how, in the last year, he had inspired them. This first wake, which was supposed to last until 7 pm, did not end until past nine. Afterward, my parents insisted that I go to dinner with them at a local restaurant across the street from the church. I could not eat, but I did drink two Tom Collins.

Curtis' parents had been adamant about holding two wakes in order to allow ample time for others to pay their respects. By the next day, at the second wake, I was so exhausted that I do not even recall greeting Curtis before the ceremonies. But I do remember noticing right away that his body looked wearier, as if it too were tiring of the sentiments, hugs, and tears. I put his black Oakley sunglasses on him in an effort to protect him from seeing the look of disbelief, grief, and hopelessness on visitors' faces just as I attempted to protect myself on this second day by wearing a large black hat.

At some point during the second wake, Annie and Tommy asked me if they could leave Uncle Curtie with some things and so I told them I knew just where we could put them. The very large and very beautiful oak casket had a secret compartment. With the bottom half of the casket closed and the top half open, as it was during the wakes so that the visitors could only view the top half of Curtis' body, one could access this compartment, for it was a drawer that came out of the edge of the bottom half. Tommy ran to the back of the church, grabbed the thin memoriam paper which was wrapped in a green ribbon and handed it to me. "Uncle Curtie wasn't able to see or read this so I think he might need it." Annie asked if we could leave Uncle Curtie with some cherry Chapstick. He had needed it applied so often the last few weeks as a result of his severely dry mouth that resulted from his struggle to breathe.

At the end of the night after the second wake, the funeral director asked me if I'd like to say a final goodbye. The casket would remain closed for the funeral on Thursday and it would not be reopened before the burial in the spring. For the last time, I leaned over Curtis. I saw the pain and sorrow imprinted on his face. He was gone; I was sure of this now. He was finally free from the suffering and physical hardship. I did not look at his body while I whispered but instead looked out toward the altar. "Thank you for allowing me to see the freedom and joy you experienced when you were first greeted by whatever or whomever came to get you on Sunday morning. You accomplished what you had set out to do. Your mind, body and soul were completely healed for at least a moment. Thank you for staying and helping me to get through the last two days. Thank you for having the strength to leave your body behind. I, too, will say goodbye to your old body. I will forever remember its lines and curves. I will never forget your smile, the fact that your eyes would change their color from blue to green and back again and the way your hand felt in mine. You had promised that we would never say goodbye. Only see ya later. I believe you, Curtis."

Finally, in the casket, on one side of Curtis' hips I laid his charcoal farm jacket to keep his old body warm and draped a small bouquet of dried flowers from our wedding across his lap.

That evening we held a healing service in West Danville; I have no memory of this event. I suppose that my mind was preoccupied with trying to figure out where Curtis had gone. I knew for sure that his soul had finally exited his body.

I was still writing the eulogy an hour before I was supposed to leave for the funeral. I wanted to be able to relay those last days of Curtis' life to all of those who had loved him. As I sat in front of the keyboard, I doubted my ability to remember exactly what had happened. The last few days had gone by so quickly, and there had been very little warning. It was that morning, the morning of the funeral, four days after Curtis' death, that it occurred to me: I had not been prepared for Curtis to die. It was also that morning when the shock began to dissipate and reality began to seep in. Perhaps Curtis really had died?

I remember choosing a red dress from the closet. Red is the color of love. I once again put on the big black hat; I needed to protect my soul. I think that I put on make-up or, at the very least, I must have applied lipstick. I am pretty sure that I wore stockings. I made sure that Woo Woo ate some breakfast, drank some water, and went outside. He, of course, would be accompanying me to the funeral.

Woo Woo and I sat in the front row at the North Congregational Church in St. Johnsbury. We stared at the closed casket in front of the altar. It had been placed in the very same spot that 26 days earlier Curtis and I had sat and declared our love to one another.

My soul ached to cry out, *"Please help me!"* but I remained silent.

I reminded myself that I had been adamant about speaking. I had to finish what Curtis and I had started: I needed our family and friends, who had traveled alongside us and supported us for the past year, to know that Curtis had fought as long as he could. I also needed to let them know that the miracle that we had been waiting for had finally occurred. And so, I read out loud to over 500 people what I had written to him:

"Dear Curtis,

My best friend. My love. My husband. It has been 96 hours since I held your breathing body in my arms. I miss touching you. But I feel you. I know that you are here with me.

I remember those last three nights. You were so afraid to fall asleep, fearful that you would not wake up beside me, that you would not wake up here on earth. Sunday night, the 19th of December, 12 hours after you had passed, I sat in your blue recliner, also afraid to fall asleep. I was so fearful that I would wake up and you would still not be beside me. I was also afraid that I would wake up here on earth and not in heaven with you. Monday morning, the 20th of December, I woke up, and reached for you. I felt you, but you were not there when I opened my eyes. I shot out of bed and stood in the middle of the room. Tricia asked me what I was doing. 'Everything,' I told her. 'We have so much to do.'

But then, I thought, I have nothing to do. No other physical body to feed, move, care for, or keep alive. I sat down. And then I shut off, but just for a minute, for then I thought of you, sitting in your chair, talking about all of the things you would do that day and asking me to do all the things you wished you could do. Curtis, you prayed for your freedom every day. And here, for a moment, my own freedom was terrifying.

A few hours later, Sandra and her daughter visited. Joe was already at the house as he had been so often before as well as after your death. We all consoled one another and recognized that Sam was taken to be your guide, for you feared the journey and prayed for a friend to be there by your side. What better man than Sam to lead you to the Kingdom of Heaven? I told Sandra, though, that it would be hard for the two of us to go on. What would we do? Joe, who was sitting, listening, the same way you would just sit and take it all in, stated, 'If you love yourself half as much as you loved Curtis, you will be fine.' And so, my dear Curtis, I will be fine. I will go on. You will also go on, inside me and beside me. I talk to you every minute. I hear you every other minute. And I am so thankful for you.

You and I would always recount our days together. I would either lie or sit beside you and we would remember the events of the past year, the past month, the past week or day or hour. We relished the fact that we had learned to live every day to the fullest. We gloated to one another that we took advantage of every minute of our time together. But the last week of your physical life, you realized that you were no longer living the life that you wanted to lead. And so, you prepared us for your journey. You always thought of others first, and in the last months you always instructed me to voice your words of care and concern for another's benefit, and, so, my Curtis, I will be your voice again and I will reassure your community that it was time for you to go and that you were miraculously healed: mind, body, and spirit.

Two Fridays ago, I awoke before sunrise. You were asleep and so I spent a rare moment alone. I witnessed a glorious winter sunrise. Deep reds and oranges and yellows covered by a blanket of bluish-gray. And on our ride down to Boston that day I remarked that sunrises always remind me of an upcoming death. When we returned home we learned that Sam had passed away earlier in the day. You were shocked and sad and yet would not speak about your loss or his family's loss.

On Tuesday, the day of Sam's funeral, I ran past their house and on my return route I stopped. There were hugs and tears but the moment I saw Sandra she said, 'I have something for you and Curtis.' She led me to their Christmas tree and took off an ornament. 'I wanted to shop for an ornament for you two last Thursday, but I didn't have time. And then, after Sam was gone, I sat down and looked at our tree and saw this one.' It was an angel with a green ribbon on it. 'Please tell Curtis that it is from him,' Sandra pleaded.

I returned to our house and presented you with your gift. You did not even smile. You were not surprised.

We attended Sam's funeral that afternoon. You asked me to wheel you to the front for communion although you could not swallow the bread. I placed the soaked bread in your mouth, and then you smiled. Neither you nor I cried during the funeral and, yet, it was the most beautiful tribute to the most wonderful man. As I led you into the elevator after the service, a friend of yours gave you the thumbs up. He told me later that for the first time he did not see anything when he looked into our eyes. Later, we wondered, why had we no feeling?

Wednesday and Thursday you were no longer sad, but you

were different. There was an acceptance, a peace within you. Thursday's healing circle was magnificent. That previous Sunday we had decided that we would like our friends in the healing circle to answer the question, 'What do you see as the next step in Curtis' healing?' And so they tried, yet during the dialogue that resulted, I realized that there are no answers. The circle determined that whether you were miraculously healed, or stayed the same physically, or if you died, the circle would continue for the circle had realized that it was healing for all. When the reporter from the *Burlington Free Press* had asked you in May what the purpose of the circle was to you, you had said for your community to be healed. And so, your community gave you their permission to go that Thursday night. You knew that the circle and the healing could continue without you here.

On Friday at 2 am, you awoke in a panic. You begged me to remove your full-face nighttime mask and replace it with your daytime nose mask. I did. You said that your nose was plugged. You asked me to try to unblock it. I tried, but couldn't. You said that your throat felt strange, as though there was mucus in it. For the next five hours, we dozed in and out of sleep, and whenever I awoke, you urged me to lay closer, to hold you tighter, but not across your chest.

At 7 am I told you that I could lie in bed forever, holding you, touching you. I asked you if you felt the same. You said no.

A half an hour later, our local doctor came and we discussed what you and I thought would someday be the last stage of ALS, before you passed away. We ironed out all of the details, all of our concerns and prepared for events that we thought were months away. That morning you felt odd, uncomfortable. You didn't want a bath, and you didn't want me to shave you. You didn't even let me take Woo Woo for a walk. You just wanted me beside you, holding you. And so I stayed. That afternoon we talked about the course of your illness. We marveled at how far the disease had progressed and about how we had coped with it. I explained to you that it was amazing: when you lost the use of any one part of you, we would mourn the loss of that part, complain about what we could not do as a result of losing that part, and then we'd say, if the disease stopped right now, we'd be okay. I asked you if you were okay now. And you said, 'No, I would not be okay if the disease stopped now.' I told you that I missed your smile, for your smile had changed since your facial muscles had deteriorated. You told me that you missed making people laugh. I reassured you that you still made people laugh, for your eye and eyebrow movements were all you needed to make others see how you feel. But you said, 'No, I miss telling my jokes and stories.' The rest of the afternoon was hard. There was no relief. You said to me, 'We're not having fun anymore, are we?' I said, 'No, honey, it's not so much fun anymore.'

At 3:30 pm on Friday I started to administer morphine. More at 4:30 pm. Another dose an hour later, and yet another at 6:30 pm. A few friends came and comforted you with their touch. Your father joined them, and then your mother. By 7:30 pm you began to relax, but you were not yourself. I read you some stories from your *Small Miracles* book, and you smiled, although distantly. On her way out, your mother asked me, 'What is the next step? What are our options to improve his breathing?' I explained again that you and I had decided that there were no options. We had gone as far as we cared to go.

You finally fell asleep for a few hours, but awoke at 1 am on Saturday in a panic. You were nervous, and kept repeating that you were scared. At 3:30 am I spoke with your doctor in Boston. He said that there was a 99 percent chance that your breathing was deteriorating, but that there was a one percent chance that you were just having a bad day and had a head cold. For the second time since your diagnosis, I asked him how much time we had. He stated, 'We're not talking months, but we're not talking days. Just keep him calm, and try to balance the morphine so that he is alert but comfortable.' You had your eyes closed when I explained this all to Mandy's mother, a nurse, who had volunteered to stay with us that night. You opened your eyes when I said that there was a chance that this was just a head cold. We tried to believe that this was the answer, although we saw the truth in each other's eyes. I told you then that it was okay if you went and left me behind. It was okay if you were taken to a place where you were not afraid to close your eyes, in fear that you would not wake up beside me.

Later that morning, around 7 am, Saturday the 18th of December, we added Valium to your system. Morphine and Valium finally relaxed you enough so that you were alert, but comfortable. By mid-morning, you felt okay to let me take Woo for a walk. On our journey, we met your father and I told him about our sleepless night and your anxiety and fears. I told him that the doctor had predicted that you had a matter of weeks to live. And then I asked your father if he could ask your mother to give you her permission to leave your physical body. You were so afraid to disappoint, and I knew that you needed to hear from her that dying was okay and that you had made her proud with all that you had accomplished throughout your life, particularly in the last year or so.

That afternoon your mother called and told me that she had a letter to read to you. She asked, 'Could I come over tomorrow or would that be too late?' I told her that I didn't know, but that she may feel better if she came right away. And so you and I, your father and your mother, sat in a circle and she read to you a letter of love. A letter that gave you permission to go, a letter that made the four of us so sad and yet happy.

At 5 pm you said, 'Go get my pants.' And so I did. As I dressed you, you said, 'I wish I were healthy. We would do something special.' We traveled out to North Danville to your Christmas party that your family had planned for you. You were on morphine, valium, and a fentanyl patch. You were alert and excited. Three large and amazing outdoor decorations of light greeted us: a green and white star of hope, a colorful Christmas tree and a beautiful guardian angel. Once you entered hunting camp, I prepared to give you your hourly dose of morphine, and you said, 'No. No more morphine.' And then, among your family and friends, their noise and laughter, you fell asleep in your wheelchair, which you used to think was the most uncomfortable thing ever.

We brought you home at 10 pm and after putting you to bed I ignored my usual two-hour nighttime routine of preparing for the next morning and just crawled into bed beside you and wrapped my body around yours. At 3:45 am you again awoke in a panic. Your nose was plugged again, and you wanted all of your machines out, in order to try to clear your air passages. It was then that I told you that I thought you did not have a head cold. I told you that I thought that your breathing was deteriorating. You said, 'I'm sorry.' And so I gave you more medicine to relieve the pain of suffocation.

You suffered for a few more hours, during which I read Deuteronomy 30 and prayed with you for comfort from God. At 6:30 am, our neighbor went home to get some sleep after her night shift of helping us. A half an hour later you were surrounded by five of us: me, Tricia, your uncle, Mandy and her boyfriend. We rubbed you, held you and talked to you. Since you were still afraid to close your eyes, I reassured you that you would either awake in my arms or in God's and either way it would be wonderful. You agreed. It was at this time that I opened the curtains and witnessed a magnificent sunrise and from that moment forward the sun shone right on you. At 7:15 am you told us that you were scared, tired, that you couldn't breathe and that you didn't want to go to the hospital. And then you closed your eyes and fell asleep. At 8 am the minister came and we prayed together. For the next few hours you slept, but five or six different times you shook your head violently and then opened your eyes and stared in disbelief. You told the five of us, 'Don't be sad.' At around 9 am, you opened your eyes and saw Tricia beside you on the bed. You whispered my name. I climbed over you and held you. You closed your eyes for the last time, and your face relaxed. You looked calm and at peace. The doctor called and I explained the change in events and he stated that it was now a matter of days. 'They will not be good days,' he had said. You would probably never be alert again for you would need a large amount of medicine to stay comfortable.

You started to turn purple, and I started calling your family. Our family and friends came, one by one, and said their goodbyes. One friend appeared unexpectedly with our dried flowers from our wedding. A bit after 11 am, with me by your side and our family and friends surrounding you, your mother began to read her story aloud to us all and as your pulse slowed I crawled as close as I could, and held on for dear life. I cried until I could no longer breathe, and then your pulse stopped at 11:30 am. You were at peace. And you were beautiful. The blisters that had been on your lips for days were gone. The marks from your mask had disappeared. All your blemishes, gone. You were perfect. As the sun shone on you, I realized that you were complete. Mind. Body. And Spirit. We had often laid in bed and fantasized what you would look like the morning you were miraculously healed. And here you were. It was a miracle. Yours was a miraculous death. It was at that moment that you became my angel. My Curtis. I stayed by your body for the next three hours, touching you, talking to you, showing you our completed wedding album. There was still a bit of you there. I shaved you right before you were transported, and I took a picture of you, for you had wanted a picture of yourself without your mask at the wedding and also because I couldn't get over how perfect you looked.

Amazingly, when I saw you again on Tuesday night in your casket, the blisters on your lips had reappeared and the blemishes were there. I believe that you were finally miraculously healed and that for at least a moment you were perfect in mind, body and spirit. I thank you for that gift of faith.

My dear Curtis, what next? As your voice, I will write my book about our journey and ALS, and I will develop our nonprofit organization for genetic ALS research. And I will go on. We never did say goodbye, only see ya later and I will see you, and someday, my dear husband, I will be placed beside you in this Danville earth that we both called home.

One of our last disagreements was over my name. I told you that I was having trouble adjusting to the loss of my last name. You said that it was because I had had no time to prepare, for after all, I did go from your girlfriend to your fiancé to your wife in just a few short weeks. I told you no, it was that I felt as though I was giving up a part of my identity. And now that you are gone, I am struggling with another loss, and although I had 12 months to prepare for your departure, I know that on Sunday a part of me went with you, but I will carry you in my heart, and I will carry on your name with no hyphen. You did win in the end. I would have never expected otherwise."

After I spoke the last words of Curtis' eulogy, I took a minute to span the sea of souls who had loved Curtis. I felt so much love. And heartbreak. I gathered my pieces of paper and walked off the altar toward Woo Woo, who had sat silently while I read. His pensive eyes had watched me the entire time. I took my seat and held him tightly. Heather began her solo of *My Heart Will Go On*. As I heard my sister's voice sing, I hoped that I would never be alone.

On the evening of Curtis' funeral, the night before Christmas Eve, we still held our usual healing circle at the Danville Inn where the circles had been held since October. The attendance that night was overwhelming. Since I had realized that Curtis' soul had left his body, I asked Julia to try to "see" where he was now. I had felt him inside of me ever since I had said goodbye to his body after the second wake, but I needed to know exactly where he was and I was pretty sure that Julia would know.

Throughout the healing circle, I felt a burning, in a positive way, a warm almost hot feeling in my chest. After the healing touch had been performed, which all of the participants had insisted be done on me, Julia whispered in my ear, "He's inside your chest. He's become a part of you." Now I knew for sure that I would never be alone.

# Curtis' Spirit

Because Curtis and I needed to believe that he could heal himself, we created tangible goals for which to strive. In September, ten months after the diagnosis, we had decided that our goal would be for Curtis to walk with a cane by Christmas. We had been realistic enough to know that he probably wouldn't be able to walk alone, but we had been optimistic enough to believe that he would be able to walk with assistance.

On a Tuesday morning, 16 days after Curtis' death, I awoke very sad because Tricia had to return to college that day, and then it would just be me and Woo Woo in the house. Woo Woo barked and scratched at the maroon front door. I opened the door to let him out and witnessed the tail end of another glorious winter sunrise. There was now over two feet of snow on the ground as a result of another six inches falling the night before. The magnificent sight of the sun's reflection on the white earth made me think that there truly was something greater in life than us. I asked Woo Woo to wait as I gathered my jog bra, running pants, and turtleneck. I grabbed my winter coat, hat, running boots, and gloves. It was too beautiful to be inside.

"Come on, Woo Woo, let's go," I yelled as I ran from the front of the house to its side. Woo Woo knew that we normally did not take our daily run until at least 10 am.

When I reached the top of the driveway, I stopped. Small circular marks about an inch and a half in diameter were imprinted in the snow. They began at the garage. I followed them down the steep, long driveway until they ended. They appeared in a single line, with a spacing of about a foot apart. Inside each circle there was a slight mark. There were no other markings anywhere that could be seen. I could not imagine what human or animal could have made these marks. And then, I remembered. Being careful not to disturb the markings, I ran back up the driveway and into the garage. I popped open the plastic top of one of the Rubbermaid containers that Tricia and I had recently filled with Curtis' things that I wanted to keep. There it was. Curtis' cane. Golden handle on one end, the circular black rubber stopper with a slight mark on the other end. He accomplished his goal only a little over a week past his personal deadline.

I did not immediately run inside and wake Tricia up for I preferred to relish in my time alone with the thought that Curtis had figured out a way to tangibly prove what I had assumed but didn't understand enough to truly believe. His journey along the path toward healing was still happening. When Tricia woke up, I asked her to put on her winter clothes and follow me outside. I showed her the markings that began at the garage and continued down the driveway.

No hesitation.

No questioning.

"That looks like Curtis' cane." Tricia's words validated what she and I had experienced together the past few days: Curtis was still, in some way and to some extent, a part of our physical world.

As I had felt at the end of the previous summer when Tricia had left Curtis and me to begin her first semester of college, I wasn't sure how I would survive without her when she left after the holiday break. I was grateful, though, that she had stayed with me since Curtis' death.

A few hours after she left, Joe, Julia and I traveled to

Burlington, Vermont, for a session with a medium that they believed could communicate with the deceased. I brought questions about which I had been yearning for answers. We met the woman in her home and I liked her immediately. She was lovely – gentle, soft-spoken, and genuinely saddened by the news that my husband had recently passed. I do not doubt that she was aware of Curtis' presence during our session for I could feel Curtis throughout the entire hour. He was definitely with us. But the medium's words were not Curtis'. I knew this to be so because I knew his language; I knew the words that he chose to use to describe his thoughts and feelings. Either she was not hearing Curtis correctly or Curtis refused to speak, and so she fabricated the language. Even though I had my list of questions in my pocket, I didn't ask most of them because I doubted that Curtis would answer through the medium, and I didn't want to hear falsified information. But near the end of the session, after the medium finished telling us what she thought he was saying to us, she asked, "Is there anything that you'd like to say to Curtis?"

"Just one thing," I said. "Curtis, would you please come home and convince your son to eat? He is starving himself again. He refuses to drink. He has had a fever for three days. He is yellow. I can not handle the thought of losing him, too."

Once I returned home that evening, I sat down at the kitchen table and spoke to Curtis myself. Other than during Woo Woo's and my runs, this was the first time since his death that I spoke to Curtis out loud as though he were sitting down next to me. In the midst of my one-sided conversation with Curtis, Woo Woo got up from where he was lying beside my feet, walked over to the blue recliner, and barked. He then stared straight at where Curtis had sat for so many months and whined. Minutes later he stopped the noise and placed his little black head on the seat of the recliner just as he had rested his head on Curtis' lap so many times. Seconds later he turned around and walked over to his food bowl, which he had not touched for days, and devoured the food.

I tried to keep myself busy after Tricia left by increasing my waitressing hours and continuing to work with the lawyer to create Curtis' foundation. But, all I really wanted to do was run. Woo Woo and I went for a run every day, and very often we exercised more than once a day. I felt closest to Curtis when I was moving, so that was how I spent the majority of the week and a half after Tricia left.

And then, I stopped.

I could not get out of bed on a Thursday in January, almost a month since Curtis' death. After a night of crying, I watched the sun rise and decided that I wouldn't get up. Woo Woo remained at the foot of my bed all day, too. By that afternoon, our neighbor came over.

"It's just the flu," I told her.

"Curtis wouldn't want to see you this way, you know," she replied.

"I didn't sleep very well. I'm just tired."

"Are you going to the healing circle tonight?" our neighbor asked.

"I don't know. I don't want to let the others down but I just don't have the strength. I really don't feel well."

Our neighbor spoke slowly. "You took such wonderful care of Curtis. You have also taken care of all of us. It's your turn, now. You need to allow yourself to be taken care of. You need to allow us to help you."

"I don't know how you could. All I want and need is Curtis."

I skipped the healing circle that night for the first time since its inception, almost a year beforehand, and for the next week I struggled. I couldn't focus. I had trouble eating. I never slept. I spent my nights crying and my days trying to recover from the nights. The only thing that got me out of bed in the morning was the fact that Woo Woo had to be let outside despite the fact that he, again, was feverish, anorexic, and the whites of his eyes as well as his skin were yellow. Our local veterinarian referred me to a specialist in New Hampshire. A week and hundreds of dollars worth of tests later, the results were inconclusive. The veterinarian believed that it could be slow liver failure but the only way to determine this for sure would be to have a liver biopsy. Also, he added, it could be depression and separation anxiety as a result of losing Curtis. "I could prescribe him an antidepressant."

I ignored his second suggestion. "And if we discover it is the liver, what can we do for him?" I asked.

"Nothing," the doctor replied.

I refused to put my boy through that pain. I brought him home to our house and held him and begged Curtis to heal him because I knew that I couldn't bear losing Woo Woo, too.

I fully recognize that the months after Curtis' death were extremely difficult for me. Looking back, reading journal entries, talking with loved ones who supported me during that time, I can say with the utmost certainty that it was a period of deep, unending, all-encompassing anguish. The sadness was unbearable. I couldn't just "snap out of it" or "make myself feel better" or "focus on the good." In addition to not being able to control my emotions, I couldn't bring Curtis back to life which is all I wanted.

Those months were almost impossible to live through. Almost. For all intents and purposes, I was most certainly depressed. The signs and symptoms were there. It was obvious. Although the year that I had cared for Curtis was physically and emotionally exhausting, I was almost always happy because Curtis was with me. After Curtis' death, during that most intense period of grief, I was surrounded by people who would thank me for taking such good care of Curtis. They would marvel at my strength.

"Loving and caring for Curtis was easy for me," I would reply. "Living without him physically by my side is not."

Throughout the months following Curtis' death, I purposefully didn't eat much because my own physical weakness allowed me to remain calm. Any energy I had was expelled in the form of sadness and anger – sadness over the fact that Curtis was gone and anger over the fact that I wasn't allowed to go with him. The less energy I had, the better. I preferred to feel nothing. But, at the time, I didn't recognize the depression. I was focused on trying to figure out how to continue to coexist with Curtis' soul.

In January, I agreed to have Julia perform an energy balance on me. She had been urging me to have one for months, and even though I didn't understand what it was or what it could possibly do for me, I had the time, now, and nothing to lose. Julia greeted me with her gentle and loving demeanor and led me into the room in her house that she used for her work. I lay on my back on a table much like one used for massage. I closed my eyes. For the next two hours, I relaxed and listened to Julia as her hands moved over me without any touching. Intermittently, she would speak.

"All of your chakras are closed except for your third eye which is your intuition and your head chakra."

"What do you mean by closed?" I asked.

"It means that most of your body is not in tune with you. It is functioning, doing what it is supposed to be doing, but you are not in tune with it. In time, if these chakras remain closed, your body will stop working."

According to the energy balance, my body was beginning the process of shutting down but my mind and intuition were busy traveling. Spiritually, I was alive and well, figuring out ways to live with only Curtis' soul. Physically, my body was acting as though it did not want to live.

While Julia was focusing on my head, I told her that before I went to sleep that past Monday night, I had asked Curtis to visit me. "Really visit me," I had said. "And, Curtis, I need to remember it when I wake up."

Then, I told her about the dream that followed. "My sister and I were lost in the woods, searching for a clearing. Fearful of going forward and becoming more lost, I considered stopping, but an overwhelming sense came over me that I had to keep moving in the same direction. A few moments later, my sister insisted that we turn around, but a voice pleaded with me to keep moving forward. I walked quickly, and when a field came into view, I began to run. I discovered a clearing surrounded by trees in all four directions. 'I'm home,' I declared. My sister was no longer behind me, but I was not alone. Curtis came from above. In other dreams, he had come to me in human form, but this night he was a spirit. Words cannot describe the magnificence of his being, which was marvelous to witness. Slowly, he approached. I stood still, waiting. His energy surrounded my whole being. I felt as though his arms were holding me. As one, we left the earth, and I felt the sensation of us dancing. It was our first dance as husband and wife. When I awoke that next morning, I felt as though he was beside me. Then, I recalled the dream. Simultaneously, I heard a spark of electricity and Woo Woo barked. In a flash, he was gone."

After I shared this experience with Julia, I felt heavy. It was as though hundreds of pounds came out of the sky and landed on me. When the session ended, I told Julia about the feeling of the weight crashing down on me.

"I felt the weight of your soul return," she said. "I had to work very hard for the rest of the time to try to redistribute it. You are not completely balanced, but you are better off than when you came in here."

When I shared the result of the energy balance with Tricia over the phone that evening, she commented, "So, you are the closest to a spirit form possible while you are still in your physical body?"

"Yes," I replied. "I suppose so. Julia and I talked about all of this after the session. It is not that I want to die. I know that I have so much to do here. But at the same time, I know that Curtis wants me to be with him. And I want to be with him. But I think that I can live in both worlds. For a while, anyhow. At least until I finish what I have to do here."

Four days later, I met with Cathy. For well over an hour, I confided in her many of my and others' experiences with Curtis' spirit. I told her about the cane markings. I told her about how he visited me in my dreams and me and Woo Woo in the house. I told her about how Tricia and I heard the sound of an electric "spark" in our home many times those first few weeks whenever we were speaking about him. I told her how Curtis' Aunt Judy shared with me her dream about Curtis in which he seemed so real and how, when she awoke from the dream, her printer randomly turned on and printed out a blank page of paper.

I relayed his brother Chad's story from his experience on New Year's Eve. "Remember when I borrowed Curtis' truck from you so that I could bring my Christmas tree up to camp? I was alone that day. I drove slowly up to camp. It was a beautiful day, snowing, calm, kind of warm. For the first time, I felt Curtis. I could have sworn he was sitting right beside me in the truck. I couldn't stop thinking of him and of all the memories up at camp. I got to camp, dragged the tree to the pile, went into camp to check it out and then got back in the truck. When I sat down in the truck, I heard a really loud whistling sound. I looked around but saw nothing. The sound started again and a shiver ran up my spine. I got out of the truck and still heard the whistle. A few minutes later, I got back into the truck and the sound stopped. I looked behind me and realized that the back window was open just a bit, like Curtis always left it. But when I put my hand out the window to see if there was a breeze, it was just as calm as it had been all day. I am not one to believe in such things, but I really do think that Curtis was with me that day."

I also told her Justin's story that he had shared with me. "On New Year's Eve, I spent the morning driving around the back roads of Danville just like me and Curtis used to do. For hours, I visited the loops that Curtis and I used to travel. I felt Curtis the whole time. He was sitting right next to me in the car. I've had quite a few dreams, too, about him but I can't remember the details. But I will say, the one thing I do know is that you were right beside him in all of the dreams."

Cathy smiled as she took all of this information in and then remarked, "You need to be careful who you tell this stuff to. I knew a woman who had similar communication and experiences with her deceased husband. She shared her stories with others, and people thought she was crazy." She continued, "I feel as though you are holding Curtis back. I think that the reason Curtis' soul is not settled is because you are keeping him here. He is worried about you. I think that he needs to know that you are going to be okay."

I did not think about it this way. I was happy that Curtis' soul was hanging around. Cathy convinced me to attempt hypnosis. She believed that perhaps it would help me to be able to understand why Curtis was still so present.

So, three days later, I sat in Curtis' blue recliner and allowed Cathy to put me into a trance. We recorded the session. Being in a hypnotic state, I felt normal except for the fact that I didn't seem to have any control over my physical movements. First, Cathy asked me what my signals would be for yes, no, and I don't know. My right thumb raised itself for "yes," my left thumb raised itself for "no" and my right forefinger raised itself for "I don't know." Then, under Cathy's direction, my left arm began to feel light and it touched my face.

Cathy continued to speak. "What I would like you to get out of this session is to figure out what Curtis needs in order to be settled. And, what do you need in order to let go of Curtis?"

I heard her words but my mind was busy exploring. And then, it found Curtis. Or, Curtis found me. I don't know how it happened, but there he was, and I felt as I had felt that night in the dream when we were in the woods, as though I was floating. The same way I had felt during the energy session with Julia before the weight came down on me. My heart was pounding, just as it had been during the dream and the energy session. Curtis' spirit was beside me. We were connected and we communicated without words. I knew what Curtis was thinking before I asked him a question. It was as if our minds and our feelings were lying on our beings, out in the open for all to see.

I continued to hear Cathy ask my subconscious to figure out what it needed to let go of Curtis.

My left thumb answered "no" twice.

So, Cathy asked, "Why are you answering 'no?' I had asked you to signal 'yes' once your subconscious came up with the answer. Please speak if you can."

While under hypnosis, I spoke, "I asked Curtis if he wanted me to let go of him and he said 'no.' Then, I asked him if he was happy and he answered 'no.' As I was asking Curtis these things, my left thumb answered 'no.'"

Curtis and I were together. And we just wanted to continue to be together, alone. But Cathy kept talking. I stopped listening; I didn't pay attention. Curtis and I traveled to the Stagger Inn. There was snow all around. We were outside, on the camp's porch, watching the bonfire and looking out like we did the day we had stood in that exact spot and talked about building a home together. Suddenly, it became fall and we were at the back farm discussing our house and apple orchard. We saw it being built. We were doing it together and I was smiling.

"What are you smiling about?" Cathy asked.

Again, I spoke, "We're up at hunting camp. We are going to build our house and our apple orchard. We can see it."

"Can you tell Curtis that it can't happen? That was your dream but you can no longer do it together." She continued, "Do you still want to do all of that alone?"

"No. But Curtis says that we can still do it together. It's possible. He's sure of this," I answered.

"How is that possible?" she asked.

"I don't know," I answered. And then, I cried, still under hypnosis.

"What time period are you and Curtis in?"

"The future," I answered.

Silence.

Curtis left.

A few minutes later, Cathy asked, "Is he gone?"

"Yes."

"Okay, I need you to focus. I need you to figure out what Curtis needs and what you need to let go.

Curtis' spirit reappeared. He brought me to the places that we had dreamed of visiting together: Alaska and Hawaii. I had never been to either location but somehow I knew that that was where we were. Then, we traveled to a familiar place. We swam by the raft at Joe's Pond. Cathy continued to ask me things. But all I wanted to do was be with Curtis.

"Where are you?" she asked again.

"Curtis is bringing me all over."

"In his world or in yours?"

"In our world," I answered.

"What world is that?" Cathy asked.

"This one. This is the one that he is in. And we're traveling. Curtis is exploring all of the places that he has not been and doing all of the things that he wanted to do. It's wonderful."

She tried to bring me back.

She just kept talking.

Curtis and I laughed at her. Cathy didn't understand. We began to get frustrated. We just wanted her to be quiet and let us be. And then, we were at hunting camp again, and we were dancing. It was wonderful. And then I realized that I was being pulled away so I asked Curtis if we could meet again.

"Tonight in a dream, perhaps?" I begged. "Can I continue to see you? Can I feel you, be with you?"

I had so much to ask him but we needed to be alone. Curtis didn't want me to go. I told him that we'd be focusing on him at the healing circle that night.

"See you later," I told him.

And, I left.

I was no longer under hypnosis.

"He is a spoiled brat, isn't he?" Cathy remarked.

"He almost always got his way," I smiled.

"Who ran the show before Curtis got sick?" she asked.

"He made the daily decisions, or at least appeared to, but I made all of the major decisions. Once he got sick, though, we always made our decisions together, both the small and large stuff."

"You are going to have to make the big decision here. Can you ask him to go?"

"No. I am not ready. He is not ready. I do not want that to happen."

That night we had the fourth healing circle since Curtis' passing. I requested that we send energy to Curtis, like we had done when he was alive, for I felt as though he still needed us. I placed Curtis' picture on a chair, and the group encircled him and held hands. While we were supposed to be focusing our energy, I opened my eyes and thought I saw his form sitting on the empty chair next to the chair that held his picture. He begged me to come to him; he needed my physical touch. I wished to break free of the two hands that held me in my place, but I was afraid of what the others would think. This was unlike me. Instead, I envisioned myself breaking the bonds, kneeling in front of Curtis, and placing my hand on his heart as I had done every other Thursday for the last eight months of his life. I knew exactly where his heart lay. I could feel Curtis smile. He knew that I did what I was capable of doing.

I woke up at 4 am the next morning to Woo Woo barking wildly. It was at that point that I realized that I had had a dream, again, and that Curtis and I had once again been with one another. I did not know how this could be possible, just as I had no idea how it could have happened that Curtis and I were together while I was under hypnosis, but I was convinced that it was not just a dream. During this "experience," we were in the bleachers at a game. I never saw the game or what it was that was being played but we were most definitely sitting together on the bleachers, surrounded by others, but totally alone. I did not recognize the other spectators. And they were not watching the game; they were watching me. I was aware that they could not see Curtis; I saw Curtis' form just as I had during the healing circle the night before.

"Can you allow me to see you, Curtis?" I asked him. "I need to be with you."

And there he was. Perfect and healthy. He could move his arms and legs, and he could smile again. He was 26 years old and healthy and wonderful. He was beautiful.

We began to speak to one another. It was not like during hypnosis when we read one another's thoughts. We were actually using words. I was aware that I had so many questions I wanted to ask him, but suddenly they didn't seem important.

"Are you happy?" I asked, finally, after just staring at his face, which didn't have a mask on it.

"No," Curtis replied.

I got up from beside him and sat down on the cold metal bench in between his legs. I began to rub his feet as I had done every day for the past year.

"Curtis, why is everyone staring at me?" I asked.

"They can't see me," he replied. "But don't worry. They don't get it."

"Curtis, did you really love me? I mean, did you really, really love me?"

No hesitation.

No questioning.

"No," he replied.

In the dream, I was not surprised by his answer but needed clarification, "What do you mean?"

"I was not capable of complete love. I tried, but I just couldn't. My inability to love completely was what kept me from being able to completely heal. But I am now learning. And now I know how to love myself and you the way that I had tried so hard to do before."

Curtis' physical form then transformed into that of an adorable young boy, about five years old. He did not resemble how Curtis looked at that age, though.

I questioned him again, "Curtis, do you really love me?"

"Yes," the little boy replied. "I love you unconditionally because I now know how."

"Why now?" I asked.

"Because you are my mother."

When I woke up that morning, I felt at peace even though I had even more questions. I opened the curtain and witnessed a spectacular sunrise. The sun was a little less than halfway over the horizon and it was so orange and so bright and so beautiful and the reflection on the snow-covered ground was splendid. Curtis' presence was so strong that I expected him to walk right out of the sun's rays.

# *Vanished*

On the first Thursday in February, feeling bare, naked, and exposed, I attended our healing circle for the fifth time with Curtis inside of me rather than by my side. At the healing circle the week before I had confessed to our friends and family that I was struggling. My courage, my strength, and my ability to get up in the morning had come from Curtis when he was alive and through him even after he had first departed our world. But now, a month and a half after his passing, I felt Curtis slipping away even though I still expected him to walk through the front door of our home and greet Woo Woo and me with his broad smile and gentle touch. I wished he would appear and wipe away the hours of tears and torment that I had been expelling and experiencing the last weeks.

At the same time, I was trying my hardest to realize that he had died. He had, right? I had seen the body leave our home in the big black bag. I had seen the body dressed in his only suit and Santa tie with his black slippers adorning his feet at both of the wakes. But even death couldn't keep Curtis and me apart. I believe that we still existed together on a plane that was neither earth nor heaven. For a little over a year, we had learned how to live while preparing to die, together. Over the course of that year, as Curtis' body deteriorated and I cared for his ailing physical self, our souls intermingled with no restrictions. We experienced a miraculous love. Our spirits did not recognize that death's barriers were slowly creeping in on us; perhaps that is because they knew that in our case death could not keep us from one another.

When Curtis was alive, the weekly healing circles energized us, but since his passing I found myself leaving the circles feeling drained and exhausted. Curtis now surrounded me whenever I was alone, but hardly ever appeared when I was with others. I preferred to be alone, in the darkness, where I could relinquish the strength that it required to remain sane, and exist with only Curtis and Woo Woo.

Although I was unable to attend this healing circle with Curtis, I didn't have to walk into the Danville Inn by myself. Feeling vulnerable is one thing; being alone is quite another. I parked our blue Chevy Blazer as close to the Inn's front entrance as possible. If it had been just me, I would have parked at the furthest possible spot from the entrance. I have always liked to have a few minutes to expel my nervous energy before entering a social situation; right after Curtis' death I realized that I needed even more time to gather my thoughts before encountering a room full of people. I had to be careful to remember not to say too much. I hopped out of the driver side, opening the left back door as Annie and Tommy tumbled out.

"Run, quickly," I advised. "It's freezing."

I watched the children sprint the 50 yards to the entrance and look back at me.

"Go ahead," I urged. "I'll be right there."

Even Annie and Tommy wondered if I would be okay alone.

I ran around to the passenger side door, opened it with all my strength (the Northeast Kingdom's wind had begun to blow fiercely that February evening; the wind chill was well below zero), cradled Woo Woo in my arms and sprinted to the entrance. I opened the first door to find Annie and Tommy standing on the porch still bundled in their winter coats, hats, gloves, and scarves.

"You ready?" Tommy asked.

"Sure, honey. Let's be as quiet as we can, though, okay. We're ten minutes late."

"Uncle Curtie would be mad," smiled Annie.

"Yes, he would be." I smiled thinking of how prompt Curtis had preferred to be.

I opened the second door that led us into the cozy restaurant and a circle of loving eyes greeted us.

"Well, now you all know the truth," I stated. "It was never Curtis who held us up; I am the one who is perpetually late."

Laughter rang through the crowd.

"We're just so glad that you are here," said a dear friend who was always there with her green ribbon displayed proudly on her lapel. In fact, almost all of our friends and family continued to wear their green ribbons as they had done while Curtis was alive.

After I helped the children with their gear, I took off my own jacket, removed Woo Woo's leash, and sat down.

"Well, let's get started," began Julia. "We spoke last week about sending energy to Curtis again this week for it had been mentioned that, perhaps, Curtis still needs us. So, let's close our eyes and concentrate on Curtis. You can envision sending him light, or love, or whatever it is that signifies positive energy to you. If, though, you believe that someone else needs your energy even more than Curtis, please send it to that person. If you believe that person is you, try to bask in your own light."

I closed my eyes and tried to concentrate. But I could not. I couldn't even focus, never mind send energy. The children were talking, Woo Woo was whining, and I swore that I saw something that resembled a shadow, but was not dark, moving quickly around the room, stopping behind each person for a split second.

I picked up Woo Woo and held him in my lap. I sat with my eyes open watching a circle of 50 people with their eyes closed trying to send energy to my deceased husband who I knew still needed them.

A good friend was the first to open his eyes, and as he did we caught one another's stare. He smiled. He knew where I was. A little over a week prior to this healing circle, on a Tuesday night, he had called and asked if he could come over. I was so happy to have company. It had been a little over five weeks since Curtis' passing and the commotion had all but dissipated. I found this to be very strange, particularly because for the year that Curtis and I had lived with ALS we had welcomed visitors with open arms and although there had been people who stopped by continuously and others who had done so rarely and still others who we had known really wanted to but didn't quite know what to say or what to do, we had never been in want for visitors. In fact, there had been times when we had wished we could just be alone. But after Curtis' passing and that initial week that will be forever defined by the two wakes and a funeral and the following week, during which Tricia lived with me until she had to go back to school, I felt very much alone. Except for when Curtis visited me.

I was thrilled when our friend knocked on the green side door that Tuesday night in January. We sat down at the kitchen table and for at least a minute we watched one another in silence and then his tears started.

"I'm sorry. I didn't mean for this to happen," he spoke.

"My tears only appear when Curtis visits, and he usually only comes home when I am alone."

"He has come to me, too."

The fact that our friend had also sensed Curtis' presence validated all of the experiences that I had had and that I had heard about from others the past weeks. Our friend was a man of the earth. He lived by the land, harvesting crops and growing Christmas trees. It was through his work with nature that he was in touch with his reality. He, like me, had not been born in Danville. He, like me, had made this quaint town his home. But, unlike many non-natives, the townspeople trusted him. Still, though, he was, and would always be, a flatlander.

"How are you doing?" he asked.

Silence.

"I'm sorry. I guess a better question is what have you been feeling?"

I had been waiting for someone who I knew would understand and who would not judge me to ask me that question. I had not known who it would be but I had wished for someone.

And so, I told him everything.

"Since his death, I've been as close to Curtis' soul as I was while he was physically with us. I've been aware of his journey ever since his last breath that Sunday morning. But, the first time I 'saw' Curtis was a week after his death, a Sunday night. Things had finally settled down. The funeral and the wakes were over. The visiting and all the chaos had passed. Mom and Dad had gone home. Finally, I could concentrate on Curtis. Tricia and I were here at the house and I was sitting at the computer typing out questions that I would ask Curtis during my visit with the medium. Tricia and I started talking and then suddenly we were talking to Curtis and we felt as though he was with us and I began asking him if he could teach me how to talk to him and then all of a sudden we heard and saw a spark. It was Curtis. I knew it. And

Trish heard and saw the same thing. And then, we no longer felt him. It was so beautiful.

The first night I slept alone was a week and a day after Curtis' death. The first two nights after Curtis' death, Heather, Tricia and I slept together in the beds that Curtis and I had slept in. When the hospital bed was taken away, Tricia and I slept in the twin bed that remained in the living room. Heather had moved upstairs. But after we finally cleaned and organized, a week after Curtis' death, I decided that I could sleep in the twin bed alone downstairs in the living room as long as Tricia slept on the couch.

After I turned out the lights and said goodnight to Tricia, I prayed that Curtis would come to me during the night and talk to me. What did not seem like long after I had fallen asleep, I awoke to a pleasant sound, almost like a laugh. At the same time, I saw Tricia raise her head.

'Tricia, did you hear that?'

'Yes,' she had replied.

'It's okay, Trish. Go back to sleep.'

For the remainder of the night, I woke up every hour and felt Curtis. At 4 am, Woo Woo woke me with his incessant barking. He had gotten off my bed and was barking at what appeared to be someone or something inside the house. An hour later, when his barking still had not ceased, I got out of bed to write. After a while, I saw and heard the spark again. I knew it was Curtis. And then, I felt him for a few minutes.

When Tricia woke up a few hours later, she said that before she heard the sound she had been dreaming that I was having a conversation with Curtis. After the sound awoke her, she was a little bit afraid. She considered getting into bed with me but decided not to because she felt as though Curtis was probably with me."

Our friend watched me with tears in his eyes as I described the first few encounters I had had with Curtis' spirit. I also spoke with our friend about how I felt that society, in general, does not allow people ample time to grieve. Curtis had only been gone a month when many people were already asking me, "So, what's next?" Or, "It is so great to see that you are doing so well." My favorite, "So, now that he's gone, are you going to use your degree?" I had also vented to our friend that I thought that people, me included, are fearful of spending time with those who are grieving because they don't know what to say to them. As a result, the griever feels isolated, especially if the deceased was the person with whom the griever spent most of his/her time. In the month or so since Curtis had died, I had received many smiles, many waves, and many looks of compassion. But I almost never got what I needed: a conversation about Curtis, an attentive ear. My mother repeated over and over, "I want to help, but I just can't relate. I have never lost a spouse." All I wanted was people to listen. I yearned to tell everyone about my experiences with Curtis since the day he had died, how lost I felt or how I was struggling to live in the world that I had helped Curtis to leave.

"Did I do too much?" I asked our friend. "If I had not been a part of Curtis' life, if I had not pushed so hard and been so damn determined, if I had just given up on us when we were kids, then maybe I would not have been part of his life when he got sick and then so much of what happened would probably not have happened. Would it have been easier?"

"Easier on whom?" our friend had asked.

"Curtis. Would it have been easier if Curtis had just been allowed to be angry? Angry at the disease, angry at the world, angry at his family, angry at anyone who wanted to help rather than really believing that it was possible to heal and remain here with us? Ultimately, Curtis was disappointed. One of the last things he said to me was, 'I'm sorry.' What was he sorry for? I knew that he was sorry for not being able to physically heal himself so that he could be with me on this earth. I felt the disappointment and the guilt. Would those feelings have been present if we had not worked so hard? Had we not believed and had faith? I believe that we did the right thing. We did everything the way it was supposed to be. But I feel so sad. He was so sad right before he left me."

Our friend and I talked for hours that night. I told him about the anger Curtis harbored, the anger that almost took control of the situation many times. But when it would begin to leak out, we would get it under control before it could do irreversible damage. I would help Curtis get his anger under control by bringing it to his attention.

"You allowed Curtis to see himself through your eyes. You showed him the person that he could be; the person that you believed he was. But, his instinct was to turn toward the anger, to allow the anger to take over. He thought that anger should and would solve everything. Anger allows one to expel the negative emotion onto another. That was what he knew. You and your experiences together this past year taught him that it didn't have to be that way. There was another way. And he embraced that new way of living, with grace, beauty, understanding, optimism, and faith. He did not want to disappoint you because you believed in him."

"I had to believe in him. I've never been able to imagine life without him. I needed him to live. I love him."

At the healing circle, once everyone opened their eyes, our friend stood, and began to speak. "I asked Julia if we could take a few minutes tonight to talk about grief and the process of grieving. I know that I am personally grieving the loss of Curtis, and I am really struggling. And maybe we all need a little help in order to figure out what this process of grief is all about and how we can aid one other."

After a few minutes, Julia, as usual, asked those of us in the room to introduce ourselves one by one and to share thoughts with the group if we wished.

Curtis' mother began, "I am Curtis' mom. I would like to read this book which, along with a cash award, was given to Curtis at his high school graduation in honor of being the leader of his class." After she read the book, she resumed. "Although I would like to keep this book for myself, it now belongs to my daughter-in-law, for she is allowing Curtis to live on through her. She is taking Curtis with her as she moves forward in life, and I am so very thankful for that."

Curtis' mom stood and walked toward me.

I stood.

She handed me the book; I took it.

She embraced me.

When I returned to my seat, I looked at the title, *Desiderata*, and the author's name, Max Ehrmann.

A visitor to our circle spoke next. "This is going to sound crazy, but during the energy session I felt a tap on my right shoulder. It came from behind me."

Three others who I had never seen before muttered simultaneously, "Me, too."

We had never before experienced spiritual intrusions at our

healing circles. When each of the four newcomers stated what they had felt, everyone else responded the way they had reacted to everything for the past year: they listened with acceptance and without questioning. I wondered if I had seen the person who was tapping these people on the shoulder?

Another friend introduced herself as she looked at me. "Last Thursday was the first time that I felt as though you were no longer strong and that you are human. I didn't know how to respond to that, although I am happy that you are finally letting go and grieving."

It was my turn to introduce myself. After last week, I had told myself that this week I would just say my name and thank everyone for continuing to support Curtis. And so I did.

But then I sat in silence.

I looked to my left at Annie and to my right at Tommy and to my feet at Woo Woo, all three of whom appeared to be waiting for the words that would make everything okay again.

Looking at Curtis' mother, I began, "First of all, thank you for this gift. Secondly, I am very sad," I whispered as I looked down at Woo Woo. "I suppose that last week was the saddest that I've ever felt. Ever since Curtis passed, my strength has slowly gone away, and last Thursday was my weakest point physically and spiritually. I never wanted anything but to go with Curtis. We worked so hard together to prepare for death. I know that I will end up where he has gone eventually, so why not go now?"

I didn't mean to say what I had said. But even as the words leaked from my broken heart, I did not receive the reaction I assumed I would get: looks of pity and concern or someone rushing over to me and begging me to not do anything drastic. No, most of these 50 people sitting in this circle knew that part of the grieving process required that I express the anguish and torment that was in my soul. They missed him, too. Curtis had matured into a figure of hope and a source of strength for the entire community and they too did not know what to do or where to go without him. With expressions of love on their faces, they sat with pure and complete understanding. It was then that I realized that one of the reasons Curtis had started this circle was because he somehow knew that it would help me find my way after his passing just as it had helped him prepare for his own death.

I continued. "Thank you all. I do believe that perhaps my strength will return. I know that it will continue to come from Curtis but it is also coming from all of you."

After the introductions were complete, we moved onto healing touch. When Curtis was alive, he had been the central focus of the healing circle as well as the healing touch. Everyone who wished to participate would encircle him, place a hand on a part of his body and attempt to send positive, healing energy to that part of his body all the while imagining that part of the body healthy and well. Since Curtis' passing, the group had decided that each week one or more persons would volunteer themselves for healing touch. Tonight the four children (two of whom were Annie and Tommy) sat in chairs in the middle of the room, accompanied by two adults also sitting in chairs, and then the four newcomers who had felt the tap on their shoulder during the energy session stood and encircled them and then the rest of the people, also standing, surrounded them.

I didn't want to participate. I stood off to the side. As I watched each person put their hands on another and with their eyes closed attempt to channel positive energy to those who wished to receive it, I, for the first time since the circle had begun almost a year beforehand, witnessed the miracle. I stood off to the side this night because I knew that I barely had enough energy to sustain my own life. I felt blessed to see almost 50 people whose sole intention was to help others. *This is what Curtis wanted. This is his miracle. Curtis no longer needs us, his wish has been granted.*

So then we were supposed to perform healing touch on Curtis again. We had done it the week before when I had expressed that Curtis was not where he was supposed to be and he still needed us but while I watched the group take part in this healing touch it occurred to me that Curtis no longer needed our touch. He only needed to know that we could and would continue on with the circle in order to help one another through the painful process of grief. When the first round of healing touch was finished, I did not remind Julia that I had wanted to concentrate on Curtis as we had done the week before.

As was customary, when the healing touch was finished, we re-formed our circle and recited the Lord's Prayer. Curtis had been the one to make this customary. On that day in February, throughout the prayer, I felt Curtis as I had felt him so often throughout the weeks since his passing but I also felt as though he was finally ready to go.

In my mind, or in my heart, I heard him say, "The circle is how it should be. You are being taken care of. Love is what life is all about. You are being loved. You no longer need just me."

*Okay.*

Simultaneously, I heard a loud whooshing sound. As the members of the circle and I spoke the words of the Lord's Prayer, "Thy will be done on earth as it is in heaven," I heard the extra large spider plant behind me rustle and I knew that a month and a half after his death, my Curtis was really gone.

Julia turned to me and witnessed the tears streaming down my face.

"I am so sorry. We forgot to send energy to Curtis tonight as you had asked."

"Oh, no, we weren't supposed to." I sobbed uncontrollably as I explained to Julia that Curtis had left. I had not shed one tear at either of the wakes or the funeral. Up until this moment, very few people had seen me cry. The tears continued to fall for many days and nights for I was now certain that Curtis and I would not exist on the same plane again until the moment of my own death.

# *Reality*

Later that night, after the circle, as I lay in bed with Woo Woo at my feet, I wondered if Curtis blamed me for not joining him just as I believed that he had been so disappointed in himself that he could not heal and remain with me. The Thursday before, after the hypnosis, I knew that I could have gone. He had wanted me so badly to be with him.

There were different forms of crying. The first could occur in public, for it did not distort my face, making me seem abnormal. A sudden remembrance or someone saying something he would have said, or swearing I saw him walking in a crowd a few hundred feet ahead of me, or sitting by myself staring ahead, convinced that he was going to appear and sit down beside me and begin just where we left off: these incidents brought a tear to my eye. Occasionally one or two drops would fall, but usually these tears were contained within my eye, my mind, and my heart.

The second type of crying only happened in private, either alone in my bed when I could not sleep or in a public setting when no one was watching me. Somehow I could cry on a long stretch of highway with cars surrounding me because the other drivers were not tuned in to who I was or what I was thinking. I was silent as the water streamed down my face. The tears didn't stop, and they coincided with the questions I was asking him with my voice that only he had known, the voice of insecurity and unreasonableness, the voice that questioned the fairness of it all, the purpose of such a nightmare. I once read that in these moments of grief a loved one's spirit is beside you. They say that because there is so much feeling between the two that have been physically separated by death, the human body of the living physically explodes with clear, raw, hurtful emotion and tears. Some nights I prayed to Curtis to help me understand, to show me the way, to appear before me in some form, just so that I knew for sure that he still existed. Other nights I spoke to Curtis as my husband and my best friend. I recollected the events of my day dryly as if he came home every night. I listed my troubles, the little things that bothered me throughout the day. Some nights I begged him to crawl into bed, even if for just a second.

"Show me a hand," I would coax. "Anything. Just so I know for sure. I just want to see you with my eyes, again. I just want to touch you with my flesh. I want to go back to where we were, what we were."

The third form of crying only took place in the darkest of hours: in the wee hours of morning or the late hours of night. The feeling came upon me with no warning. Sounds escaped me that I had never before heard. I shook uncontrollably. I screamed, I yelled, or I remained silent, except for the sobbing. My body rocked, the words tumbled, and the tears fell. My body was no longer mine; I was no longer responsible for my words. I blamed him for my loss. I yelled that he took the easy way out, "You never had to suffer like this. You never had to be alone." I wished that he could comprehend my pain. I was screaming, demanding that he come home to where he belonged, "How dare you leave me?" I couldn't breathe.

I struggled for breath as I tried to slow my heart rate. I felt as though I had just been on a roller coaster ride, but the fear of falling would not subside. I felt like I had just missed a head-on collision, but I thought that the car was still ahead of me and I might still hit it. I was suspended between reality and a nightmare. I was so tired. My body slowed its shaking, my shouts became a whisper, and one last tear fell. I curled up inside of myself, held my legs to my chest, my arms wrapped around my shivering body. And then my body was still. My voice was silent. There were no more tears. I awakened the next morning; I had made it through another night. I made it through the next night and the one after that. For many months, almost every night was exactly like the one before.

In February, I accepted a job offer to return to Middlebury College as the women's assistant tennis coach but I was not ready to leave our home in Danville, so Woo Woo and I commuted the two hours to Middlebury and back again almost every day. I continued to waitress at Vinny's and also accepted a job to wait tables at the Danville Inn; Woo Woo was allowed to come to work with me at the Inn.

In late April, a few days after the tennis season ended, I flew out to California to spend some time with friends from college. My mom thought that I should get away so she offered to take Woo Woo for me. While on the west coast, one Sunday, I visited a beach in Marin County. After a few hours in the sun, I knew that I needed to run. And so I did. I ran up the steep cliffs until I reached the top of the range. And then I stopped and looked out in all directions. The view was magnificent. The Pacific Ocean was directly beneath me. The sky appeared to melt into the ocean. I felt as though I could see eternity. And then I realized that I had been there before with Curtis. We had witnessed the same view together while I had been under hypnosis in January. And he was with me again this Sunday in April. The landscape, the ledge, the deep blue ocean, the light blue sky, the fact that Curtis was with me again was all so miraculous. But on the plane ride home I wrote in my journal, "*I am ready to go home to my Woo Woo and my memories. They came with me on this trip but not as much as I would have liked. It has been nice not to cry all the time, but sad too. I look forward to once again being immersed in Curtis' presence, or at least my memory of his presence.*"

In May, a few days after returning to Vermont from California, I sat down with Cathy for my second hypnotic session because I desperately needed to connect with Curtis again. As time moved forward, I felt Curtis slipping further and further away. My mind was spending more time preoccupied with everyday issues and less time flirting with the time and space in which Curtis existed. I missed the wonder and calmness of Curtis' new world. As spring overtook winter, I began to dream of another summer with Curtis, and I knew that I needed to return to the realm of the subconscious in order to communicate with him. Before Cathy helped me go into a hypnotic state, she asked me where I would like to visit once I entered the altered state. I told her that I wished to understand more about what had happened the night of the healing circle in February when I had felt Curtis' spirit leave.

The following is a transcription of the taped hypnotic session with Cathy that day in May.

Me: "Curtis is behind me. Most of us in the circle have felt him walking around this evening. He has stood behind each person and has said goodbye to them in his own way. He has already said goodbye to those who aren't at the circle this night. As he is behind me, he tells me that he's bored. He's done what he's needed to do. It's no fun anymore being where he was, now that he's changed.

It's different and he needs to go. But he's nervous for me."

Cathy: "What happens?"

Me: "He continues to hang out, right there behind me. I can feel his love and his concern and his anxiety. I can feel the intensity of his spirit. Curtis convinces me that we have a lot of work to do, but right now he has no power with us, or with God. He's caught in between the two spheres. He can't come back, and he has yet to go up to God, but he can, and that is what he would like to do. I tell him that I can't comprehend what he is telling me; I hear him but my mind has limitations. I do not know what it all means. He says that it's okay; he doesn't really expect me to understand. As he waits behind me with his hands on my shoulders, the group is reciting the Lord's Prayer as it does every week in order to conclude the session. When the words 'earth as it is in heaven' are recited by the crowd and me and through Curtis, everything makes sense. Curtis is going to do in heaven what I am going to do on earth. At this precise moment, I know this to be true. If and when I doubt it as time goes on, I'll just have to remember this conversation. It's the only way that he can tell me. With the strength that I can gather as a result of Curtis holding onto me from behind, I tell him that it is okay to go. In typical Curtis fashion, he does not hesitate. With my permission, he leaves. There is no time to change his mind. I no longer feel his presence behind me. He is gone."

Cathy: "Now what's happening?"

Me: "I feel empty for a second, but then I feel him again, in a different way. He's not as close. I tell him that I don't understand. He tells me that I have to remember and believe. He'll always be right here, beside me. I cry because I am happy, but I can't see where he is, and this is disturbing."

Cathy: "Do you have a sense of knowing where he is now?"

Me: "Yes."

Cathy: "And that's fine?"

Me: "No. It's not fine."

Cathy: "How would you describe it?"

Me: "It changes from a field, to flowers, to a brook. He can create what he wants to create, but he can't bring us up there, and this makes him sad."

Cathy: "How do you feel?"

Me: "It's okay for a while. I know that I have a lot to do here, and he's guiding me."

Spending time with Curtis while in a hypnotic state reignited our connection. We visited one another in my dreams night after night, again. I awoke wonderfully exhausted from our adventures and depressingly amazed when I remembered morning after morning that he was dead. By the end of May, I felt the need to flee Vermont once again to evade the heavy feelings. I flew to Alaska with my parents. My father had been invited to a conference and he really wanted my mother to go with him but she didn't want to go because he was going to be in meetings all day. Because my sister offered to take care of Woo Woo, because I didn't want my father or my mother to be alone, and because I needed to elude the suffocation of my memories, I offered to go with them. Reliving our shared memories and trying to create new ones through hypnosis had morphed from a way to try to cope into an addiction and like any addiction, there were times when I craved it and times when I desperately needed to escape its life threatening hold. We flew into Anchorage, and as we drove south to Seward, the site of the conference, I realized that I had been there before, too, with Curtis, that same day in January during my hypnotic session. Curtis was everywhere; he was always near me.

Throughout the spring, I continued to work to establish Curtis' foundation, a nonprofit corporation whose purposes included public education and funding of research for a cure for ALS and providing assistance to the victims of the disease and their families. Curtis, of course, had feared the day that another member of his family would be stricken with the disease. And he and I would be forever grateful to the generous people who had given us resources so that we could spend the year learning to live while preparing to die rather than worrying about money. Thus, our foundation would give money to others suffering from ALS without the need for them to fill out mounds of paperwork or wait months for approval. We would strive to fill a void so that they could continue to live a certain quality of life while they still had the time.

Our first fundraiser took place in late spring, six months after Curtis' death, and it was the outdoor wedding reception that Curtis and I had planned, complete with dinner and dancing. It was held at the Joe's Pond recreation area, which is directly behind my family's cottage, exactly where we had always dreamed of spending the evening of our wedding. It was an emotional time – I felt overjoyed to be raising money for our foundation and overwhelmed by the continued support of our family and friends. I missed my Curtis that night. His uncle danced the first slow dance with me that evening; I held on to him for dear life.

The next morning we planted Curtis' apple orchard at the back farm in North Danville. For 100 dollars, a person "bought" a tree. A percentage of the money went to the cost of the tree and the rest went to the foundation. Family and friends purchased the trees in memory or honor of a loved one. Inscribed plaques were later placed on a large wooden sign that stands on one edge of the orchard. We planted over 100 trees that spring Sunday. I knew that Curtis' soul was right beside me, inside me, that entire weekend. We made our dream come true. And we did it together. Neither one of us could have done it alone.

I survived the summer by waitressing 50-60 hours a week and teaching tennis in Danville. I kept myself busy running from job to job. I had asked Curtis' aunt and uncle when they would like me to leave our home so that they could move into their house. They had wanted me to have one last summer. Before I could leave, I had to take care of all of Curtis' things so I spent that summer also sifting and sorting through stuff, none of which I wanted to throw away but all of which only made me miss him more. I also had to find a place to live. Mostly, though, I spent my time that summer trying to find the light.

Becoming a widow is a strange thing. It's almost unthinkable, almost unimaginable. One does not prepare to be a widow. Death sweeps upon the survivor like a gale-force wind. It blindsided me. One day my husband was alive, the next second he was gone, and yet I was still here, alive. Alone. Although we understood that there was no cure for his disease and that the progression would be fast, his death surprised me. I couldn't believe that he had actually died, and I was shocked that I didn't go with him.

After they took Curtis' body to Boston, and for most days following, I bundled up in my Vermont gear, grabbed Woo Woo's leash, and we walked, hoping to find Curtis. For the next year, anytime I was looking for Curtis and expected that I could find him if I just looked hard enough, I walked. Up hills. Down hills. In the woods. On the main roads. To the cemetery. In the apple orchard. Past the house that he grew up in until he was eight. To the house he lived in from the time he was eight until he moved in with me. I walked to find him and to lose myself. I was no one without Curtis; that is what it feels like to be a widow. Here, but gone. Alive, but dead. I heard Curtis. I felt Curtis. I walked with Curtis. I breathed Curtis. I slept with Curtis, for it was only in my dreams that I could see him, feel him, hold him, and make love to him. And I lived like that for a while. But was it life? Or was it death? If you had asked Curtis during that last hour of his life if he was experiencing life or death, I believe that he would have answered, both, but neither. It is all one existence. How does a widow go on? Did I want to love another? Could I?

The thought of loving another never crossed my mind until the numbness wore off and my body recovered from the shock. Six months after Curtis died, my body once again desired physical love. I was alone, so I loved myself. I broke down afterward and was grateful that it had been me and not another man for it would have killed me to be loved by another and it may have destroyed the other man. All I thought about was Curtis. All I felt was Curtis. How much longer would this go on? How much longer could I bear it?

As a widow, I was treated strangely. People who barely knew me treated me like a fragile waif who, when bumped or whispered about, would break. Most people who knew me thought that I was a piece of steel. I could not break, could not bend, and would not relent.

But steel drowns. Fast. One minute it's up, the next it's gone.

I believed that no one understood me because I thought that Curtis and I were the only ones who had experienced helplessness, the kind of fear that is felt when things are out of your control, the kind of fear that only comes at life's end, before the calm and peacefulness take over. Panic. Awesome panic. I experienced panic many times throughout the last year of Curtis' life; when he turned to me in our blue Chevy Blazer and wished that we were going to the Red Sox playoff game instead of to the hospital for a feeding tube, when he wished that we could have a child. "Faith" would have been her name we had decided. Actually, we had chosen the names for all five of our children: Faith, Joshua Curtis, Katie Elizabeth, Geoffrey Lee, and Adelaide Courtney.

I experienced fear very often as Curtis' widow. Fear lives in a lonely place where there is no hope, no breath, no smell, taste, or touch. After his passing, Curtis had begged me to find the light but I continued to search for him in the darkness. I was attracted to the dark for the light would force me to go on and I couldn't imagine life without my Curtis. But I didn't let myself drown in the darkness because I feared seeing the blackest of black and then the ray of light and then Curtis passing by, "See what you have missed." I feared that if I took my own life, I wouldn't be reunited with Curtis. This fear was solely based on fear itself; I am thankful for that fear, though. I think it saved my life.

There were moments that first year after Curtis' death when I thought that I really did want to die, when all I wanted was to be with my Curtis. I recall lying in my bed, crying so desperately for Curtis, and remembering that his handgun and shotguns were upstairs. I almost never got out of bed to look at them. Except for once. I opened the closet door and stared at the shotguns. Curtis had taught me how to fire one years back while we were partridge hunting. Then, I opened the bureau drawer and stared at the handgun. I had no idea how to shoot that one. Woo Woo appeared by my side. He looked up at me and barked. I walked downstairs, crawled back into bed, and thought about the weapons the rest of the night as well as many nights after. I remember driving to work thinking about what would happen if I just swerved the car off the road. It seemed so simple. But then I thought of Woo Woo and my family. I knew how horrible it was to live in this world without a person I loved so much. I couldn't knowingly and willingly put those I loved through that horror. Most often, though, I thought of my Curtis, who had fought so hard to live. How could I give up so easily? How could I not take advantage of the fact that I had a healthy body as well as a sound mind?

Change is not easy. You're lucky if you get a second chance. Could I chance a change? Could I change and take the chance to live a life without Curtis? Could I take the chance to love another?

Although I still prayed for a life with my Curtis, a life here without him that used to seem impossible became just sad as time wore on. And I was tired of being sad. He was tired of seeing me sad.

In my dreams, he told me that he was okay. "Stop protecting me. You need not care for me anymore," he said. "Take care of you. Live, again," he continued.

"But we learned how to live, together. And we prepared to die, together," I replied.

"Have you been listening to me?" he said. "It took me so long to learn, so long to trust you, to figure out how to give of myself without the fear that I may never get that part of myself back. You have time to live and to love others as I learned that I could."

Life is a continuum, a cycle of light and dark. Curtis was my light. ALS introduced us to the darkness and taught us how to live. We learned to bask in the light and experienced tremendous hope and powerful love. We learned to live in the moment. The darkness enveloped me the moment that Curtis left the physical world. It suffocated me. Together, we once again started to crawl out of the darkness.

# A Season of Miracles

At the end of the summer, I moved out of Curtis' aunt and uncle's house and into my parents' cottage on Joe's Pond. This move was temporary. I could only stay at Joe's Pond until I could no longer withstand the cold or the pipes froze. Woo Woo and I continued to wait tables at the Inn until we woke up shivering one October morning, ten months after Curtis' death. According to the thermometer, it was almost freezing. I called my parents and asked them if I could come home. Just for a while.

I spent that fall in Connecticut working on Curtis' foundation, writing, sleeping, and running with Woo Woo. I spent most of my time with Woo Woo, remembering, processing and trying to figure out where I had been and where I was going. One night I looked through old photo albums. Of myself. An infant. A baby. A toddler. A child. My yellow blanket. I wandered upstairs to the hall closet. Stored in the back, crumpled into a ball, I found my tattered yellow blanket. A few durable strings held it in one piece. *I thought Mom had thrown it away.* Back downstairs. More pictures. Elementary school. Eighth-grade graduation. 15^th^ birthday. *Was I really that young when we first met? What if Laurie hadn't come over? It took me forever to call! What if I hadn't called?* Afraid to disturb the silent household, I tiptoed up the stairs, got a glass of water and crept back down the stairs. Brushing my teeth, I stared at my reflection. I did not know the person looking back. Gaunt, pale, shallow. Old. *Who am I?* I silently asked the person in the mirror. *Curtis' widow?* The last time I had checked, I was a recent college graduate who was still trying to find her place in this world. Under the crisp, chilly sheets, I forced my eyes shut and clutched my old yellow blanket to my naked skin.

That fall I began to realize that I was still alive. One night, I sat on the couch in my parents' basement with my ankles crossed upon the Lane cedar trunk that I had bought at an antique store; I needed something to harbor our physical memorabilia. Woo Woo rested his chin on the locked trunk. His dark Chinese Shar-Pei eyes peeked up at me through his black hair. The trunk held some of Curtis' belongings, which I couldn't give or throw away because he was a part of me. While Curtis' body rested beneath the Vermont ground in a solid coffin, Woo Woo and I rested on a solid oak trunk that held my husband's leftover tangible things. Curtis' possessions were useful, even after he was dead, because things, unlike memories, can be held and smelled and cried upon forever.

My slippered feet left their perch atop the trunk. As I leaned forward and turned the key, I feared that I had forgotten what was inside. Representations of his and our life lay in an orderly cramped fashion. My eyes fell upon the ivory satin beaded headpiece and purse, both of which my mother had made for my wedding day. An embroidered white linen handkerchief, which Bubbles had given me at my bridal shower, lay folded inside the satin purse. "Something old," she had said. "Your grandfather's mother gave me a similar handkerchief on my wedding day. I gave your mother one on her wedding day. Your great-grandmother had embroidered many so that all of the generations could have one on their special day. This one is yours. Hold onto it. You will always remember Curtis' face and his words 'I do' each time you see the hanky."

My eyes glanced at the handkerchief, but my hand was afraid to reach for it. My heart feared going back, but if I wished to move forward, it must. I unfolded the hand-knit hanky. The delicate stitching around the edges reminded me of how fragile Curtis was on our wedding day. I remembered how the others and I had to wipe the tears from his face throughout the ceremony. He had cried out of happiness. I hadn't cried at all. I couldn't. One of us had to stay strong and since Curtis had been the stable one in the beginning, it was my job to keep us from crumbling in the end. With the handkerchief draped over the palm of my hand, I saw through it to my flesh, the way that I had been able to see through Curtis' skin to his bones those last few months. Curtis rarely spoke about the loss of his physical self. His mind was untouched, allowing him to remember and continue to see himself as he had always been: a large, strong, dominant boy. Most importantly, the disease allowed him time to find the soft, gentle man inside the large body. Gentleness, which for so long he had been afraid to reveal, is what shone through on his face on our wedding day. Gentleness that I had noticed the day I met him that first summer. Yes, Bubbles was right; Curtis was in this handkerchief and he was beautiful.

I leaned over and picked up one of the five photo albums that lay on the carpet to the left of the cedar trunk. I flipped to the two pictures of Curtis and me on our wedding morning. One of the pictures captured me leaning over Curtis, re-strapping the Velcro on his mask strap. With my back to the camera, all you could see of me in my green negligee, a bridal present, was my bare shoulders and calves as I finished buttoning Curtis' white tuxedo shirt. My hair was pulled back and bunched up in a bun with a ponytail holder. Curtis was sitting up straight with the help of my right shoulder. Even in this picture, which was poorly lit and taken from afar, I noticed his thin legs that looked like twigs wrapped in black fabric. The muscles and his physical strength were gone; in their place were the core ingredients of a human body: skin, bones, and blood held together only by the sheer will to live. The picture also revealed the strain on his face. He had just gotten back his air. I only faintly recognized myself. My bones showed through my skin, too. My legs looked like sticks, jutting out from under a green canopy. Again, the core ingredients of a human body held together by the sheer will to live.

Weeks after rediscovering the white linen handkerchief, I wandered back downstairs to the basement of my parents' home. As he always did, Woo Woo waited at the top of the stairs until I reached the bottom step. Just before I took my first step onto level ground, he barreled past me. I imagined that he wanted to encounter the danger before it could harm me, but maybe he was simply competitive just like me. Just like Curtis. Like the puppy he had been, he raced toward his green and white yarn chew toy, grabbed it in his teeth and nuzzled it against my leg. I switched the lights on and we played catch, or what I considered catch. He never quite mastered the real game as it was described in the various "How to raise a healthy, happy puppy" books that I had purchased before getting him at the age of nine weeks. His version of catch was getting the toy, standing in the same spot that he had retrieved his toy, waiting until I wrestled it away from him and me throwing it for him once again. We played this game until he noticed the cedar trunk.

Immediately, Woo Woo sat near the trunk. His eyes urged me to join him. Curtis lived inside of him, too. Together, we opened the trunk, which was unlocked this time. Across the top rested Curtis' red and black metal cane with its black rubber stopper at the bottom end and its wooden handpiece on the top. As the recessed lighting hit the cane, it appeared to glow as brightly as the moon's shadow on Joe's Pond. The cane was stored at its smallest size, but when I pushed down on the golden button and pulled the handle up and the black stopper down, it once again looked familiar. Yes, this was the right height for Curtis.

The black and red cane was the first piece of medical equipment that Curtis had bought, and it was the only disabled person's item that Curtis purchased by himself. The credit card receipt is still in the fourth drawer of my solid oak filing cabinet, along with hundreds of receipts, bills, and insurance statements from the year that Curtis was ill. I keep the receipts for my records and for his signature. Curtis' handwriting is precious; it reassures me that he was alive. The cane represents Curtis' independence. The day that he bought it was the last full day that he spent alone. And the cane reminded me of the day, two weeks after his death, that the markings of the black rubber stopper miraculously appeared in the snow outside our home in Danville.

After leaving Vermont in October, I drove up north from my parents' home almost every weekend during the months of November and December. Woo Woo and I needed to feel Curtis. We needed to be home with him. We stayed with Curtis' parents and slept in Curtis' bed that remained in his boyhood room, visited with Chad, his wife, and the children, and we spent time with Joe, Julia, and their daughter. But most of the time Woo Woo and I walked. We felt closest to Curtis when we were at the gravesite, the apple orchard, or just moving in the natural world.

Curtis' family decided to go on another Caribbean cruise in December, one year after Curtis' death. It would be a time to remember, a time to celebrate his life. They asked me if I would like to go with them. I told them "yes" and asked them if Tricia could accompany me. That week was difficult. Being surrounded by Curtis' family forced me to realize that talking about Curtis with them, although therapeutic and wonderful, was limiting. I was grateful to be surrounded by people who wanted to talk about Curtis, but many of them did not speak of the things that I most fondly recalled: how he had learned to live every moment to its fullest, how he had appreciated simple acts of kindness and how his soul, through his eyes even when he could no longer move any part of his body, told me how much he loved me. The memories they spoke of and the stories they told most often included him acting as though he didn't have a care in the world. I, too, remembered the boy he used to be, but we had grown up together, the year that we lived, day by day, with ALS and it was the memory of the man whom he had become that I wanted to hold on to forever. Curtis and I shared a lifetime of experiences throughout the year that he was sick; we were no longer kids when he died. ALS might have taken away my youth and my innocence, but it also gave both Curtis and me an amazing perspective on life – and death.

And being surrounded by Curtis' family almost killed me. His brothers, each in their own way, reminded me of Curtis with their work ethic, wit, humor, gait, and smile. Their company reminded me too much of what I had lost, of what I was missing. I couldn't take it anymore. I had to go. After the cruise I returned to Connecticut and ceased driving up to Vermont every weekend. Over the years, I have kept in touch with Curtis' family, as well as friends with whom Curtis and I spent so much time that year, but I realize now that I removed myself from the life Curtis and I shared in Vermont because it was too painful to be there without his physical being.

On Christmas night, a little more than a year after Curtis' passing, while experiencing my first real sleep in almost two years, I found him. I had to once again travel deep inside myself, and it was there that I found the part of me that had been buried ever since Curtis left. Along with the rediscovery of a part of me, came Curtis: real, alive, full of love and laughter and tears. He reminded me of who I was, how vibrant I had been, how full of love and hope and peace and wishes and dreams. How alive. I cried when I felt, saw, revisited the person I had been. He was the one who found that person originally, who helped develop her and who crafted her into what others thought I was: a beauty, an angel. His love for me helped to make me who I was. My love for him helped to make him who he was. When I found that part of me again it felt wonderful to see her smile, hear her laugh sincerely, to feel her heartbeat out of love and compassion rather than fear, anger, suspense, or anxiety.

Throughout our experience this time we talked. He was full of speech, anxious to get through to me. I could tell that he had been waiting for me to take the time to figure out how to hear him again.

"All you have to do is listen," he reminded me once again. "I am always here inside of you. I am in the depths of your soul."

He was warm, accepting, full of love, and compassion. He commented that he, his grandmother and others were proud of my efforts as far as ALS was concerned. He told me that it was beautiful where he is now.

"Beauty that you can't even begin to imagine. Incredible.

Unbelievable," he said.

"I am preparing for you," he said. "But you must not concentrate on that and neither can I. I have a job to do and so do you. I help others transition from life as they know it to life as I now know it. I will greet you. I will be the first one when it is your time. I can't wait. The time will come. Do not rush. Do not waste. It will be here before too long."

He told me how much he missed Woo Woo but that he, too, will go to where we will all meet again, soon.

I told him how happy I was when I was with him and that my fear was that should I remain here on earth I would never feel that way again.

He told me not to be afraid of intimacy. "It's okay if you are not who you were. It's okay if you never feel what you felt with me. You will learn to love another way, other ways. Different people will enter your life and you will embrace them in new ways. I wouldn't want it any other way."

One day soon thereafter I woke up and felt lighter. I don't recall exactly when or how or why. It just happened. Although inexplicable, I sensed something beyond the past. Not tomorrow, or the next hour but at least I saw the present.

*I saw your soul, Curtis. I loved your soul. Is that love? If I truly love you, I will let you go. If you truly love me, you will let me go. Let it. Go. And we will fly away.*

I could see it. I was not ready, yet, but I would be soon. One day I would walk to our gravestone and lay the three red roses across the base and tell him that I had found someone who would care for me and hold me and tell me that everything would be okay. Someday. And then I would reassure my Curtis that when it was time for my soul to leave this earth I would wait for him to take me home.

# Birthday Wishes, Again

Later that winter, I bought clothes of only the brightest colors: a striped, short-sleeved stretch shirt with red, orange, yellow, and black stripes and a misty blue shirt of a similar stretch material. Blue like the sky, or a tear or heaven. For the simpler days, I purchased two long-sleeved, 100 percent cotton T-shirts. One was purple, the other orange. And, despite the season, I purchased a simple, elegant, brand-name white cotton dress shirt, tailored in a petite style, with three-quarter length sleeves and a neckline that would attract looks but not beckon stares. I cut off the tags, wrote the style, size, and description on the packets that held the extra buttons so that when I lost a button I would know where to find the extra, although I would never get around to sewing it on because I do not know how to sew. I hung my new clothes on hangers and slipped them into my closet. The vibrant colors shone brightly. Over the past two years I had accumulated a dark wardrobe. Mostly black. Gray. Brown. The new clothes shouted, "Notice me!" I was ready to be noticed. I wanted people to see me again. I needed to talk again. I still spoke mainly of the past, but that was okay. I am the past and the past is part of me, but I was once again aware of the present, and I had an inkling of the future. My future. Vibrant orange, yellow, and red. But still, always, a stripe of black.

Over a year after Curtis' death I spent the late winter and early spring traveling across the country holding events for our foundation. My friends wanted to help me on my mission of spreading the word about and raising money for ALS. And so we held events at bars, which is where many of my 26-year-old friends spent their weekend nights. Bands played, we held live and silent auctions, and I spoke about my love for and my loss of Curtis. A few of my friends had a mission of their own. They asked me if I was ready to date. I didn't think I would ever be ready but I did toy with the idea. I met one guy in San Francisco who was very nice, but I assumed that distance would be an issue. I met another guy in Chicago who was thinking of moving back east, but I knew that he wasn't quite right. I met a third guy on a plane coming home from Chicago and I actually agreed to go on a hike with him in Connecticut. That way Woo Woo could come with us. Woo Woo didn't like him.

I met a fourth guy at my gym in Connecticut.

He approached me and asked, "Is that your black dog hat you're wearing?"

Curtis and I had baseball hats made with a black Chinese Shar Pei embroidered on them. I wore mine often and was wearing it that day at the gym.

I was confused and surprised that this man knew that I had a black dog.

"Yes, it is. How do you know I have a black dog?"

He looked at me and smiled, "I didn't know that. I asked if it was a Black Dog hat?"

I wasn't aware of the Black Dog brand until he explained that it was an apparel company out of Massachusetts. We laughed about the confusion, talked for a while and then he asked me out on a date.

I hesitated. Then I thought about how Woo Woo's hat sparked our conversation and said, "yes."

We went out on a date without Woo Woo. Throughout the

evening I wished that I didn't need words to help this man get to know me. I yearned to be able to open my soul and say, "Here I am." It felt silly to explain things about myself and it confused me to not be able to express these things the way in which I knew them to be. If I had allowed myself to talk about Curtis then perhaps the dinner wouldn't have been so awkward and silent. Curtis and I were still so connected and intertwined that in order for anyone to understand me they had to also get to know Curtis. But I didn't think that another man would want to hear what I really wanted to say.

At the end of that first date, he walked me to my parents' front door and hugged me. Even though I wasn't sure if I even really liked him, I longed to invite him downstairs, to my room, where I could ask him to hold me. At dinner, I had failed in my attempt to communicate with words and, thus, my mind begged to say, *lie with me tonight and then you will know me.* Curtis and I communicated by touch. Our bodies willingly and naturally showed one another how much we cared. *Just hold me,* I longed to hear my voice say, *then I will know if you are capable of protecting me, of caring for me, of loving me unconditionally.*

After a way too long hug, he kissed me. He opened his mouth way too wide, forced his tongue into my mouth, and held me tighter. I pushed him away as nicely as I could and as I struggled to fit the key into the lock of my parents' house, I told him that I had had a good time and that I'd call him. I closed the door behind me before he had even turned to step off the front stoop. I flicked off the front light, ran down to my bedroom in the basement, and threw up.

That night I wrote in my journal, *"I do not look forward to dating. I do not wish to risk not being heard, or expressing myself incorrectly. I know how to be who I am and give the other person the best chance to see me for who I am. It requires true, blunt, clear honesty."*

A few days later my uncle invited me to a happy hour at a bar in downtown Hartford. He told me that it would be like a blind date, but with four eligible bachelors. He said that it was a birthday happy hour for a young man who worked at his firm and this particular guy, along with three other single and available men with whom he worked, would be there. I didn't want to go. After the disastrous date the few nights beforehand, I had convinced myself that it would be a very, very long time before I would ever be intimate with anyone again and it would most certainly have to be with someone much older, probably a widower, maybe a divorcee. I kept telling myself that it had only been 15 months since Curtis' death and I was crazy to think that I was ready to even get to know someone well again let alone attempt a physical relationship.

But Mom urged me, "Just go. Have fun. What's the worst that can happen?"

I reluctantly went with my uncle to the Standing Stone, a bar on Allyn Street that was known for the peanut shells strewn all over the floor. An hour or so later in walked Paul, the young man for whom the party was being held. I immediately noticed his dirty blonde hair, confident yet humble stature, athletic build, and sheepish yet real smile. I remained where I was until my uncle's friend introduced him to me as he had done with the other three bachelors. While I was talking with Paul, I saw a hint of his soul in his green eyes. Looking back at that moment, I wonder – if I had been fully living in the present would I have known right away that he was the one? I wasn't able to make those important judgments; a large part of me was removed from the ordinary, everyday existence. I was aware that I was intrigued by the little piece of himself that I noticed, though.

"I am a 26-year-old widow," I stated after just a few minutes of conversation. I guess that I had decided that I wasn't going to waste any time on anyone who couldn't or didn't have any interest in knowing the real me.

Paul, two years younger than me, replied, "Oh. I would love to hear your story."

Paul and I exchanged email addresses that night, and we emailed and talked for hours every day for a little over a month. He invited me to join his work's soccer team, we played a lot of tennis, and we even went out for dinner. Paul's gentle humor and easy-going character made me feel at ease. Like me, he enjoyed listening to others. Our relationship began with me telling him about Curtis and him trusting me with his feelings about his mother, Martha, who had been diagnosed with cancer the summer before his senior year of college. At the time that Paul and I met, she was still living but he had many unexpressed emotions about her illness.

From the beginning, although he fought him for the front seat of our car, Woo Woo liked Paul very much. One night, a few weeks after we first met, we ate Chinese food and watched a movie at his apartment. At the end of the night, Paul walked me to my car. He said a quick hello to Woo Woo who was waiting for me in the passenger seat. When it wasn't too hot or too cold, I preferred that Woo Woo be near me even if it meant that he had to hang out in the car for a bit. Woo Woo hated for me to leave his sight and he didn't get depressed or neurotic when he was in the car by himself rather than at my parents' house without me. As I turned to walk around to the driver's side of the car, Paul took my hand and pulled me toward him. He took my face in his hands and kissed me. He wasn't hesitant but he was careful. He kissed me on my lips once or twice and then I kissed him. That night, as I drove back to my parents' house, I cried in awe over the fact that kissing Paul had felt so good and so right.

A few nights later Paul asked me to a Red Sox game. His parents had given him tickets for his birthday. I accepted. On the car ride back home to Connecticut, I told him that he could just drive us to his apartment. While Paul was brushing his teeth, I undressed myself and climbed into his bed. Looking back upon that moment, I suppose I thought that it was going to be hard enough for Paul to try to love someone who he knew had been loved so deeply by another; so the easier I could make it for him the better. And, I needed to know that I could physically love and be loved by him.

Since I had met Paul, it felt as though I could give and receive love, but I needed to know before either one of us invested too much. I would be lying if I said that I didn't think of Curtis that first night that Paul and I were intimate. But, my thoughts were entirely different than I assumed they would be. Just as Paul had first kissed me tenderly and, yet, passionately, he first touched me with care and desire. It reminded me of how I had touched Curtis: protectively and, yet, with such fervor. Paul took things slow, just as Curtis and I had learned to do as a result of ALS. Paul seemed to savor each moment, each step. Afterward, I told Paul that I loved him. It was a different kind of love than what I had felt for Curtis, but it was just as intense and just as real. I felt as though our souls had been lovers for a lifetime already, but this was the first moment that we had been allowed to physically touch. I told Paul that I didn't expect him to love me, yet. How could he? We had only known one another for one month and one week. I was a 26-year-old widow whose husband had been dead for less than 17 months and I had loved my husband completely since I was a teenager.

Eighteen months later, on an unusually warm November day, Paul asked Woo Woo and me to go for a run along the Connecticut River. This was not unusual. As we ran, he told me that he thought there was something wrong with Woo Woo's leg and that he'd check it out.

"Go on ahead," he said.

I continued to run but then stopped and turned around. Woo Woo was running toward me and when I bent down to greet him, I noticed a string tied around his green collar. A black box was attached to the string.

Before I knew it, Paul got down on one knee.

"You would make me so happy if you would agree to spend the rest of your life with me," he said.

Paul and I were married a year later. Ten months after that, I was told that Woo Woo should be put down. He stayed for two nights at the veterinarian hospital where he was diagnosed with Familial Shar-Pei Fever (FSF), a recurrent episodic fever disorder. The FSF had led to kidney failure. FSF explained Woo Woo's 107-degree fevers over the years. FSF explained the jaundice and his periodic refusal to eat and drink. The average lifespan for a Shar-Pei with this genetic disease is five years. Woo Woo was five years and eight months old.

Earlier this same day, I had purchased a small pink box from the pharmacy. Paul and I had been trying to start a family and I had miscarried a few months prior. Immediately after I got off the phone with the vet, distraught over Woo Woo's seemingly failing health, I went into the bathroom. Minutes later, I was overjoyed when I saw the two pink lines. This explained everything. My and Curtis' baby would go home to his father, and Paul and I would start our own family.

The next day, Paul and I drove Woo Woo the three hours north to Curtis' apple orchard where we waited for the local veterinarian; he had been Woo Woo's doctor when we had lived in Danville and he knew how much the orchard meant to us. I sat on Woo Woo's green dog bed which we had laid on the ground and held my baby in my lap as I rubbed his head and behind his ears. Woo Woo tried a few times to get up and walk around his favorite place. He was too weak to do so. Paul drove back into town to the local hardware store which allowed me time to spend with Woo Woo and Curtis' spirit, alone. I sensed Curtis in the air, the trees, the wind, and the sun. I imagined that he was behind me, his spiritual form holding and supporting me.

Once Paul returned with a shovel, a tarp, and some rope and while the veterinarian prepared his supplies, I spoke to my Woo Woo as I held him and gently stroked his soft, black fur one last time, "I love you so much. I will miss you so much. You brought so much joy to your father and me. I don't think I would have survived that first year without you. I owe my life to you. Go. Find your father. I will see you both soon."

With Paul's hands on my shoulders, I held my hand on Woo Woo's heart until it stopped beating. And then I sobbed.

I held Woo Woo's body for quite some time before I nodded toward Paul as I released my arms from around Woo Woo, and slowly stood up from the ground while still holding Woo Woo's head until I slipped my hands out from under him. Paul squatted, gently picked up Woo Woo's dog bed with Woo Woo on it and carried him to the center of the orchard. Paul and I, with Curtis' father's help, for he had come up to the orchard after seeing Paul at the hardware store, buried Woo Woo in the earth at the center of the apple orchard at the back farm in North Danville.

Nine months later, Paul and I welcomed a baby girl to our world. Martha "Mattie" Grace blessed our life, and we named her in memory of Paul's mom, whose spirit had left her 58-year-old-cancer-riddled body a year earlier, two months before Woo Woo's passing. Less than two years after Mattie's birth, Ava Kathleen joined us, then Caroline Mae followed almost three years after that, and four years later, James Ryan completed our family. The love I felt the moment I found out I was pregnant each time, the love I felt the first time I held each of my children, and the love I feel every minute I think about or am with them reminds me of when Curtis, in a dream, assured me that I would experience different and amazing kinds of love.

The love I feel for my children is deep, raw, pure, intense, and natural. It is effortless. It's as though I knew their souls before they were each born. I am grateful for the experience of being a mother. The year that Curtis and I lived with ALS prepared me for the practicalities of caring for my children as newborns. More importantly, my and Curtis' experience with ALS and learning to live while preparing to die gave me the perspective that above all, spending time with Paul and my children will always be my priority. I know how short life can be. I know how life can change completely and forever in an instant.

It took many, many years but I eventually wrote the first rough draft of Curtis' and my story. Throughout the process, there were days and nights when I left Paul and the girls so that I could write. I needed to be completely alone, with Curtis, in order to try to remember a moment or a day that Curtis and I had shared that my mind had kept at arm's length in order to protect my soul. I was so grateful for the extensive and raw journals that I had kept and for the countless pictures and few videos that I had taken throughout the year that Curtis was sick. My words and the vivid photographs helped me to recall some of the most wonderful, as well as some of the most painful, times. And, then, when I would return, it was apparent that Paul could see the toll that traveling back had taken on me. It wasn't remembering the details of Curtis' and my time together that hurt me the most; it was facing the dreams of a life that would never be that drained me every time.

The first time that I returned from writing for a few days, I asked Paul why he had decided to love me.

"I have never questioned my decision to love you because there was never a decision to be made. It just happened," he said. "All that matters to me is being with you."

Still, though, I can only imagine how hard it is for him when I speak of Curtis, as I often still do. I think of Curtis daily as though he is a permanent fixture in my life, and when I really need to talk to or be with Curtis, I run. As my body moves, my mind travels to wherever he is or because I am alone and listening, I am once again aware of the fact that he is always with me. Always. I believe that Curtis is happy that I have remarried and rejoices in the fact that Paul and I have created a family.

I also believe that Curtis is proud of so many of his immediate and extended family members who, over the past two decades, have educated others about ALS, helped raise money for ALS research, and participated in various ALS clinical trials. Since

Curtis' passing, four additional members of his family on his mother's side have died of ALS. The first was one of his aunts, the woman who so graciously and generously gave us her and her husband's home so that we could have a place of our own to live in the year we lived with ALS. Like Curtis, she chose not to extend her life with a ventilator and lived about the same length of time with the disease as Curtis had before passing on. The second family member is one of Curtis' mother's cousins, and he lived with ALS for three years with the aid of a feeding tube and a ventilator.

The third family member, Curtis' beloved uncle, died a few months before the 15th anniversary of Curtis' death – and in the midst of the ALS Ice Bucket Challenge, an activity that involved pouring ice water over a person's head in order to promote awareness of ALS and encourage donations to research. Reportedly, the challenge helped raise over $220 million worldwide. During the years after Curtis' death and before his own diagnosis, Curtis' uncle painstakingly built a stunning log cabin by hand on one edge of the apple orchard at the back farm in North Danville. I don't know if he knew about Curtis' and my dream of building a home near our orchard. I do know, though, that it took so many of us to make that dream come true. At one point in time, I gave money to Curtis' uncle for the roof; I knew that Curtis would have wanted me to help in that way. I imagine that the sight of the magnificent log cabin brings joy to Curtis' soul as it does to me, but I also imagine that it breaks Curtis' heart, as it does mine. Although it symbolizes faith, hope, and love, it also stands as a constant physical reminder to me that our moment of sharing a home together was fleeting, just as was our dream of raising a family and growing old together in this lifetime.

I saw Curtis' uncle a few months before his death, at the yearly Orchard Celebration that Curtis' family puts on in order to help raise money for ALS research. The first celebration was in 2000 during which we planted the trees. The second one, in 2001, occurred just a few months after I had met Paul. I asked him if he would accompany me; I wanted him to meet Curtis' family and our friends. I needed him to feel the sense of community and love that had surrounded Curtis and me for the year that Curtis was sick.

Paul came and afterward let me know that he couldn't attend again, "Now I have felt the love that existed between the two of you and throughout this town. Now I understand even better than I did when you told me about it. I am so glad that you had that in your life. I just can't bear to feel it for myself again."

This particular time, in 2014, when I attended the Orchard Celebration so that I could see Curtis' uncle, I brought my son who was six months old. The older girls had soccer games back in Connecticut. I introduced James to Curtis' uncle; he was so pleased to meet him and to see me. Seeing Curtis' uncle experiencing the effects of ALS was extremely difficult for me. We spoke very little that day. I sat beside him for a while, though. Each time we looked at one another, our souls communicated without words. He now knew how Curtis had felt. We were both a part of a group that neither one of us would ever wish anyone else to join.

As I prepared to leave that day, I gave him a hug and as I held him close I whispered in his ear, "Please tell Curtis and Woo Woo when you see them that I love and miss them."

He nodded.

On the day of Curtis' uncle's death, a few months after the

Orchard Celebration and about a year since his diagnosis, Curtis' mom wrote to me in part, "He talked of you today as he decided to do as my sister did and go into the hospital with sedation and lie flat in bed. He wanted to die at home as Curtis did but the doctor told him that without sedation it would be difficult. He said that he loved you and was happy for you and your family and would be doing something that he promised you he would at the Orchard Celebration."

The fourth family member, Judy, Curtis' youngest aunt and his mother's second sister to suffer ALS, was diagnosed in March of 2019 and passed away in February of 2020. Judy and I kept in touch during her illness just as we had kept in touch via email and social media over the years. In fact, in 2011 she had come down to Connecticut and spent the night with Paul, me, and the girls. As she spoke about living with ALS twenty years after Curtis had, I was amazed at how some things associated with ALS had become more modern. For instance, she recorded words when she could still speak clearly so once her words became too mumbled, she was able to communicate with her recorded voice. I was just as amazed at how some things had stayed the same since our experience in 1999. Judy participated in a clinical study just as her brother had done, just as her sister had done, and just as Curtis had done. I am grateful for the opportunity for hope but disappointed that none of the four different experimental drugs stopped the progression of ALS.

Four months after Judy's diagnosis, I visited with her. It was very difficult for me to see her living with ALS as it had been heart-wrenching to see Curtis' uncle with ALS. She told me that she was excited to go to heaven and meet her mother who she didn't remember – Judy was just two years old when her mother, Curtis' grandmother, died of ALS in 1962. Even though I knew that it would be many months before Judy would complete her journey here on earth and pass on, I asked her to give Curtis and Woo Woo the biggest, most grand hug and kiss from me. And, I asked her to please let me know once she was okay.

One evening in February 2020, I heard from Curtis' family that she had passed. The next morning, as I was running my two dogs, Bruin and Bauer, in Connecticut like I do almost every day, I looked up and saw two bald eagles flying above me. Over the previous five years of running on this particular land almost every day, I had seen one bald eagle once in a while, but never two at the same time and I had never witnessed two circling above me. I stopped and watched the bald eagles for almost five minutes. Perhaps they were circling for prey that was in the woods. Perhaps it was just a coincidence. I believe, though, that it was a sign from Judy that she and Curtis were flying, their ravaged bodies free from ALS, together.

I have spoken about Curtis with my children ever since they were each born. They have met Curtis' family, they have visited the apple orchard and I have brought them to the gravesite in Danville where they have seen my name engraved next to Curtis'. I have always wanted Curtis to be synonymous with someone who they've felt they've always known. In order to really understand me, one needs to know Curtis. I hope that they will read this story of Curtis and me and that they will take from it what I believe to be the truth: This life is all about love and faith.

The fear of losing those whom I love is still very real for me. I believe that it always will be. The thought of Paul dying has overwhelmed me more than once. Early on in our relationship, I almost walked away from him because I figured it would be easier to leave him rather than risk losing him later. I remember one morning in particular. We had just met a few months prior and he had to go out of state for business training. I surprised him by showing up at his hotel room. That morning, when I woke up in the hotel's king-sized bed, I realized that I was lying practically on top of him, like I had had to do with Curtis so that he could motion for me with his head. I was mortified and wanted to run out of room, out of the hotel, and out of Paul's life. He asked me to stay. A bit later, he got out of bed, and because he kept the bathroom door open, I heard the shower as though I was right there with him and then watched him shave as I lay in the bed. I marveled at how he could shower himself and at him shaving his own beard. The scent of Gillette gel for sensitive skin traveled out of the bathroom. I breathed it in slowly. My heart rate increased, and I became light-headed. I would likely have fainted if I had been standing. At that moment, I imagined that something terrible would happen to Paul soon. Again, though, he asked me to stay.

Paul always kept me near him by telling me that I made him feel alive and I knew that I depended on his unconditional love, support, depth of understanding, and his ability to receive my love and give me love to live. In his eyes I see the person that he believes I can be. I do not wish to disappoint him. He and our experiences the past two decades have taught me that there is another way. I've embraced that new way of living with grace, beauty, understanding, optimism, and faith. I've landed in a place that is magical, mystical, and real. I'm living. Again. In addition to being eternally loved and protected by my Curtis, I am also loving and being loved by Paul, as well as my children, who have given me the gift of being their mother and whom I love with all of my being.

The fear of losing any one of them lies in wait. The darkness that enveloped me for so long now only occasionally becomes greater than its forever state of brewing. I make the conscious choice to keep it at bay by concentrating on the sliver of light. Even in darkness, there's always at least one ray of hope. I took a chance and chose to live a life surrounded by love and am aware that by choosing so I may experience all-encompassing and life-altering grief again. For me, love is, and will hopefully always be, more powerful than fear.

# Acknowledgments

To Paul, thank you for your courage, kindness, love, and support. You are my everything. "Our day. Our time. Our life."

To our four children and B & B, thank you for allowing me the time to complete this labor of love. You are also my labors of love. I love each of you with all of my being.

Curtis, I shared with you everything I have ever felt – there's nothing that was left unsaid. "In him there are the eyes that have the gift to see what must be seen in me to be alive." We never did say goodbye. Just "see ya later." It feels like yesterday when I last touched you. It will seem like tomorrow when I next see you.

Woo Woo, my first baby. Thank you for seeing me through my darkest days and nights.

Mom and Dad, thank you for your unconditional love and support and your unwavering belief in me.

To my sisters, thank you for always being there.

To Curtis' mom and dad, thank you for bringing Curtis into this world and for loving him so deeply. Thank you for welcoming me into your family.

To those who helped me care for Curtis, we will forever be grateful for your time, love, and deep care. You know who you are.

To family and friends who supported me before and after Curtis' illness, and both of us when Curtis was sick, I hope that I have thanked you in person and that you know what your kindness, friendship, and generosity mean to me.

To the Danville, West Danville, and North Danville communities, thank you for making me feel at home.

To all of my writing and English teachers at Loomis Chaffee, Middlebury, and Dartmouth, thank you for sharing your love of the written word.

To Audra and Liz and all those associated with Green Heart Living Press, thank you for helping me to finally make my dream of publishing this book a reality.

# Epilogue

Familial ALS (f-ALS) makes up approximately ten percent of all ALS cases. In 20 percent of these familial ALS cases, a genetic mutation (A4V) has been identified on the SOD-1 chromosome. This is also an extremely progressive form of ALS. Typically, a person with ALS can live three to five years without the need for medical intervention; the projected lifespan for someone with the A4V mutation on the SOD-1 chromosome is six to 12 months.

Curtis died of f-ALS. He had the A4V mutation on the SOD-1 chromosome. Before his diagnosis, though, at the age of 25, the fact that ALS ran in his family was not clearly understood. His mother and her family knew that their mother (Curtis' grandmother) had died of an illness that slowly paralyzed her body from the arms down and caused her to die in less than a year. It had been labeled progressive bulbar palsy. She was 40-years-old. Her sister died of what was labeled progressive muscular atrophy. The disease slowly paralyzed her body (from the legs up) until her death in less than a year. What the family didn't fully comprehend was that progressive bulbar palsy and progressive muscular atrophy are both motor neuron diseases and actually both women died of amyotrophic lateral sclerosis (ALS), also known as Lou Gehrig's Disease.

At the age of 25, Curtis began to experience weakness and odd physical symptoms in the late summer/early fall of 1998. We searched for answers as to what could be wrong with him. After four months of tests at two different hospitals, Curtis was diagnosed with f-ALS and we discovered that Curtis' maternal great-great-great-great grandfather, Samuel Farr, born in 1804, died of what was referred to as a "creeping paralysis" in 1865.

Massachusetts General Hospital had medical journals from the 1800s in which the Farr family was recorded; the disease had been referred to as Farr's disease before it was labeled familial ALS and/or Lou Gehrig's disease after the famous New York Yankee. Farr's disease has affected approximately 50 percent of every generation of Curtis' ancestors and family since Samuel Farr and his brother, who died at age 40 of ALS, and his sister, who died at age 54, of the same disease. Out of Samuel Farr's eight children, four of them died of ALS. His daughter was only 27. His three sons, one of whom was Curtis' great-great-great grandfather, all died in their 40s of the disease.

Since Curtis' death in 1999, his mother's cousin, two of his mother's sisters and his mother's brother have all died of f-ALS. Curtis' mother has lost seven immediate family members to f-ALS: her mother, her aunt, her son, her cousin, two sisters, and her brother. I am in awe of her strength and proud of her determination and hard work to advocate and raise money for ALS research.

Curtis and I worked to get the word out about the f-ALS genetic mutation in his family. We wanted to express that it was not a family curse; it was genetics. We wanted to explain its history with the hope that if it were understood, it may still be feared but it could also be explained. Curtis and I decided to create a nonprofit foundation before he died. Every day that he lived with ALS, he wished for a cure and we knew that more research was needed. Curtis' foundation was born out of the idea that it would help support ALS research as well as provide monetary assistance to those living with ALS. It was officially created in 2000. I spent many years raising tens of thousands of dollars, enough to help a few people who were currently living with ALS continue to live a certain quality of life while they still had the time and to help support ALS research at Massachusetts General Hospital and Johns Hopkins University. As time marched forward, as it always does, I realized that I was only one person and couldn't do it all at the same time. As my family grew, I poured myself into my husband, our children, my development career at independent schools, and this book. The foundation suffered and, as of today, it is no longer a viable entity. Perhaps, someday I can resurrect it and continue to raise money for ALS.

Since 2000, many members of Curtis' family have actively advocated on behalf of ALS in order to continue to raise awareness of ALS, and many have worked hard to fundraise and donate the money to continued research of the ALS SOD-1 gene. Many members of his family have also donated their skin and blood for the purposes of ALS research. Some have participated in other testing.

To learn more about ALS, see the Amyotrophic Lateral Sclerosis (ALS) Fact Sheet from the National Institute of Neurological Disorders and Stroke here:

https://www.ninds.nih.gov/health-information/patient-caregiver-education/fact-sheets/amyotrophic-lateral-sclerosis-als-fact-sheet

For more information on how to help support ALS research and those currently living with ALS, please visit:

https://www.massgeneral.org/neurology/als

# Bibliography

*ALS Association.* "What Is ALS?" Oct. 2008. 11 March 2009 <
http://www.alsa.org/als/what.cfm?CFID=2711051&CFTOKEN=8dac4efea9bb
8acd-9E91ABE7-188B-2E62-803091F3E1BFA468>.

*ALS Association.* "Who gets ALS?" Sept. 2008. 11 March 2009
<http://www.alsa.org/als/who.cfm?CFID=2711051&CFTOKEN=8dac4efea9b
b8acd-9E91ABE7-188B-2E62-803091F3E1BFA468>.

Amyotrophic Lateral Sclerosis (ALS) Fact Sheet | National Institute of
Neurological Disorders and Stroke (nih.gov).

Andersen, P.M., Sims, K.B., Xin, W.W., Kiely, R., O'Neill, G., Ravitas, J., Pioro,

E., Harati, Y., Brower, R., Levine, J., Heinicke, H., Seltzer, W., Boss, M., Brown,
R. (June 2003). Sixteen novel mutations in the Cu/Zn superoxide dismutase
gene in amyotrophic lateral sclerosis: a decade of discoveries, defects and
disputes. ALS and other motor neuron disorders, 4, 2, 62-73.

*Bible Gateway,* "Deuteronomy 30 (New International Version)." 1984. 11 March
2009<http://www.biblegateway.com/passage/?search=
deuteronomy%2030&version=31>.

*Clavis Pharma,* "Terms/Glossary." 11 March 2009
<http://www.clavispharma.com/page?id=1008&key=18278>.

Donkervoort, Sandra. "Genetic Testing for ALS." April 2008. 11 March 2009
http://www.alsa.org/als/genetics.cfm?CFID=2664714&CFTOKEN=81645290f
a85117b-75A70CF9-188B-2E62-80E0B97A6AC9051A>.

Goldstein, L.H., Atkins, L., & Leigh, P.N. (Sept. 2002).

Correlates of Quality of Life in people with motor neuron disease (MND). ALS
and other motor neuron disorders, 3, 3, 123.

Hecht, M., Hillemacher, T., Grasel, E., Tigges, S., Winterholler, M., Heuss, D.,
Hilz, M., Neundorfer, B. (Dec. 2002).

Subjective experience and coping in ALS, <u>ALS and other motor neuron disorders</u>, 3, 4, 225.

*International Ventilators User Network*, "Information about Ventilator Assisted Living." 2005. 11 March 2009 <http://www.ventusers.org/edu/vabout1.html>.

*TPALS*, "Using a BiPAP." Apr. 2001. 11 Mar. 2009 <"http://tpals.org/bipap.htm>.

# Notes

[1]http://www.alsa.org/als/genetics.cfm?CFID=2664714&CFTOKEN=81645 290fa85117b-75A70CF9-188B-2E62-80E0B97A6AC9051A

[2] Sixteen novel mutations in the Cu/Zn superoxide dismutase gene in amyotrophic lateral sclerosis: a decade of discoveries, defects and disputes, Andersen, PM, Sims, KB, Xin, WW, Kiely, R, O'Neill, G, Ravits, J, Pioro, E, Harati, Y, Brower, R, Levine, J, Heinicke, H, Seltzer, W, Boss, M, Brown, R, "ALS and other motor neuron disorders," June 2003, Vol. 4 Issue 2, p.62, 12 p; (AN 10404680)

[3]http://www.alsa.org/als/what.cfm?CFID=2711051&CFTOKEN=8dac4efe a9bb8acd-9E91ABE7-188B-2E62-803091F3E1BFA468

[4]http://www.alsa.org/als/who.cfm?CFID=2711051&CFTOKEN=8dac4efea 9bb8acd-9E91ABE7-188B-2E62-803091F3E1BFA468

[5]http://www.alsa.org/als/what.cfm?CFID=2711051&CFTOKEN=8dac4efe a9bb8acd-9E91ABE7-188B-2E62-803091F3E1BFA468

[6] Correlates of Quality of Life in people with motor neuron disease (MND), by Goldstein, LH, Atkins, L, and Leigh, PN, ALS and other motor neuron disorders, September 2002, Vol. 3 Issue 3, p. 123.

[7] Pg. 126.

[8] Pg. 126-127.

[9] Pg. 127.

[10] Subjective experience and coping in ALS, Hecht, M, Hillemacher, T, Grasel, E, Tigges, S, Winterholler, M, Heuss, D, Hilz, M, Neundorfer, B, "ALS and other motor neuron disorders," December 2002, Vol. 3 Issue 4, p. 225.

[11] Pg. 229.

[12] http://www.clavispharma.com/page?id=1008&key=18278

[13] http://www.ventusers.org/edu/vabout1.html

[14]http://tpals.org/bipap.htm

[15]http://www.biblegateway.com/passage/?search=deuteronomy%2030& version=31

# About the Author

Born and raised in Hartford, CT, Heidi Erdmann Vance McCann graduated from the Loomis Chaffee School where she learned about the power and importance of the written word. Heidi has been a keen observer of the human condition since she was a child. Her high school experiences helped her find her voice as well as her ability and desire to lead. She graduated from Middlebury College where she honed her writing skills as well as her athletic competitiveness on the tennis and squash courts.

Heidi worked in the field of development and coached tennis for over a year. When her longtime boyfriend was diagnosed with ALS, Lou Gehrig's disease, Heidi left her jobs to care for him. They spent a year learning to live while preparing to die and raised a Chinese Shar-pei, Wofosi. They married 22 days before his death. Together, they created a nonprofit foundation in his name.

Heidi went on to earn a MALS degree with a concentration in creative writing from Dartmouth College and reentered the development field at Loomis Chaffee where she currently works. Heidi loves to teach and has tutored for over two decades. She lives in Simsbury, CT, with her husband, Paul, and their four children: Martha, Ava, Caroline and James, and their dogs, Bruin and Bauer. Heidi loves to watch her children play sports and relishes in the time they spend as a family. Heidi sets aside at least one hour a day to physically move her body during which she often reconnects with Curtis' spirit. This is when ideas, words, and sentences of future books enter her mind.

# About
# Green Heart Living Press

Green Heart Living's mission is to make the world a more loving and peaceful place, one person at a time. Green Heart Living Press publishes inspirational books and stories of transformation, making the world a more loving and peaceful place, one book at a time.

Whether you have an idea for an inspirational book and want support through the writing process – or your book is already written and you are looking for a publishing path – Green Heart Living can help you get your book out into the world.

You can meet Green Heart authors on the Green Heart Living YouTube channel and the Green Heart Living Podcast.

**www.greenheartliving.com**

Made in United States
North Haven, CT
08 October 2022

25175181R10183